Principles of Marketing

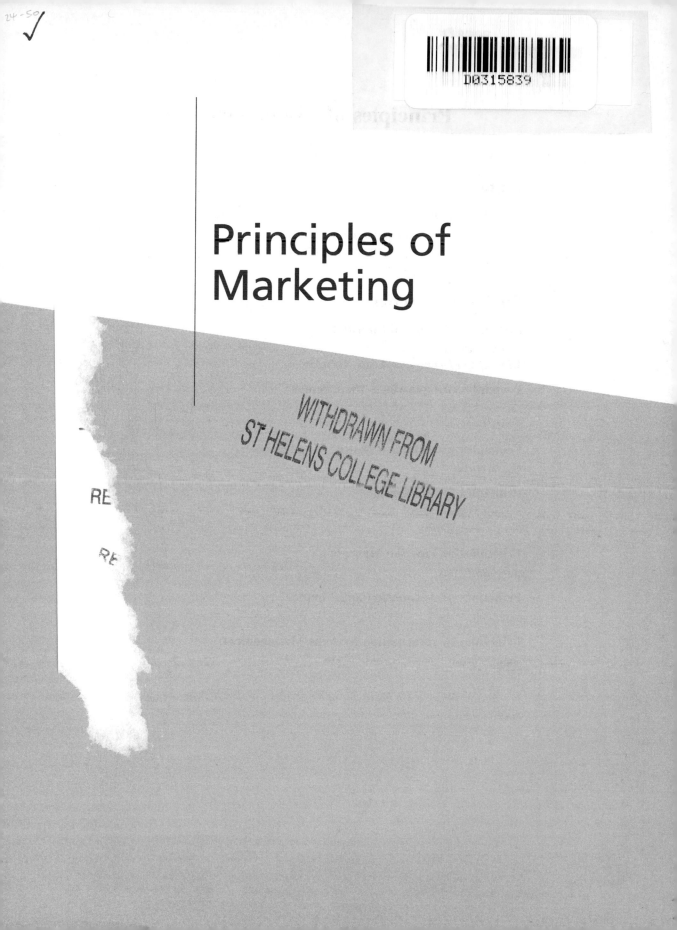

24-50 ✓

RE

RE

Principles of Management Series

Editor

Joseph G Nellis
Professor of International Management Economics
Cranfield School of Management, Cranfield University

Books in the series

Principles of Applied Statistics
Second Edition
Michael C Fleming and Joseph G Nellis

Principles of Operations Management
Second Edition
R Les Galloway

Principles of Human Resource Management
David Goss

Principles of Marketing
Second Edition
Geoffrey Randall

Principles of Law for Managers
Anne Ruff

Principles of Accounting and Finance
Peter Sneyd

Principles of Information Systems Management
John M Ward

For further information about any of these titles, or to order inspection copies or purchase books, please visit http://www.thomsonlearning.co.uk

Principles of Marketing

Geoffrey Randall

THOMSON

LEARNING™   Australia • Canada • Mexico • Singapore • Spain • United Kingdom • United States

THOMSON

LEARNING

Principles of Marketing – 2nd Edition

Copyright © 2001 Geoffrey Randall

The Thomson Learning logo is a registered trademark used herein under licence.

For more information, contact Thomson Learning, Berkshire House, 168–173 High Holborn, London, WC1V 7AA or visit us on the World Wide Web at: http://www.thomsonlearning.co.uk

British Library Cataloguing-in-Publication Data
A catalogue record for this book is available from the British Library

ISBN 1-86152-668-7

First edition 1993 Routledge, reprinted 1994 and 1996
Reprinted by International Thomson Business Press 1997

This Edition 2001

Typeset by Techset Composition Ltd, Salisbury, Wiltshire
Printed in Great Britain by TJ International, Padstow, Cornwall

Principles of marketing

Principles of marketing offers a comprehensive overview of marketing. Geoffrey Randall relates the central principles of marketing to the practice of management, covering marketing information, research, segmentation, product policy and development, the elements of the marketing mix and considering the marketing of services, direct marketing, business-to-business markets and the international framework. He shows how these elements can be drawn together in the development of strategy, its implementation and control. Adopting a fully integrated approach, he relates the concepts to the actual decisions managers have to take. By looking at a wide variety of industries and the skills that are needed in different contexts, Geoffrey Randall shows the extent to which marketing is a central part of any type of organization.

Geoffrey Randall is an independent consultant specializing in marketing training and management education. He runs in-house training courses for major companies and has wide teaching experience at various levels. He was head of the business school at the University of Greenwich and served on several national bodies in the field of business education as well as working in industry for ten years. He is author of five other books, including *Trade Marketing Strategies*, *Branding* and, with Andrew Seth, *The Grocers: the rise & rise of the supermarket chains*.

Contents

Figures in main text

Figures in main text

x

Tables in main text

Preface

In the eight years since the first edition of this book was published, a great deal has changed. The main impact has been that of new technology, in particular from computing, telecommunications and their convergence in the Internet. In this edition, therefore, there is a completely new chapter on e-commerce and marketing, and frequent references throughout the text to computer applications and relevant websites. Developments that have sprung from the new technologies, such as data warehousing and data mining, and customer relationship management are also covered.

The other major change is the shift in the focus of marketing activity, from transactions to relationships, and the resulting concentration on customer value. Chapters 1 and 2 discuss these developments. Chapter 1 also debates the rise of the so-called 'new marketing', and draws some conclusions as to how much is really new.

Of course, much remains the same. The basic principles of marketing have not changed, and – as the bursting of the dotcom bubble showed – neither have the rules of business. In the rest of the book, references and examples have been updated where necessary, but much of the content has been retained. The aim is still to present the fundamentals of marketing in clear language, and in a concise form, for people studying the subject for the first time within the context of a business or management programme.

Geoffrey Randall
March 2001

Chapter 1 | Introduction

What marketing is and is not: definitions

Marketing is one of those terms which can arouse strong feelings, and on which many people hold strong views – but which is not yet very well understood. In Europe marketing is a relatively recent phenomenon, having come to prominence only in the last fifty years; indeed, many firms have yet to adopt it in any formal way. Like any human activity, it is constantly changing and is therefore difficult to pin down.

Before looking at some definitions of what marketing is, let us clear away some misunderstandings, and say what it is not. Marketing is emphatically not the business of persuading people to buy what they don't really need. This view, widely held by marketing's critics (usually from outside the business world), does not stand up to examination. In practice it is extremely difficult to persuade people to buy a product. Think of yourself as a consumer or as a manager: how easily do you part with your own or your firm's money? We all purchase goods and services which in some way meet our needs, and which do so better than the alternative. As we shall see, the decision process may be complex, with multiple objectives and trade-offs between different factors (price, quality, convenience, for example); but in the end, we all buy those things that suit us best.

This is not to say that marketing effort does not help to influence buying decisions, particularly the choice between competing brands. Nor is it to say that heavy advertising cannot persuade people to buy something once. But if a purchase does not give satisfaction in some way, the consumer will not buy again.

Similarly, marketing does not create needs which did not exist before. Such an argument, which accepts that consumers buy to meet a perceived need, also assumes that marketing has enormous power to alter the way people feel. Again, careful examination of the case suggests that the argument is based on a falsehood, and is supported by little evidence. The falsehood is a supposed dichotomy between needs and wants – needs being acceptable, and wants somehow rather discreditable. 'Real' needs are really very few: food and water, some clothing and shelter. The great majority of people – in the industrialized world at least – can assume that these necessities are available; beyond the basics, they begin to exercise choice, and personal preferences come into play.

Most purchases are made to meet a combination of need and want; trying to separate them is impossible, and unhelpful. This is really what is meant by phrases such as 'the market will decide': businesses will produce what they see fit, and the sum of the individual choices made by consumers will decide what products survive. Thus the market decides which products best meet consumers' needs.

The only alternative to this system is for some central person or body to decide what people need. We have seen what results this system produces in the formerly centrally planned economies of eastern Europe.

Evidence that marketing can make us want things we did not realize we needed seems at first sight rather stronger. The number of products now available which simply did not exist forty years ago would appear to indicate that we can be influenced. This view, too, depends on how we define needs. Sixty years ago we did not know we 'needed' television; thirty years ago we did not 'need' a video-cassette recorder. On the other hand, we have always needed entertainment, and we always will. Technology – and marketing – may offer us different ways of satisfying that need. If we choose not to have television – and many do – we can find entertainment in other ways. Business will always try to find new and better products and services; the market – the total buying decisions of all customers and consumers – will decide whether a new product is better, that is whether it better meets our needs, than the existing ones.

At a more detailed level, marketing is not just about advertising, or selling, or creating an image, although all three may be activities contained within marketing. What then is it?

Peter Drucker, the single most influential writer on management, has defined marketing in the following way:

True marketing starts out with the customers, their demographics, related needs and values. It does not ask, 'What do we want to sell?' It asks, 'What does the customer want to buy?' It does not say, 'This is what our product or service does.' It says, 'These are the satisfactions the customer looks for.'

(Drucker 1979: 59)

This is as good a definition as any of the 'marketing concept', which can be distinguished from what marketing people in a firm actually do. The marketing concept is about how the business as a whole operates. As a British writer put it:

The marketing concept is a philosophy, not a system of marketing or an organizational structure. It is founded on the belief that profitable sales and satisfactory returns on investment can only be achieved by identifying, anticipating and satisfying customer needs and desires – in that order.

It is an attitude of mind which places the customer at the very centre of a business activity and automatically orients a company towards its markets rather than towards its factories. It is a philosophy which rejects the proposition that production is an end in itself, and that the products, manufactured to the satisfaction of the manufacturer merely remain to be sold.

(Barwell 1965: 3)

The same point was made more pithily by the then chairman of Carborundum, a company which used to specialize in producing carborundum grinding wheels. After discovering marketing on some personal road to Damascus, he said: 'Customers don't want grinding wheels, they want metal removed.' What may appear a trivial form of words in fact signalled a fundamental shift in the way the company viewed its business and how it could serve its customers.

Such quotations serve to underline the point that the marketing concept applies across all types of companies and market situations. (How its applications vary will be discussed later.)

More recent definitions of marketing have sought to broaden the concept to include organizations other than businesses, and transactions other than purely commercial ones. Typical of these is that of Kotler, author of one of the world's best-known textbooks on marketing: 'Marketing is a societal process by which individuals and groups obtain what they need and want through creating, offering and freely exchanging products and value with others' (Kotler 2000). Such a definition can be applied to non-commercial organizations, such as local government or the National Health Service, and can sometimes illuminate business transactions too. The idea of exchange – that both parties are giving and receiving – can help to clarify what is important in a situation, and how it can be influenced. In particular, this formulation may help to balance the superficial view that marketing is about giving people what they want – an approach which would quickly bankrupt a company, and which has clear dangers, for instance, for a healthcare provider.

What all these definitions have in common is a focus on the customer and consumer: that is what is meant by a marketing orientation. What it means in practice will be examined next.

Marketing as a management function

Turning from the conceptual level, to what marketing means as a function in a firm, we find the American Marketing Association defining marketing management as 'the process of planning and executing the conception, pricing, promotion and distribution of ideas, goods, and services to create exchanges that satisfy individual and organizational goals'. In Britain, the Chartered Institute of Marketing defines marketing as 'the management process responsible for identifying, anticipating and satisfying customer requirements profitably'.

The CIM's definition introduces two important new ideas: the management process, and profit. The idea of management process is important because marketing does not just happen: someone must be responsible for making it happen. The idea of profit is even more important.

It is worth repeating that marketing does not involve just giving people what they want, but rather adjusting what the firm can profitably provide to what customers want.

This leads to the concept of matching:

Marketing tries to match the firm's resources and capabilities to customers' changing needs and wants, at a profit.

Every company cannot meet every identified need, even within its current chosen market sectors. It cannot meet every need at a profit; it has to choose the best match.

The other factor so far omitted is that no company operates in isolation: it has competitors. In virtually every market, there are several companies identifying customer needs and trying to satisfy them. What your competitors do can crucially affect your profit. An extreme view even suggests that a customer orientation can be fatal if it ignores competition:

> Would identifying, conceptualizing, and communicating [customer needs] help American Motors compete successfully with General Motors, Ford and Chrysler? Let alone Toyota, Datsun, Honda and the rest of the imports?
>
> Let's say American Motors develops a product strategy based on identifying customer needs. The result would be a line of products identical to those of General Motors, which spends millions of dollars researching the same marketplace to identify those same customer needs...
>
> Why do the hundreds of definitions of the marketing concept almost never mention the word *competition*? Or suggest the essential nature of the conflict? The true nature of marketing today involves the conflict between corporations, not the satisfying of human needs and wants.
>
> (Ries and Trout 1986: 3–5)

The authors exaggerate to make a point, but it is a vital point: marketing must operate in the interface between the company, its customers and consumers, and its competitors (see Figure 1.1).

All this discussion, however, is rather general. The definitions suggest that marketing is concerned with all or most aspects of a firm's activities, and at the conceptual level this is true; it leads to certain potential conflicts within the organization, which will be discussed later. It still does not tell us about the actual *content* of the marketing function.

Clearly, it follows from the definitions given that marketing people must be concerned with studying markets and customers, with selecting particular parts or segments of markets, with helping to decide what products should be offered to which customers, and with helping to design those products. In these activities, they will co-operate with other management functions.

The domain which is entirely or mainly that of marketing is known in shorthand as the 'four Ps': product, price, promotion and place. These are the tools which marketing managers have at their disposal.

The four Ps will be expanded on at length in the course of this book. At this stage, we will go on to look at how marketing fits into the firm as a whole, in terms of overall

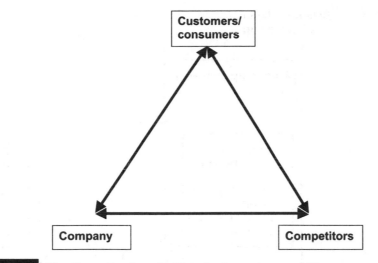

Figure 1.1 The three Cs of marketing: the importance of fit

strategy and organizational structure, before returning to the topic of how definitions of marketing change over time.

Marketing's role in corporate strategy and planning

As a function, marketing must contribute to the company's strategy in the same way as other functions such as manufacturing or finance. At the conceptual level, it could be argued that marketing has a pre-eminent role: a firm will survive only if it meets the long-run needs of customers. It was, after all, a marketing writer, Theodore Levitt, who brought the question: 'What business are we in?' to the forefront of management thinking (Levitt 1960). At one time, in the 1960s, it did indeed appear that marketing would dominate strategic planning, especially if one looks at the USA and at the literature; the reality in many European companies, however, has always been different.

Even amongst the large multinationals which seemed to be adopting a marketing-led approach, there were difficulties in really implementing the concept. From other directions, there were criticisms of the effect of marketing domination, suggesting that it led to unnecessary product proliferation, inflated costs, unfocused diversification, and a weak commitment to R&D (Hayes and Abernathy 1980). We have already noted criticism from within marketing itself that an exclusive customer orientation could be dangerous. Other influences on strategy formulation, from management consultants and industrial economists, began to take over.

Figure 1.2 shows one view of how marketing's role in strategy has changed. From its domination in the 1960s it declined in influence, but began to recover again in the 1980s. Some writers (Day and Wensley 1983) suggest that the marketing function:

- initiates,
- negotiates, and
- manages acceptable exchange relationships with key interest groups, or constituencies,
- in the pursuit of sustainable competitive advantages,
- within specific markets, on the basis of long-run consumer and channel franchises.

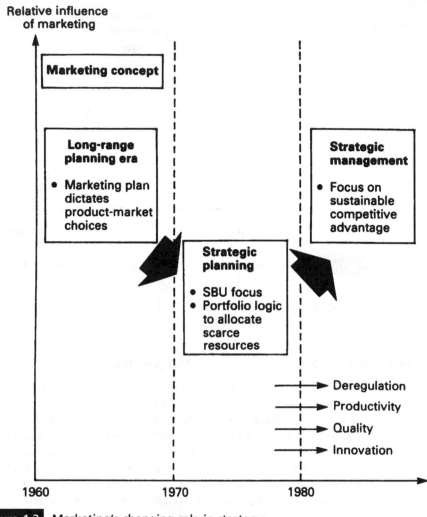

Figure 1.2 Marketing's changing role in strategy

The notion of sustainable competitive advantage was key to much strategic thinking in the 1990s. Readers will study this topic in greater depth elsewhere. At this stage, it is sufficient to underline the fact that competitive advantage can come not only from the marketing function, but from elsewhere. Porter's work, particularly on the Value Chain (Porter 1985) shows how all the firm's activities, and the linkages between them, and the linkages between the firm and its suppliers and customers, are potential sources of competitive advantage. In recent years it has seemed unlikely that sustainable competitive advantage is a tenable idea, as competitors catch up increasingly quickly. The core competences approach (Prahalad and Hamel 1990) focuses attention on the knowledge and skills, often technological, which will support long-term superiority.

The other notion alluded to above is that of constituencies. This recognizes that in real life a firm is a collection of sub-units with differing interests. There are coalitions of interests both within and outside the firm. Each functional area within the firm tries to achieve its own objectives, which involves ensuring an uninterrupted flow of resources from the appropriate external coalition (Anderson 1982). Each functional area is in some sense in competition with the others, and is constrained by them. Marketing tries to maximize consumer satisfaction, but is constrained by finance or manufacturing. (This issue is returned to later.)

Recognizing this reality, what then should marketing's role in strategic planning be? Obviously, the political power of the various functional areas in a particular firm at a particular time will determine how influential marketing's voice is. The marketing input to strategy may be logically imperative, but it has no divine right to dominate other factors. Anderson suggests that marketing has three major activities within strategic planning:

> First, at both the corporate and divisional level it must identify the optimal long-term position or positions that will assure customer satisfaction and support. An optimal position would reflect marketing's perception of what its customers wants and needs are likely to be over the firm's strategic time horizon...
>
> [Second it] involves the development of strategies designed to capture its preferred positions. This will necessarily involve attempts to gain a competitive advantage over firms pursuing similar positioning strategies...
>
> Finally, marketing must negotiate with top management and the other functional areas to implement its strategies...marketing must take an active role in promoting its strategic options by demonstrating the survival value of a consumer orientation to the other internal coalitions.
>
> (Anderson 1982 p. 17)

There are two advantages to this formulation: it preserves the primacy of the market – customers and consumers – as the final arbiter of survival and success, but it recognizes the political reality that marketing is only one function within the firm and has to argue its case with the other functions and top management.

The other point to stress is that at the strategic level, marketing people must lift their eyes from what is happening today to concentrate on what is likely to be happening in five or ten years' time. Today's consumer attitudes may be less relevant than demographic and social trends, for example. The interaction between technology and consumer and customer behaviour must be taken into account. These issues will be returned to when we look at planning in more detail, in Chapter 18.

Challenges to marketing

The idea that marketing is important, and that firms need to think about it, has never gone unchallenged. Many companies and professional firms, particularly in Britain, are still reluctant to embrace it. Over the last decade, even where it had been adopted, it began to come under fire. In 1993, the reputable *McKinsey Quarterly* published a hostile article, quoting many chief executives' dissatisfaction with marketing's performance. Other articles, both in the UK and the USA, reflected widespread criticisms from chief executives and other directors. The complaints fall under a number of headings.

- *It doesn't work.* Some marketing people, unfortunately, tend to make extravagant claims for what they can achieve. Producing dramatic transformations in company fortunes is difficult, and in reality happens seldom. External events, and competitive reactions, often conspire to defeat grand plans.

- *You can't measure it.* Finance directors, especially, mistrust managers who spend large sums of money for a return that is difficult or impossible to measure (we discuss how it can be measured in Chapter 12).

- *It is too expensive.* This is related to the measurement issue: if we could show what return the company would make on its marketing spend, it might not appear expensive at all. Advertising budgets in particular are very visible, and if they show little or no short-term return, they are open to criticism, and to cuts. (We should note that the effects of other large expenditures, for example on IT or training, cannot always be measured either; marketing is not alone in this.)

- *Marketing people don't stick around.* There is a tendency in marketing for managers to move jobs quickly, both within and between companies. If the average job tenure is 18 months to two years, there is little chance to build up depth of knowledge, and personal relationships.

- *Marketing people are different.* In one study (Baker 2000), senior non-marketing managers described their marketing colleagues in these terms:

  'You're not accountable'

  'You're (a touch) arrogant'

  'You hold meetings over lunch'

  'You're always in meetings'

  'You work a shorter day'

  'You're unaccountable, untouchable, slippery, expensive'

  These are unflattering, to say the least, and suggest that marketing has a considerable challenge in marketing itself inside the firm.

- *It is taking over our lives.* This is a criticism, not from within business, but from a wider societal perspective. Writers such as Naomi Klein (2000) have articulated it persuasively. She sums up the first parts of her case as 'No Space' and 'No Choice'. We have no space because marketing has taken over every corner of our lives. Everything is branded or sponsored – not just products, but sports, music, education, everything. In the USA, advertisements appear even in the lavatories of universities, and the institutions reach collaborative agreements with large corporations that provide funds in exchange for exclusive product distribution (of soft drink brands, for example). In both America and Britain, schools accept 'teaching materials' from firms, because they are short of money, but the materials are relentlessly branded. The 'No Choice' argument is that, with everything branded and sponsored, and with the range of suppliers reduced by the continuing trend to take-overs and mergers, we have a decreasing amount of real choice of what we buy and how we spend our time and money. The arguments may seem extreme, but are well documented and demand to be taken seriously.

Organizational issues

It became clear during the first part of the chapter that marketing must be seen within its organizational context. In this section we will explore some of the issues involved.

In general terms, management theorists have gradually come to the conclusion that there is no single best way of structuring an organization.

A central problem for marketing will always be the potential conflict between its overarching claims to strategic direction and its probably less powerful position politically.

In many firms, marketing is a relatively recent arrival in any formal sense, particularly in companies dominated by manufacturing or finance, as many British firms have been. A typical development of a functionally organized firm is shown in Figure 1.3. Originally, marketing does not exist; then it is introduced as a service element within the sales department. Achieving equality at management or board level often takes many years, and does not of itself necessarily mean that marketing has the influence it would like.

In many middle market companies, marketing is still seen as something that happens after the product is made, rather than as a philosophy which guides major decisions. It still has to argue its case, and demonstrate to the other

a) Simple functional structure, no marketing

b) Functional structure, marketing as service

c) Marketing as subordinate function

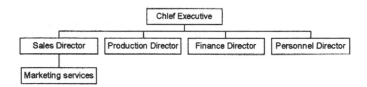

d) Marketing as parallel function

Figure 1.3 Development of a functionally organized firm

functions that it brings a new and valuable perspective to the firm. Once it has achieved strategic credibility, issues of structure can more easily be tackled.

At these later stages of development, the firm is likely to be larger and more complex; simple functional structures may no longer be appropriate. The marketing organization which has been adopted in consumer goods firms is that of the product or brand manager. The introduction of this position was a response to the perceived need to co-ordinate the wide range of activities which affect the final delivery of a branded good: market research, advertising, product formulation, packaging design, distribution, promotion and so on. In its extreme form, it was sometimes claimed that this form of structure made the brand manager 'managing director of the brand'. This was never true, but in companies in which marketing achieved power and a high profile, it was sometimes believed. It led to the classic problem of responsibility without authority: the brand manager might claim to be responsible for any activity which affected the brand as delivered to the consumer (which covers an awful lot of ground); in practice no brand manager ever had much authority over the production function, or the credit terms granted to distributors, for example.

Still, for many consumer goods manufacturers the brand manager system offers real advantages.

The development and maintenance of the brand is the main task of marketing, and having one person whose role is to concentrate single-mindedly on a single brand (or a small group of brands) is vital.

A typical structure of a brand management system is shown in Figure 1.4. Even within apparently similar structures, there will be considerable variation in the amount of power and authority wielded by brand managers, depending on the firm's history and environment.

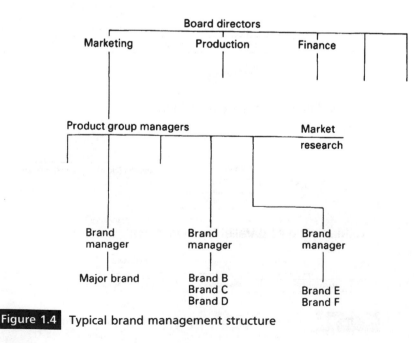

Figure 1.4 Typical brand management structure

In some situations a brand management system may be inappropriate, and a market manager system will be adopted. Where a company operates in markets which are separated by nature of buyer, technology or geography, it may make more sense to have one person (or a team) overseeing the marketing of a range of products to each market, rather than one person concentrating on each product regardless of its markets. A market manager structure is often found in large companies with a wide product-market spread, but may also be encountered when there are a few very large buyers. If you make a range of components for the car industry, for example, it may be sensible for market managers to look after Ford or General Motors.

The problem with any organizational structure is that once adopted, it tends to persist for some time. Unfortunately, the environment changes, and old structures may become outmoded. In recent years, for consumer goods manufacturers in particular, major changes have brought new challenges to organizations. These challenges will be dealt with in more detail later, but may be summarized in terms of technology, international competition, and the power of the retail trade.

Very briefly, new technology and new methods of manufacturing have made obsolete many long-held beliefs – about the economies of scale and the problems of making variants, for example. International competitors can gain significant scale advantages and pose new and unexpected threats. In most countries, the concentration of power in the hands of a few retail chains has transformed the nature of the relationship between manufacturers and retailers (Randall 1994). In this new situation, the existing brand management structure may no longer be able to respond adequately.

There are two levels at which companies need to develop new organizational forms: international and domestic. Companies operating internationally need to develop means of co-ordinating and harmonizing marketing strategies. This will be dealt with in more detail in Chapter 17; at this stage it should be noted that, although it may appear that most marketing activity is local, there will increasingly be an international influence at the strategic level.

The challenge from retail power may have most impact in the short term, as the buying power of the multiples brings sometimes brutal pressure on the supplier. The only logical response in organizational terms is to recognize the new challenge and find ways of responding. This must mean more co-ordination between the various functions which together deliver customer service: not just sales and marketing, but also manufacturing, accounts, physical distribution, computing.

The most progressive firms are moving towards a form of business team, which embraces all the relevant functions and is led by a business manager, who may come from any functional area. This innovation may herald the end of the brand management dominance and lead to a more flexible, more open structure (Figure 1.5).

For many firms who have not even reached the brand manager state, such discussion may appear rather abstruse.

For any firm, the design of its marketing organization must reflect its environment and the overall strategy that top management has decided on. It must reflect the level of resource available, and the tasks that have to be carried out.

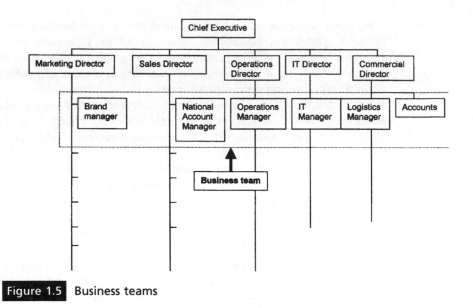

Figure 1.5 Business teams

The real lesson, perhaps, is that the marketing function should be reviewed to check that it can still respond in the way that is required for survival.

Marketing in different contexts

Although much of the discussion so far has been general, as if marketing were monolithic, always the same, it is clear that there are differences between firms and that this must affect marketing's place within each. Much textbook treatment of marketing applies mainly to very large, multinational companies; a great deal of the material available refers to consumer goods, and much to the USA. This is inevitable, given the historical development of both practice and academic study of the subject. It remains true that multinational consumer brand manufacturers are frequently at the leading edge of marketing practice, and that what they do now many smaller firms adopt later. It therefore remains worthwhile studying them, but this should not blind us to the fact that in Europe, many things are different, and that everywhere there are many different contexts in which marketing takes place.

It is the thesis of this book that marketing principles remain the same whatever the context, but that marketing practice should reflect the local situation. It is also my view that there is a convergence between the consumer and industrial branches of marketing practice, which were once seen by many as being quite separate. The similarities and differences will be explored in more detail later, but to take one example: industrial marketers traditionally dealt with a small number of large buyers, with whom they managed a long-term relationship, while consumer marketers dealt with branding and marketing to a mass market of millions of consumers. Now, however, consumer marketers are having to cope with managing relationships with a few powerful buyers (retailers), while many industrial marketers are adopting the branding expertise of their consumer counterparts.

The size of firm and the position on the consumer-industrial spectrum are likely to make the most difference to local marketing practice, though every industry will have its own particular characteristics. Generally, the major difference is likely to be in scale and power: the larger the organization and the nearer to the consumer end of the spectrum, the more resources will be available to marketing, and vice versa. The importance of the elements of the marketing mix (sales force, advertising, exhibitions, price and so on) will also vary dramatically according to context, as will be seen. What remains the same is the basic discipline of marketing thinking.

At a further remove is the situation of not-for-profit organizations. Only relatively recently has it been argued that marketing applies to them at all, and often it is difficult to see the relevance. If one defines the marketing concept broadly enough, however, it applies to all sorts of situations, including personal relationships. It is not very helpful to take it that far, but there is room for discussion in relation to, for example, healthcare, local government and voluntary organizations. Recent political developments have introduced a more overtly commercial element into some of these organizations, but the main thing which separates them from businesses is the lack of profit as an objective and measurement.

There is considerable debate as to whether profit is, can be or should be the main objective of a business; but it is nevertheless a motive which is present. With, for instance, the National Health Service, the problem of marketing becomes more complex. It was argued earlier that the market, defined as the sum total of buying decisions by all customers, would decide between the rival product offerings of competing firms; that logic cannot apply to the NHS. Although an internal market is now operating, which may produce greater efficiencies, it is difficult to extend that concept to the service as delivered to consumers. This is not a political point, but an analysis of the current situation, and it applies to similar public-service situations such as local government. Marketing techniques can be applied: the use of market research to assess consumers' preferences, for example, or the idea of market segmentation to offer different products to different groups. To apply the marketing concept wholeheartedly, however, leads to difficulties. The political dimension means that major decisions on priorities and resource allocation may, and indeed perhaps must, be made without reference to market considerations.

What can be said with some confidence is that any organization would benefit by thinking carefully about who its customers are, what they really want, and how they could best be served. Marketing thinking, and some marketing techniques, could help to achieve the organization's objectives more effectively, and more efficiently.

Development of marketing thinking: old and new marketing

Since marketing tries to adapt the organization to its changing environment, it is not surprising that marketing itself changes over time. There has been a lot of talk in recent years about something called 'the new marketing'. What do people mean by this, and how does it differ from old marketing? The first problem is that different people use the term in different ways. For convenience, we will examine three phases: old marketing, old-new marketing, and new-new marketing. (The impact of the Internet and related technologies is so important that it will be treated separately.)

Old marketing

One analysis of marketing thought distinguishes no less than twelve different approaches (Sheth *et al.* 1988). In approximate order of age, they are:

- Commodity
- Functional
- Regional
- Institutional
- Functionalist
- Managerial
- Buyer behaviour
- Activist
- Macromarketing
- Organizational dynamics
- Systems
- Social exchange.

The detail of all these is not relevant here, but we should note that the literature discussing the earlier schools of thought date back to the first few decades of the twentieth century: there have been many new marketings.

The dominant school in recent decades has been the managerial, or what Ambler and Styles (2000) call the neo-classical or 'Math' approach. This is characterized by an analytical view of markets, and sees the marketing manager's job as being to develop the marketing mix that will optimize return on investment in chosen market segments. It is typified by the Bible of marketing textbooks, Kotler (1967–2000, particularly the earlier editions), and concentrates on the famous Four Ps of Product, Price, Promotion and Place.

Old-new marketing

From the 1980s on, some critics were beginning to suggest that this model was out of date. Increasing recognition of the importance of services in the advanced economies produced suggestions that the Four Ps need to be extended, with the addition of People, Physical evidence and Process.

More radically, some said that they should be replaced entirely:

Four Ps	*Four Cs*
Product	Customer solution
Price	Customer cost
Place	Convenience
Promotion	Communication

(Lauterborn 1990)

More generally, there seemed to be a shift in perceptions of what was important:

From	To
Transactions	Relationships
Sales	Customers
Market share	Customer lifetime value
	Customer retention
	Customer service
Mass	One-to-one

This shift was partly crystallized in the phrase *relationship marketing*, which recognized that most firms have continuing relationships with their customers, and that these are worth preserving and enhancing. In reality, of course, many companies, especially those in business-to-business markets, had always known this. What has happened is that consumer marketers have recognized it too. What it has meant is a new, sharper focus on customer needs, and new ways of measuring marketing success.

The other aspect that changed in this period reflects changing technology. For physical products, new, flexible manufacturing systems meant that the old drive for maximum standardization (to achieve economies of scale) was no longer so important. In many industries, 'mass customization' became possible, at least in theory. Your personal computer is assembled to your own detailed specification, your jeans can be made to your measurements, your car will be assembled according to your individual choice of components and packages. Exactly how much this can be done without unacceptable cost increases varies from industry to industry (and perhaps from firm to firm). So far, it remains more a promise than a reality.

The other technological change was the arrival of cheap computing power. This allowed the capture (through scanning and other methods) of very large amounts of data, these can be stored in large databases and data warehouses, and analysed, in ways that were previously impossible or unaffordable. This permits – again in theory – the one-to-one marketing that is the ideal. We are still in the middle of this development.

Pulling together the new power of data and the focus on customers, many firms adopted *customer relationship management* (CRM). So far, this has been mainly software-driven, with suppliers offering competing packages that claim to tie together all the various data within the firm's systems that relate to a customer. Again, we are early in the development of applications; Chapter 2 treats this in more detail.

New-new marketing

While old-new marketing can be seen as adapting and improving old marketing, new-new marketing claims that the old ways simply do not work any more, and that new methods are needed. In one formulation, Haeckel (1999) says that we must create 'sense-and-respond' organizations. What he means is that the classical approach was, however theoretically consumer-focused, essentially 'make-and-sell'; it assumed a fairly predictable environment in which a firm could set objectives, develop plans, and implement them through a command and control system. Now, he claims, we live in an era of unpredictable (and very rapid) change: we need to have an adaptive organization that responds flexibly to external signals. Alan Mitchell (1999) used the analogy of the supertanker and the cat. The old marketing approach was like a supertanker, gathering masses of data, analysing it slowly, and changing course only gradually and in small increments. The cat hunting a mouse, by contrast, gathers no data: it waits, in complete readiness, and pounces at the right moment. Firms that exemplify this approach, it is claimed, include Virgin and The Body Shop.

The other major argument is that consumers have changed. After the Baby Boomers came Generation X and Generation Y, and their counterparts outside the USA. Members of this new generation are sophisticated in marketing practice: they know what the marketing companies are trying to do, and can deconstruct a campaign with devastating insight. They are sceptical of overclaiming, and want transparency and even truth. They are hedonistic, iconoclastic and informal, and they expect their suppliers to reflect these attitudes.

This view is summed up by a passage by one of the practitioners of 'alternative marketing', Sean Pillot de Chenecey (2000: 2).

Young people have simply begun to refuse to be walking billboards for brands in our consumerist society. Their concern for the environment, for ethical working conditions, an anti-GM food stance and a search for the authentic, real and unique in a branded world; are causing utter confusion for corporations who've got only too used to dividing people up into ABC1 this and C2D2 that. 24 years old – oh you're a young person says the ad man, 25 and you're over the hill. In a world where we've seen an explosion in brands, media and advertising targeting young people, everyone's become so marketing literate (and we've been saying this for nearly a decade), that advertising itself is becoming less and less effective, something that's giving huge cause for concern.

According to New York based Brand Futures Group, 'Marketers' biggest fear is that technology will empower consumers to keep companies out of their lives – meaning no banners, no interstitials, no email, no ads of any kind getting through'. They recently identified an increasing irritation with a 'Nowhere to run, nowhere to hide' life, where there's no escaping corporate messages as marketers make advertising out of everything from toilet walls, golf holes and cornfields, to cows wearing branded plastic jackets. We then see advertisers using ever more extreme measures to cut through all this media clutter and 'Data Smog'. Hence the immoral and (failed) advertising used by the likes of Benetton with their pseudo 'We Care' shock advertising featuring dying AIDS patients and Death Row inmates. The fact that the advertising industry still relies on outdated research to develop this communication, is giving everyone concerned nightmares.

If this view is correct – and it is powerfully argued by Naomi Klein in *No Logo* (2000) – then marketing has a real challenge ahead. We might also note that, while *some* young people are reacting in the way described, many are still perfectly happy to act as 'walking billboards', and are clearly responsive to marketing campaigns whether old or new. What we need to decide is whether the minority represent the future: after all, 'Green' concerns seemed peripheral ten years ago, but Shell and others have discovered that they are now mainstream.

John Grant is one of the founders of St Luke's, a new advertising agency in London that is consciously different, and his book *The New Marketing Manifesto* (1999) is a handy summary of the new approach. He thinks that new marketing is more advanced in Britain than elsewhere, though the phenomenon is widespread. His argument rest on four planks.

1 'New Britain' has seen a creative renaissance in politics, art, music, fashion, design and marketing.

2 New marketing is led by a new generation of people in their twenties and thirties. They are part of Generation X, and different from the older, traditional Baby Boomers.

3 Although new marketing started in 'youth' markets, its influence has spread, and corporate culture is changing even in traditional firms such as Procter and Gamble and BT.

4 New marketing reflects the new, post-traditional society. His solution is to set up *The 12 Rules of New Marketing*.

1 *Get up close and personal*, e.g. Nike, who gets close to its consumers through community programmes such as building basketball courts in deprived areas. (It is interesting that Nike is one of the darlings of the commercial end of new marketing, and also one of the main targets of critics such as Naomi Klein; see case study at the end of this chapter.)

2 *Tap basic human needs*, e.g. Gucci re-positioned from a niche luxury brand to one offering glamour to many.

3 *Author innovation*, e.g. Tetley overthrew 35 years of PG Tips brand leadership by introducing round tea bags.

4 *Mythologize the new*, e.g. as Clark's shoes mythologized a new middle age ('Act your shoe size…').

5 *Create tangible differences in the experience*, e.g. in the beer market, widgets in cans or ice beer.

6 *Cultivate authenticity*, e.g. MTV Unplugged.

7 *Work through consensus*, e.g. the AIDS awareness campaign that tried to get shy couples talking about condoms.

8 *Open up to participation*, as Sainsbury's did with its recipe campaign.

9 *Build communities of interest*, as Oddbins do with their store design, staffing policy and Wine Club concept.

10 *Use strategic creativity*, e.g. Gap using dance to communicate the qualities of khakis.

11 *Stake a claim to fame*, as Richard Branson does for Virgin.

12 *Follow a vision and be true to your values*, as IKEA does.

As we will note later, many of these do not seem very new at all.

Some other forms of new marketing

Apart from new marketing (and its sub-set one-to-one marketing already mentioned), other new phrases have been coined. Some of them, with explanations, follow.

Guerilla marketing: the use of unusual tactics to gain publicity or blindside rivals. Examples include direct attacks on the competitor (easyJet on British Airways' launch of Go, its low-fare airline), press or e-mail campaigns spreading damaging accusations, or blanketing televised stadium events with your posters, when your rival is the official sponsor.

Cause-related marketing: using a good cause to associate your brand with socially desirable ends, such as Tesco's computers for schools campaign.

Permission marketing: asking for explicit permission before contacting a prospect (especially important when 'spam', or unsolicited e-mail, is upsetting many recipients).

Viral marketing: an Internet-based version of word-of-mouth (known to some as word-of-mouse), in which people are encouraged to forward messages to their friends and contacts.

Post-modern marketing: the term 'post-modern' is used in a variety of ways in different contexts, and its application to marketing is by no means self-explanatory. It appears to reflect the view noted earlier, that the new generation is genuinely different from their predecessors, and therefore needs to be researched and approached differently, using a variety of methods. Advertising may be allusive and self-referential, mocking its own cultural framework, as in the Boddington beer ads which consciously subvert previous conventions. Going further, some campaigns adopt the anti-advertising attitudes of the new generation, as in Nike's 'I am not a target market. I am an athlete', or Sprite's 'Image is nothing'. In these we see marketing reacting to criticism, and trying to absorb and reflect essentially anti-marketing attitudes.

How new is new marketing?

The question we must ask is how much of this is really new and different. Some of Grant's examples of the failure of old marketing are simply old marketing done badly, and some of the new marketing successes are simply old marketing done well. Brooke Bond had the technology to make round tea bags before their rivals launched them; they had not bothered, whether from complacency or from a belief that 'If it ain't broke, don't fix it'. There seems nothing new about developing a product improvement and getting it to market before your competitors. Similarly, developing the widget so that canned beer was closer to the draught experience is classic marketing, and hardly new.

On the other hand, some things are different. The main ones can be summarized.

- The younger generation is different in important ways from its predecessors, and must be addressed appropriately. This may demand new ways of researching the market, and new ways of communicating.

- All consumers are becoming more demanding, and have higher expectations of quality, service and response.

- People increasingly want companies to stand behind their products. They would like their suppliers to act responsibly, and to be transparent.

- Some markets are so volatile that a sense-and-respond approach is the only way to stay in touch.

- New technologies do allow new, more finely focused ways of identifying and targeting segments.

- New media are proliferating (not least, of course, the Internet), and old media are fragmenting. There is an increasing need to find a way of integrating all marketing communications, especially when they may be produced by different people in different parts of our own organization, and by different agencies outside.

- Old methods in stable, mature markets, will simply not produce the growth that companies need. Procter and Gamble, previously the most admired marketing firm in the world, probably, has discovered this to its cost.

If all this is to say that marketing firms must understand their customers, and provide what they want (at a profit), then it is merely to re-state what marketing has always been about. If the New Marketing is a wake-up call to firms that had grown smug, complacent and arrogant, who were stuck in old ways of doing everything, then it is valuable and to be welcomed.

These issues will be examined in more detail in subsequent chapters.

Nike: Just Do It – but not like that

Nike can stand as the epitome of new marketing. The result of one of the late twentieth century's most successful branding campaigns, it has been a hero of new marketing prophets. Partly as a result of this success, it has also been the target of the most sustained and detailed attacks by critics.

Nike first became successful by catering to the jogging craze with its high-tech running shoes. When that fad started to subside in the 1980s, it had to reinvent itself. Phil Knight, Nike's charismatic CEO, formulated the new vision: Nike would transform itself into 'the world's best sports and fitness company'. The way it did this was, initially, to choose a few very high-profile sportsmen and promote them as individuals and types: supreme achievers, who represented the ideals of sport in its purest form. The best-known of these in Britain – indeed, probably the best-known sportsman in the world before Tiger Woods – was Michael Jordan. Sports personalities as sponsors and presenters were not new; what was different about the Nike campaign was the use of the best movie and commercial techniques – freeze frames, close-ups, jump cuts and so on – to create 'the first rock videos about sports' (Klein 2000). The Nike campaigns made Jordan into a superbrand in his own right (itself a source of later problems), and the branding as a whole aimed squarely to associate Nike with the idea of individual achievement through sports – 'Just Do It'.

The brand could then be extended from running shoes through basketball to tennis, baseball, to every other sport. Nike tried to identify itself totally with sport by, among other things, starting its own sports agency, buying the Ben Hogan golf tour and re-naming it the Nike Tour, creating a college football team, and even sponsoring the attempted transformation of two Kenyan runners into cross-country skiers (it failed). Brand extension continued through clothing, and identification through the famous 'Swoosh' symbol. So successful has this been that not only Nike employees, but ordinary people have gone so far as to have the swoosh tattooed somewhere on their bodies.

Another creative approach was the opening of Nike Town shops. There are few of these (Nike is not, for obvious reasons, in the business of competing directly with its distributors), and they are temples to the brand and to the idea of sport. They are dedicated 'to all athletes and their dreams', and inspirational quotations about 'Courage', 'Honor', 'Victory' and 'teamwork' are inlaid in the floor (Klein 2000). What these showcases do is to add further glamour to the brand, some of which will rub off on the more down-to-earth transaction of buying an item in the shopping mall or local shop.

More recently, perhaps in reaction to the criticisms discussed below, and to some backlash against the extreme aggression of some of its advertising, Nike has developed its marketing further. They have tried to become what John Grant calls 'up close and personal' (Grant 1999): their series of commercials showing children swinging a golf club and saying 'I'm Tiger Woods', for example, or their sponsorship of 'have a go' urban running road shows and local soccer tournaments.

In the USA, Nike has gone furthest in trying to get close to the community on which it depends. From its Michael Jordan ads onwards, Nike has always been closely associated with urban black youth, for whom success at sport has offered one of the few ways out of the ghetto – and who are the source of much teenage fashion not only in the USA but around the world. Nike staff take new designs into the inner cities on what are called 'bro-ing' expeditions: they show the designs to the inner-city kids and ask, 'Hey, bro, what do you think of these new Jordans – are they fresh or what?' (Klein 2000). They also use philanthropy to increase brand exposure, by building or re-furbishing basketball courts in poor areas of the city; the court has a very large swoosh built into its surface.

All this relentless and pervasive branding was enormously successful well into the 1990s. In the six years to 1993, Nike's sales went from $750 million to $4 billion, and it emerged from the recession of the early 1990s with profits 900 per cent higher. Part of the reason for this was their realization that their central task – their key success factor – was marketing. As Phil Knight put it,

> For years we thought of ourselves as a production-oriented company, meaning that we put all our emphasis on designing and manufacturing the product. But now we understand that the most important thing we do is market the product. We've come around to saying that Nike is a marketing-oriented company, and the product is our most important marketing tool.
>
> (Willigan 1992:92)

With such a neat summary of the marketing concept, and its impressive financial results, it is not surprising that Knight and Nike became heroes to many marketing people.

The new philosophy also contained the seeds of future problems. The logic of the new orientation meant that Nike no longer needed its own manufacturing skill base; it would be cheaper to have the shoes and clothing actually made where production costs were lower. It became a pure marketing company, responsible for branding, the product concept, design and advertising; all production is out-sourced to contract manufacturers around the globe. It is not alone in this, of course, but is one of the models of a new type of virtual business unencumbered by large investments in factories. This is much admired by many in business, but has attracted criticism from others, not only the trade unions whose members lose their jobs when plants are shut down. Nike, because of its very success in making its brand pervasive, has been one of the most prominent targets. The attacks centre around the sweatshop conditions in Third World countries in which so many of the branded products are made. Not only are wages extremely low by western standards, but working conditions are frequently appalling (see, for extended descriptions, Ortega 1999 and Klein 2000). Nike, along with other targets, initially denied that it had any responsibility for its subcontractors, or indeed any knowledge of what went on in their factories. In fact, Nike was for some time protected from the effects of the attacks by its powerful base among the young black population of America: African-American heroes from sportsmen to rappers had been endorsing the brand for a decade, and it remained an icon to teenagers.

Protesters therefore worked through this faithful audience, by demonstrating to them that, for example, the workers in Indonesia who produced the shoes earned $2 a day, and that it cost Nike only $5 to make a shoe that they retailed for between $100 and $180. It is, to say the least, ironic that it is among the poorest section of a wealthy society that a very expensive brand of shoes is the most desirable (and there are many stories of teenagers being beaten up or even killed for their new trainers). Protests such as the dumping of hundreds of old Nike shoes in front of the prestigious Nike Town store in New York by African-American youths finally led Nike to respond. In 1998 and 1999, it issued a number of statements and policies designed to improve conditions for its subcontracted workers, and there was some progress.

The effects on Nike, however, were significant. After years of uninterrupted growth in sales and profits, both began to falter, and its stock price reflected those trends. It began to recover in 1999, but its sales were still suffering in comparison with Adidas, one of its main rivals. It may seem unfair that Adidas has adopted the Nike model too, but has avoided much of the criticism. Nike is the victim of its own success: as market leader, it had flown highest, made the loftiest claims, been most successful in imprinting its image on the world's consciousness. As one its most cogent critics, Naomi Klein, put it, 'Nike was the most inflated of all the balloon brands, and the bigger it grew, the louder it popped'.

There are many lessons here for marketers.

■ Fierce focus on getting inside the minds of target consumers, and staying there, will bring enormous rewards in sales and loyalty.

■ Aggressive efforts to extend the brand, carefully directed, can capitalize on a powerful initial position if the central brand proposition is itself broad enough.

■ The determined commitment of large resources to marketing, using creative techniques and genuine innovation, can build a global brand, recognized (and bought) by millions.

■ But there are dangers to unfettered aggression. Nike did well to recognize this, and try to become more human, more 'up close and personal'. It may not be enough.

■ Consumers – at least, many of the most influential ones – want companies to stand behind their brand. That means taking responsibility for all its operations and their effects, wherever they are. The bigger and more successful the brand, the greater target area it provides.

■ Complacency is a perpetual danger. Nike got it so right for so long that they began to believe that they could do no wrong, that they were invulnerable.

Key learning points

■ **Marketing as a concept suggests that a company will succeed by focusing on what customers want rather than on what the company thinks it can produce. This focus should inform all the company's strategies and operations.**

- Any one company will choose which customers to serve, and which of those customers' needs it can meet profitably.

- As a management function, marketing identifies markets and tries to establish what buyers in that market want: what benefits and satisfactions are they seeking? Taking account of what competitors are offering, it helps the company to design products and services which will be attractive to buyers, and which have *sustainable competitive advantage*.

- It is then marketing's role to make sure that the products are known to customers and are available to them at the right time, in suitable quantities and at an acceptable price.

- Increasing competition will ensure that only firms which respond to changes in the marketplace will survive; marketing thinking will be essential to that response.

- Although the principles of marketing remain the same, its practice will vary according to context. It also changes and develops to meet new challenges.

Further reading

Klein, N. (2000) *No Logo*, London: Flamingo.
Kotler, P. (2000) *Marketing Management*, Millennium edition, Upper Saddle River, NJ: Prentice Hall.

Case study: Alderson's

Alderson's is a medium-sized Midlands firm, founded in the 1930s. Originally a typical 'metal-basher' carrying out subcontract work, it grew rapidly during the 1960s, making components and body parts for the motor industry. A garden furniture line was set up, which was reasonably successful, and the company has experimented with hand tools and related equipment such as wheelbarrows.

The founder retired in 1990, and his daughter has been chair and managing director since then. Younger members of the family are working their way up through the firm. One of them, Harry, has recently been on a management development course, and has learned about marketing. He is keen to put his ideas into practice, but fears that he will meet resistance from the established managers.

Harry has done some preliminary work: his notes are summarized below.

- Sales peaked in 1993 at £30 million; they are now £25 million.

- Major customers in the car industry have cut back; the outlook is not good in the short term; 35 per cent of sales.

- Other engineering also affected by slowdown in manufacturing industry in the late 1990s: 20 per cent of sales.

- Garden furniture doing all right, especially considering there is no sales force. DIY seems to be a growing market – could we get in there?

■ No information on profitability of the various lines.

Questions

1 How would you recommend that Harry proceeds?

2 Draft the outline of a report that Harry might prepare for the board, setting out the arguments in favour of adopting a marketing approach. What benefits might Alderson's expect from this new way of doing business?

3 Take your own organization: how well (if at all) is the marketing function carried out? Who is responsible for marketing? What changes would you like to see to make the organization more responsive to customers' and/or consumers' needs?

Chapter 2 | Marketing strategy: delivering customer value

Customer value

Without customers, a business does not exist. What customers buy is value. It follows that:

the central function of a business is to create and deliver customer value.

What marketing must focus on, therefore, is what our chosen customers want, what they value, and how we can deliver it better than competitors. We must judge this value *from the customer's point of view*, not from our own. It is very easy – and extremely common – for people to become focused on the internal details of the company's operations: to develop fixed ideas about what customers want, and how well our products or services deliver. What is important is not technical details, or what our experts tell us, but what potential buyers perceive.

Value is the difference between total cost and total perceived value delivered. For a simple product, this would be the price paid, and some holistic, probably qualitative judgement of perceived value: we pay 28 pence for a bar of chocolate, we enjoy it, and are satisfied. Products that are more complex need more explanation, since we do not always buy the product at the cheapest possible price; we take many things into account. One model (Kotler 2000: 35; see Figure 2.1) suggests that we can break down value and cost into four elements. The value of a product centres on its functional benefits, but we may also take account of service elements, such as advice from a salesperson, or availability from stock. We may gain personal value because we have a long-standing relationship with the seller. Finally, we may derive some benefit from the image of the brand or supplier. Standing at a smart bar with our friends, we may gain considerable value from the designer label on our jeans; but when we are clearing out the garage, we are happy with a cheap, own-label pair.

Similarly, the total cost is based on the money we pay, but there are other costs too, notably the time and energy it takes to buy and use the item. There may be psychological costs, such as the risk. The more complex the buying decision, the more we need to elaborate beyond simple price and value judgements.

The value of customers

The other side of the coin is that customers have value for the firm. As we noted in the previous chapter, the last decade has seen an increasing recognition of how much a customer is worth over the time they stay with a supplier. Even for ordinary purchases such as groceries, a loyal shopper can be worth a substantial amount. If someone shopping for a family spends £100 a week in a supermarket, for 48 weeks a year, then over a ten-year period their custom would be worth £48,000. The lifetime value of a loyal car buyer would be very much higher (in all such examples, we would discount future cash flows using the

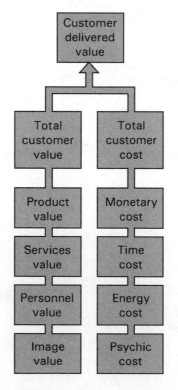

 Figure 2.1 Determinants of customer-delivered value
Source: Kotler (2000)

techniques you will have learned in accounting). Even if the accounting system does not allow exact calculation of costs and revenue, rough estimates will show how much a customer is worth.

The value is enhanced by the relative cost of retaining existing customers against the cost of finding new ones. It costs at least five times as much to recruit a new customer as to keep an existing one, and on average, firms lose 10 per cent of their customers a year (in some fields, such as mobile phones, the loss or 'churn rate' is very much higher). To clinch the argument, evidence shows that reducing the rate of loss by 5 percentage points can raise profits by 25 per cent to 85 per cent, according to one estimate (Reichheld 1996), or by 35 to 95 per cent according to another (Reichheld 1994; see Figure 2.2; Zeithaml and Bitner 2000: 145). What is surprising is not that some firms now focus intensely on serving customers well, but that others have apparently not yet realized how vital it is.

Customer satisfaction

If we deliver value to customers, we assume that they will be satisfied. It is important to us that they stay satisfied, so that they repurchase, so we need to measure satisfaction and dissatisfaction. Satisfaction results from comparing the consumer's perception of value delivered with their expectations. If we have low expectations, then we are satisfied with relatively low performance, especially if we have little choice of alternatives. At the other end of the scale, if our expectations are high, then even a reasonably good product or service may leave us feeling dissatisfied. If we pay a high price for a meal in a restaurant with a good reputation, we would be dissatisfied with food that, in a different context, we would find quite acceptable.

Satisfied customers are what firms should aim for, but we should enter one note of caution. You need to be very careful about measuring satisfaction, and interpreting the

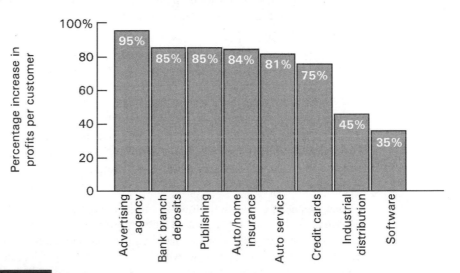

Figure 2.2 Profit impact of 5 per cent increase in retention rate
Reprinted with permission from *Marketing Management*, published by the American Marketing Association, Frederick E. Reichheld, 1994 vol. 2, no. 4.

results. In California, the insurance companies might have felt very happy that they received satisfaction ratings of over 95 per cent – but soon afterwards, the same customers voted overwhelmingly for Proposition 103, which forced an immediate 20 per cent reduction in insurance rates (Aaker 1991). Clearly, the way that satisfaction was measured somehow missed a huge well of resentment and frustration.

There are five ways that we can measure satisfaction.

1 *Complaints.* Many companies still hate complaints, and prefer to ignore them. Others actively encourage their customers to complain, which seems perverse. However, you can learn a lot from the nature and trend of complaints. It is important to encourage them, because, as you will know from personal experience, most complaints go un-made: we simply cannot be bothered to go through the process. Unfortunately, the evidence shows that those who feel dissatisfied but do not complain are the most likely not to repurchase. Those who complain *and whose complaint is resolved* are actually most likely to return, even more than those who are moderately satisfied (Zeithaml and Bitner 2000).

2 *Free telephone lines, Internet.* Many firms offer a free telephone line (0800 numbers in Britain) for customers to use, or encourage them to contact the company through the Internet. A dialogue will provide help when it is needed, perhaps head off problems before they arise and build the relationship.

3 *Surveys.* Surveys can either be of the self-completion type, or conventional market research. Self-administered surveys are familiar from the short questionnaires placed in hotel rooms, restaurants and aeroplanes. These can be useful, but suffer from a problem of low completion rates. More formal surveys (see Chapter 6) will provide a more accurate picture, but of course cost more. The advantage of a formal survey, apart from its accuracy, is objectivity: people answering questions from a neutral research company are more likely to give unbiased responses than if they know they are talking to the firm itself. Many firms use customer panels, that is respondents who agree to answer questions on a regular basis. These provide data on trends, but may be less unbiased than objective surveys.

4 *Mystery shoppers.* These are people employed to buy a product or use a service as if they were ordinary customers, then provide a structured report back, for example rating various elements of the service. They are commonly used by airlines, hotels and similar services, but may also be valuable to find out, for example, what advice shop assistants give to prospective buyers of consumer durables.

5 *Lost customer analysis.* All businesses lose customers, but as it so important to minimize the rate of loss, it makes sense to try to find out what makes them leave. This can be done by personal interviews (similar to the exit interviews with staff leaving an employer), or by surveys.

None of this is a substitute for keeping in close personal touch with customers. All marketing people – and arguably a selection of everyone in the firm who contributes to the delivery of customer value – should have regular contact with real customers, preferably in their home, place of work, or wherever they consume the product or service. Information derived from such contact may be qualitative and unrepresentative (it should be checked against more reliable data), but is rich and alive.

Relationship marketing

In Chapter 1, we noted that the new emphasis on customers led to the development of what was called relationship marketing, but noted also that the approach had been common for many years in business-to-business markets. Indeed, in Europe, a group known as IMP (the Industrial Marketing and Purchasing Research Group) has been publishing their findings since the early 1980s. They recognized that, in industrial markets, there was *interaction* between buyers and sellers, and what was then taught as consumer marketing was not appropriate for such relationships. What relationship marketing has done is simply to adopt this perspective for consumer markets.

We should stress that not all markets are necessarily suitable for relationship marketing, nor do all firms want to act in that way. Some markets remain predominantly transaction-based, particularly those that deal in commodities. Many buying situations in business-to-business sectors focus on price, and the relationship between buyer and seller is adversarial, with buyers playing suppliers off against each other. Both buyer and seller need to determine with whom, and when, a relationship approach would be more beneficial, and with whom to stay transaction-oriented.

Where a relationship is appropriate, the aim is to bring together the three areas of the firm that were too often treated separately: quality, customer service and marketing (Christopher *et al.* 1991: 4; see Figure 2.3). Quality had been the preserve of total quality management programmes, and often, customer service was divorced from the marketing function. Bringing them together recognized that only by working as part of one overall unit could the firm as a whole measure what customers wanted, design and deliver the product/service package, measure the levels of customer satisfaction and feed the results back into corrective action.

The aim of the co-ordinated effort is to move customers up the *loyalty ladder* (Figure 2.4). The further customers are up the ladder, the more the company's emphasis is on retention, developing and enhancing the relationship; at the lower, transaction-based end, the emphasis is on finding new customers all the time.

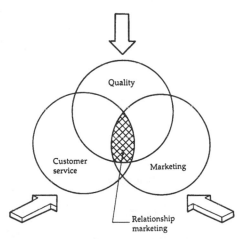

Figure 2.3 The relationship marketing orientation: bringing together customer service, quality and marketing
From *Relationship Management* by Christopher, Payne and Ballantyne. Reprinted by permission of Butterworth Heinemann Publishers.

Figure 2.4 The loyalty ladder

To manage a relationship, the firm must understand all the interactions between itself and the customer. Once this is done, through flow chart analysis of the process, it is possible to identify contact points, product and information flows, and potential blockages and bottlenecks. Some firms (and indeed textbooks) seemed to think that the only contact point was that between the salesperson or account manager and the buyer – the so-called 'bow-tie model' (see Figure 2.5). In practice, many others are involved, including technical people, accounts, operations, IT and logistics. It is this sort of analysis that leads to the development of business teams mentioned above: only a team, acting together, can deliver customer satisfaction.

As this approach grew, alongside it developments in computing became more relevant. Database analysis enabled customer data to be tracked, so that future marketing campaigns could be more finely targeted. New company-wide systems attempted to standardize and link together all the different functions and their reporting systems (Enterprise Resource Planning software). From this is a short step to *customer relationship management* (CRM) software, which tries to bring together all the data that affect the delivery of customer value. In theory, this is excellent, but the practice has not always lived up to the promise.

CRM has been essentially software-driven, with different suppliers trying to sell their own particular approach. The problems of implementation arise from the fact that it is

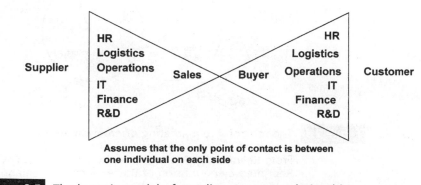

Figure 2.5 The bow-tie model of supplier–customer relationships

usually the IT person, such as the Chief Information Officer, who leads the introduction – but its success depends on co-operation from people in operations, marketing and other functions. This may involve real culture change.

Steve Diorio, principal of Stamford, Conn.-based IMT Strategies put his finger on the problem with a lot of CRM practices today: 'I feel like a marriage counselor when I go around to a lot of these companies. Over the past six months I've been with 30 companies' CIO and marketing guys, and the level of co-operation now looks like kids in a street fight' (*Best Principles to Practice for Effective CRM*, 2000: http://adsections.businessweek.com/care/relationships/crm_effective.htm).

The way to improve rests on several principles.

1 *Involve top management.* This is fundamental to any such organizational change, and little will happen without it.

2 *Restructure employee compensation to reinforce CRM priorities.* Much of the problem, of course, is a company pushing a new set of customer-centric priorities while the old set of compensation practices remains the same. In other words, not 'walking the talk'. Cisco Systems, for example, rewards employees based on whether the company hits customer satisfaction targets.

3 *Concentrate on customer lifetime value.* We have seen how looking at lifetime value changes our perception of the value of an individual customer. This must remain the focus, and enhancing it the purpose of the CRM system.

4 *'Bulldoze goat paths, don't pave them'.* Insight Technology Group's Jim Dickie says,

> Time and again, I have heard executives lament about how they started focusing on technology too soon in the process. If you use 21st century technology to pave a goat path, you will end up with a really smooth goat path. But, it is still a goat path. If your process is fundamentally flawed, technology may give you boost, but more likely it will end up helping you do inefficient or ineffective things faster than ever before. (Ibid.)

5 *Provide training and support. Prepare for continuous improvement.*

   ■ Train new employees. New employees will require the same level of training as your existing personnel.

   ■ Maintain adequate system support. For example, if you are asking your sales teams or channel partners to manage their business through a CRM system, you must give them a fast, easy way to get support.

   ■ Plan appropriate enhancements and upgrades. You will continue to improve the way you sell over time, so your system will need to be enhanced accordingly. Budget for that now. (This and much else on CRM can be found at http://adsections.businessweek.com/care/relationship/. Case studies of CRM applications can be seen on the Websites of the software suppliers, such as www.sas.com/news/success/, www.ibm.com/e-business/crm/, www.quadstone.co.uk, www.siebel.com/eBusiness Applications/Marketing Application, www.oracle.com, www.sgi.com/software/mindset/.)

CRM is still developing, even in the USA (which, as in so many other fields of management theory and practice, is leading Europe: to keep up with developments, see the website www.crmguru.com).

Marketing strategy: delivering customer value

So far, we have seen that customers look for value, and that is what firms must try to offer them, better than competitors. We have looked at the importance of customer lifetime value and therefore customer retention; and we have described the growth of integrated systems of relationship marketing. What draws all these together is marketing strategy, which is the way that a firm decides how it is going to compete in a given market. Following our argument, strategy is about choosing the value to be delivered, and how to provide it to customers.

- *Choose the value.* This involves:

  — segmentation of the market (see Chapter 7)
  — selection of the segments to serve
  — choice of a particular value positioning (see Chapter 8).

- *Provide the value.* This covers:

  — product and service development (see Chapter 10)
  — pricing (Chapter 11)
  — operations design and implementation
  — communications development (Chapters 12 and 13)
  — channel design (Chapter 14).

The process of strategy development and implementation consists of the main stages of:

- *analysis* of environments, markets and buyers (Chapters 4 and 5)
- *strategy development* (this chapter, below)
- *development of the marketing plan* (Chapter 18)
- *implementation* (Chapter 18).

The rest of the book will explore and amplify each topic in turn.

What do we mean by strategy?

Strategy has become an over-used word in business literature and discussion, and this over-use has weakened and blurred its meaning. Let us return to its roots. The *Oxford English Dictionary* shows its derivation from the Greek word for the office of a commander or general, and defines it as:

The art of a commander-in-chief; the art of projecting and directing the larger military movements and operations of a campaign. Usually distinguished from *tactics*, which is the art of handling forces in battle or in the immediate presence of the enemy.

Strategy is therefore broad in scope and looks to the overall pattern of events, the big picture. It cannot, however, make sense on its own, without some context and, more particularly, some clear objectives. As Clausewitz, the great writer on military strategy, pointed out, war is the continuation of diplomacy by other means – but both diplomacy and war need a defined goal and a set of objectives otherwise it is impossible to choose an appropriate strategy.

The two ideas – of an overriding goal and of a commander-in-chief's broad direction of affairs – are directly applicable to business (and other types of organization).

It is up to the chairman/chief executive to set the organization's goals and broad strategy: where do we want to go, and how do we get there? Although logically the goal comes first, the strategy being merely the means of achieving it, in practice the two interact, and the process of strategy development (as of all planning) is iterative: the strategy which the organization is capable of adopting may affect the goals it is aiming for.

A problem with business is that the firm may be very large, with many divisions, hundreds of products, and scores of subsidiary companies. The idea of a single strategy becomes blurred. It is helpful to distinguish between different levels of strategy. One such division is as follows:

■ **Corporate strategy** The determination of the businesses in which a company will compete and the allocation of resources among the businesses.

■ **Institutional strategy** The basic character and vision of a company.

■ **Business strategy** The determination of how a company will compete in a given business and position itself among its competitors.

(Hamermesh 1986)

We are concerned here with the further level in the hierarchy, in which business strategy is translated into function or departmental objectives and strategies, as in the wheel illustrated in Figure 2.6. In anything other than a small organization, there are bound to be several levels in the hierarchy; what is a strategy at one level becomes an objective for the next level down. Thus market share may form part of a higher-level strategy, but becomes the objective of a lower one; the marketing strategy at this level will need to incorporate the means of achieving market share goals.

Ansoff defined strategy as, 'A set of decision-making rules for guidance of organizational behaviour' (Ansoff 1984). The marketing strategy of a company will therefore be a broad, relatively long-term description of how the company will compete in its chosen markets and segments; it should guide the tactical decisions which will have to be made as circumstances change throughout the implementation phase, ensuring that the organization does not stray too far from the desired path and that it keeps moving towards its defined goals.

Types of strategy

The best-known categorization of strategies is that of Porter. He suggested that a firm's strategy could be defined on a matrix in terms of its competitive scope and its competitive advantage (Figure 2.7).

Porter suggests that, as an example, within shipbuilding Japanese firms follow a differentiated strategy, offering a wide range of ships of superior quality at a premium

Figure 2.6 The wheel of strategy

price. Korean yards offer good but not superior quality over a wide range at a lower price (cost leadership). Some Scandinavian firms concentrate on a few specialized types of vessel of high quality and price (focused differentiation); while emerging Chinese yards offer a narrow range of simple, standard ships at very low cost (cost focus) (Porter 1990). The force of Porter's argument is that only one of these 'generic strategies' will be successful: a firm must choose one and only one, or they will be 'stuck in the middle' and vulnerable to better-focused competitors. This contention, it should be said, is not universally accepted, but the model is useful in forcing top management to think deeply about the overall competitive positioning of the firm.

The relationship between a firm's marketing strategy and its overall generic strategy is similar to that between objectives and strategy. Logically, the marketing strategy must follow on from and serve the overall strategy; but the analysis of what is possible in marketing terms may affect the overall objectives and generic strategy. Thus the firm might decide to be a low-cost leader: this might demand market leadership (in order to gain the necessary economies of scale), but if the company's current position were only third or fourth, rigorous market analysis might suggest that leadership would not be attainable in reality; the objectives and generic strategy might then have to be revised. This is particularly true when corporate objectives are set in purely financial terms (growth in profits, return on capital employed, earnings per share, etc.). Merely setting an objective does not make it feasible, and it is frequently marketing's task to find growth to fill the gap between what the current business can achieve and what the new objectives demand.

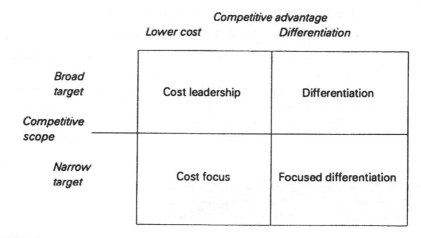

Figure 2.7 Porter's matrix

Since most corporate strategies demand growth in most if not all their businesses, marketing strategies must follow. The product-market matrix comes into play once more (Figure 2.8).

The iterative loop between marketing and corporate strategy will determine the product-market scope: in which markets and with which types of product the company will compete. The marketing strategy will then have to determine how to achieve the targets in each market segment: how to develop further penetration of existing markets, how to develop which new markets, and so on.

The types of marketing strategy available can be categorized in broad terms only:

- Mass market, or niche
- Offensive or defensive
- High-quality, premium priced, or cheap and cheerful

Mission \ Product	Present	New
Present	Market penetration	Product development
New	Market development	Diversification

Figure 2.8 Ansoff's matrix
Reproduced with permission

- Broad or narrow, deep or shallow product line
- Consumer-based pull or channel-based push.

Most of these strategies will be discussed in subsequent chapters. The last needs a brief explanation. A pull strategy is one in which the differentiated benefits of the brand, supported by heavy advertising, creates consumer demand which 'pulls' supplies through the distribution chain. A push strategy concentrates on pushing stocks into the channels, whose efforts are relied on to sell the products out to buyers and/or consumers. In reality, of course, many firms use a combination of both strategies.

Fitting the strategy to company, market, channels and competition

The first question concerns the company's current strategy, or perhaps whether it has a strategy at all – a coherent set of rules for tackling its marketing tasks. If such a strategy can be identified, is it appropriate?

It may of course not be sensible to talk of a single strategy. The firm may have a wide range of products and markets, and different strategies may have been adopted for each. A single overall marketing strategy might be adopted, for example, a company could have the following stance:

- **Objective** Number one or two brand in defined consumer markets.
- **Strategy** Each brand must have a functional differentiation from competitors and be of superior quality as measured by blind product tests; it will be supported by heavy advertising (competitive parity or greater) and as little trade promotion as possible.

Such an objective–strategy approach could be very effective if followed rigorously (it looks very similar to that adopted by, for example, Procter and Gamble); but it would lead to hard decisions about product deletion, and demands large financial resources as well as determined discipline. On the other hand, if markets are narrowly defined and the company is a niche player, a similar form of strategy could be suitable.

Thus, the company must start from where it is; the strategy must be feasible for this company in this market now. This is not to say that objectives should not be ambitious and stretching, but to stress that they should be realistic. To go from 2 per cent market share to 30 per cent in two years is extremely unlikely (without a revolutionary new product which no one can copy), and no strategy could achieve it. However, to go from 10 per cent to 15 per cent over several years may be much more achievable, but even then the strategy must be one which the company can afford and can implement.

This suggests that each strategy, whether a single overall marketing strategy for the whole company or one of a series aimed at a group of product-market sectors, should be tested against a set of questions.

1 What will it cost? How will this be financed?
2 How different is it from existing strategies?
3 If very different, what effect will it have on existing channels and consumers?
4 How will competitors react?
5 What changes in behaviour, by whom (channel buyers, users, consumers) is required?

What does the strategy do to encourage such changes? What are the barriers to those changes?

6 What are the critical success factors for this strategy? Which do we control?

7 What will happen if any of the assumptions we have made (about the environment, markets, customers, consumers, competitors) turn out to be wrong? Is the strategy sufficiently flexible to cope?

8 What skills are needed to implement this strategy? Do they exist, or can they be developed in time?

Experience suggests that some of these questions (particularly 4, 5, 7 and 8) are not asked, or are answered superficially.

A strategy is long term, and should be adopted only after the most thorough analysis; it cannot be changed at every turn of events without severely weakening its impact.

In arriving at a strategy, the managers concerned need to have used all the available information, to have evaluated it objectively, and to have avoided wishful thinking about themselves, the rest of the company, and competitors. Ideally, they should also have injected some real flair and creativity into the strategy, giving it the power to engender enthusiasm in colleagues, partners such as channel members, and buyers. This is a challenge, but marketing should be challenging!

The other major problem is that implicit in question 1: will the company provide the resources needed? Unfortunately, many marketing strategies which demand the investment of major amounts of cash find themselves crippled half-way through implementation by the slashing of budgets. It could be argued that this is the fault of the marketing people for not convincing top management of the absolute necessity for continuing support. Political reality in many firms means that such arguments are more often won by cautious accountants taking a short-term view; they can be won by marketing only if very good evidence is presented which proves that investment now will definitely lead to greater profits soon – and as we have seen, very good evidence of the effects of marketing action is rare.

To summarize, a good strategy will fit the company and its resources, will consistently target the chosen market segment, will differentiate itself from competitors, and will offer real benefits to intermediaries and final consumers; it will, it goes without saying, meet the company's objectives. It should specify how the chosen segment will be targeted and outline the roles of the different elements of the marketing mix.

Key learning points

- **The central purpose of a company is to deliver customer value.**
- **The company needs to recognize customers' lifetime value.**
- **Customer retention is often more important, and more profitable, than finding new customers.**
- **The firm should measure customer satisfaction regularly.**

- **In many sectors, relationship marketing is the best approach to keeping customers.**
- **Marketing strategy is about deciding which segments to target, and how to deliver value to chosen customers.**
- **Strategy is broad in scope and looks to the overall pattern of events. It exists to achieve an overriding goal.**
- **Marketing strategy is informed by the overall corporate strategy, but should in its turn help to shape that strategy.**
- **Marketing strategy needs to be matched to the company itself, and to its markets, channels and competitors.**

Further reading

Lanning M.J. (1998) *Delivering Profitable Value*, Oxford: Capstone.
Knox S. and Maklan S. (1998) *Competing on Value: Bridging the Gap Between Brand and Customer Value*, London: Financial Times.

Case study: Welcome Hotels

Edith Seth is head of marketing for the Welcome Hotels group. Welcome has two main chains: one (Executive) of three- and four-star hotels near major cities, aimed at business people and better-off independent travellers; and one (SpeedRest) which consists of budget motels close to motorways and main roads. Both cover several countries in Europe; Welcome's market share varies by country and by chain, from market leader in a few, to fourth or fifth in many. Competition is increasing, both from local companies and from international groups. Customer expectations are also rising, fed by competitive offers and marketing efforts.

Welcome has tried to measure customer satisfaction, although Edith is not satisfied that their method, which relies on customers filling in cards left in rooms, is entirely reliable. She thought that their satisfaction levels, at around 80 per cent, were good, but has recently heard at a conference that one of their rivals achieves 90 per cent. On a visit to Canada, she had been impressed by the customer care delivered by the chain she stayed in, and thought she could apply some of their practices in Europe.

Questions

1 How can Welcome deliver better customer value, in both the Executive and SpeedRest chains?

2 Assuming that Welcome's aim is to continue to grow sales at ten per cent a year or more, outline a marketing strategy.

3 Examine the way that your employer delivers customer value. Do you measure customer satisfaction? How? (If not, how should you go about it?)

Chapter 3 | E-commerce and marketing

Introduction

The last five years of the twentieth century saw one of the fastest and potentially most profound of all the changes our world has seen – the growth of the Internet and the World Wide Web. Jack Welch, CEO of General Electric, and probably the most admired businessman of his time, called it the most important development he had witnessed in his career. To cope with it, he called on his managers to '*destroy your business*', so that they could rebuild a new model for the different world that was approaching. As a priority, he said, e-commerce ranked number one, two, three and four (*Business Week*, June 1999). The sad story of one famous brand illustrates the wrenching change that the new world can produce.

Encyclopaedia Britannica, the most famous encyclopaedia in English, started in 1768. Moving to America in the 1920s, it went from strength to strength: its comprehensive and authoritative content was allied with aggressive marketing to build what seemed an unassailable position. The peak was reached in 1990, but since then, sales have fallen by over 80 per cent. *Encyclopaedia Britannica* had been overtaken by a new technology – the CD-ROM. Whereas a full set of *Britannica* cost the consumer at least $1500, a CD-ROM rival cost only $50, and in practice was increasingly bundled 'free' with a PC. The new encyclopaedias were not serious competitors, in breadth or quality of content, but to consumers they were apparently good enough.

Britannica dithered, at first refusing to treat the newcomers seriously. As sales continued to plummet, they then considered producing a CD-ROM version of their own, only to find that their forty million words would not fit on to one disc, at least with illustrations and interactivity. When they produced a text-only version, the sales force revolted, as the CD-ROM could not produce anything like the $500–600 commission they were used to on the printed volumes. The company bundled the disc with the printed set, and sold it separately for $1000. Sales continued to fall, and the company itself was put up for sale. The price of the CD-ROM was reduced to $125, but eventually, in 1999, the company recognised the inevitable, and put the whole content on the Web, free.

(Evans and Wurster 2000, www.britannica.com)

There are several lessons here. The most frightening is that a two hundred year old brand, in a seemingly impregnable position, can be destroyed in just five years – and by a technically inferior product (though Christensen (2000) argues that this is just what happens with a disruptive technology: see Chapter 10). The management lesson is that a strong company culture, developed over many years of success, may be a formidable barrier to rapid and decisive action, when radical change demands it. The management knew – or certainly ought to have known, from their research and from years of experience – that the *Britannica* brand was about aspiration and parental guilt. Parents bought the encyclopaedia to do something for their children's education, but the average set was opened less than once a year. The product was grossly over-engineered for its actual use. When the world changed, parents could buy a PC for their children; the PC, its software, and the Web provided all the help the children needed, and the fact that *Encarta* (the Microsoft CD-ROM encyclopaedia) was part of the package removed the last vestige of need for *Britannica*.

The final lesson is that, even when managers recognize and respond to the changes, there may be little they can do. They are saddled with an obsolete business model, and with assets that once held real value, but are now worthless. The *Britannica* sales force was superbly effective in its day, but now had no purpose. The magnificent content remained, but no one wanted to pay for it. It is significant that Evans and Wurster, who tell this story in their enlightening *Blown to Bits: how the new economics of information transforms strategy* (2000), thought that there was a happy ending. 'But there is hope', they wrote (p. 7):

> Britannica under its new management has produced a moderately successful CD-ROM product. It goes far beyond its competitors ... The brand guarantees, as do few others, the seriousness and reliability of the content. The hope is to rise above the clutter and mediocrity that have proliferated in the early years of the Internet and build anew something of permanent value.

As we know, even that model did not work, and it is unclear whether *Britannica* will survive in any form.

Not all industries, and not all brands will suffer so dramatically. The challenge for managers is to look ahead and try to discern, however dimly, what the likely effects on their industry will be. There are two mistakes in forecasting the future: to assume that *everything* will be different, and to assume that *nothing* will be different. This chapter will examine what functions the Internet performs, and how marketing will be affected.

Some underlying concepts

The Internet is different in some ways from 'old economy' businesses, though what marks it out is a combination of factors, some of which we also see elsewhere. The first idea is one it shares with some more conventional industries, in that it is information based. Information, unlike physical products, does not lose its value by being used by one buyer: it can be used again and again by different people (although the value of certain sorts of commercial information can be increased by restricting it to one or a small number of buyers).

More importantly, the Internet benefits from the *network effect*, through which the value of a system increases as a multiplier of the number of members. One telephone on its own has no value. Two telephones that can communicate with each other begin to be valuable, and the value of the network then increases as a multiple of the number that can communicate with each other. Three telephones produce three potential links, four produce six, five produce 10, and so on. As the number of people using the Internet has risen into the hundreds of millions, the number of potential connections has risen astronomically, to produce a network of previously undreamt of size and richness.

What makes communication possible between all these members is the existence of *standards*. The invention of the World Wide Web and its associated protocols enabled computers using different operating systems and languages to talk to each other, allowing non-expert users to move freely around the Web with clickable hyperlinks and unique addresses (URLs, or Universal Resource Locators). A common language (currently HTML, or HyperText Mark-up Language) for Web pages allows any suitable browser, such as Netscape or Microsoft's Internet Explorer to read any of the billions of pages posted on the Web.

Another effect which we see in many other areas of contemporary life is known as '*winner takes all*': competition for the very best – or most popular – singer, football player, or even top manager, is so fierce that the few individuals at the apex of the pyramid can command huge rewards, seemingly out of all proportion to their efforts or to what others, only slightly less good, receive. It seems likely that the most popular Website in a particular field will gain an increasing lead over rivals, as users will want to go only to the one 'best' site. Amazon.com, for example, was early into the field of selling books over the Internet, and through aggressive expansion has built up such a lead over later arrivals that it seems unlikely ever to be caught. The number of so-called e-tailers who have merged with rivals, or failed, suggest that the effect is real (though of course over-supply and hopelessly optimistic forecasts of what business would be available have contributed too).

Finally, what marks out the Web as special is *speed of development*. It only started to become a commercial proposition in around 1994. Estimates are necessarily inexact, but one authoritative source puts the number of people online in September 2000 as 377 million, of whom 105 million are in Europe, and 161 million in Canada and the USA (www.nua.ie). This is a staggering rate of growth, and the pace at which Internet access has penetrated society is very much faster than any previous new technology. Anyone who wants to keep up to date has to do so on a weekly basis, if not daily, as Websites appear (and disappear) with bewildering speed. All we can do at a fixed point of time is to try to discern the general patterns that are emerging, but we have already seen many confident predictions proved false, so we must accept that really, no one knows exactly what the future holds.

Classifying Internet business

Amongst the vast array of Internet businesses, we can distinguish two major categories, and two lesser ones (Figure 3.1). Business-to-business, or B2B, is now and will remain by far the largest in revenue – around 70 per cent of the total. The Internet can dramatically reduce the costs of searching for suppliers, getting information, and buying industrial goods and services. Purchasing in many industries has already migrated largely to the Web, and this seems certain to be the major trend affecting B2B marketing. The shift is happening very quickly: 46 per cent of UK suppliers had e-commerce solutions to sell more efficiently to their business customers in place by Autumn 2000, compared with only half that only six months previously (*Marketing Business*, October 2000: 5). No business selling to other organizations can afford not to be Internet-aware, and ready to do business over the Web. The current trend is for industries to set up exchanges that allow all participants to buy and sell. A typical example is Covisint, set up by the major American car manufacturers and joined by some others. Such exchanges have proliferated, but it is not clear how many will survive. Assuming that they pass regulatory scrutiny (competition officials in both Europe and the USA are concerned about possible monopoly effects), then exchanges offer great potential benefits of cost and efficiency. The winner-takes-all effect is likely to ensure that only one survives in each field, and indeed the first casualties have already appeared. Supply chain management in general will become more efficient as time and cost are squeezed out by the instant availability of information.

Companies can also use the Internet to offer additional services to their customers, by allowing access to information on stocks, sales and likely future needs, for example. Even small and medium-sized firms can use the Web, as it is much cheaper and easier than the previous proprietary system, EDI (Electronic Data Exchange).

B2C has been the most hyped area, but has also been the scene of the most dramatic rise and then fall in valuations. In the late 1990s, venture capital for start-ups was freely available, and new ventures were announced daily. Dot-com billionaires were created by initial public offerings that were bought in a feeding frenzy by investors desperate to get a share of the action; valuations of companies with no profits, and sometimes no sales, were crazy. A necessary correction came in 2000, and many of the companies went bankrupt. Investors and analysts began to take a more realistic view, and looked for a real possibility that a company would make profits within the foreseeable future. This shake-out seems likely to continue. We return to e-tailing in more detail below.

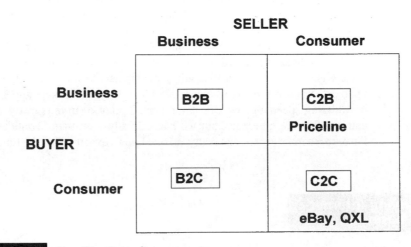

 **Figure 3.1** Classification of e-commerce

The other two categories both use the Internet to offer auctions. One of the most successful launches has been eBay, which sets up a huge auction site on which individuals can buy and sell. In many ways, this is applying the unique features of the Web to local classified advertising and specialized collecting: you can now buy and sell anything, not just within your local area, but across a whole country, or continent, or even the world. eBay is now moving from its American base into Europe, and although it is not clear how many people will want to go on using the service once the novelty has worn off, it is still growing, and, unusually, is profitable. At present, it seems to be taking share in Europe from the local player, QXL, so the winner-takes-all effect may also be working here.

C2B takes two forms, reverse auctions and buying groups. In a reverse auction, an individual posts the price he or she is willing to pay for something, say a flight from London to New York, and airlines bid for the custom. Priceline.com is the main proponent of this model, and was one of the most hyped businesses. In late 2000, doubts began to appear. Attempts to extend the service from air travel to other sectors failed, and the airlines were preparing to launch their own system. It may be, too, that regular flyers, who must make up the bulk of customers if the business is to succeed, become unwilling to accept the conditions (not knowing which carrier you would fly with, or what the take-off time would be or what changes there might be).

Buying groups are another idea that only the Internet makes possible (or rather, greatly expands the potential of). An individual will usually expect to pay more for an item than a group – so why not use the Internet to assemble a group, then negotiate with the supplier? Companies such as LetsBuyIt.com offer this service, but again, it is unclear whether enough people will want to use the service often enough to make a profitable business. At the beginning of 2001, it seemed doubtful if either Priceline.com or LetsBuyIt.com would survive.

Who will buy over the Web?

Early users of the Web were often characterized as nerds or anoraks; they were certainly mainly young, male, white and college educated. As the market has matured, this profile has changed; in the USA, and increasingly in Europe, more women are logging on, and the age spread has widened. At present, though, access is still highly skewed to the higher socio-economic groups. Any numbers quoted will necessarily be out of date, and the estimates of Internet use are notoriously imprecise, but as we saw, by September 2000, there were probably over 360 million people world-wide with online access: (Nua 2000) www.nua.com/surveys/. Table 3.2 shows a more detailed breakdown by country (Nielsen/NetRatings 2000: www.eratings.com/). Outside the USA, which still leads, the Nordic countries (Denmark, Finland, Norway and Sweden) are the most advanced, with Britain and Germany leading the rest of Europe, and Australia, New Zealand and Singapore well developed elsewhere. Table 3.1 shows the proportion with access at home and at work. Patterns of online browsing and shopping by country are shown in Table 3.2. In the 'advanced' countries, around 10 per cent of the population shop online, and about twice that number use the Web for gathering information on products or services.

Table 3.1 Per cent with Internet access at home and at work

	% Access at Home	% Access at Work
Australia	43	28
Austria	29	24
Belgium/Luxembourg	32	20
Denmark	47	35
Finland	43	37
France	13	5
Germany	23	18
Ireland	33	22
Italy	23	13
Netherlands	48	26
New Zealand	44	28
Norway	53	40
Singapore	50	22
Spain	14	12
Sweden	49	36
Switzerland	39	41
United Kingdom	42	24

Source: Nielsen NetRatings May 2000

Table 3.2 Per cent browsing and shopping online

	% Browsing	% Shopping
Austria	22	10
Belgium/Luxembourg	10	4
Denmark	32	11
Finland	23	9
France	5	2
Germany	19	10
Ireland	11	4
Italy	7	2
Netherlands	19	5
Norway	25	10
Spain	5	1
Sweden	34	17
Switzerland	25	11
United Kingdom	16	9
Europe	13	9

Source: Nielsen NetRatings May 2000

The general view is that most buying is of:

■ Books

■ Computers and software

■ CDs and music

■ Travel

■ Financial services

One estimate of the proportion of UK retail sales that are currently going via the Internet, and the likely pattern in the future, is shown in Table 3.3. Some commentators put the penetration higher: for example, Forrester believe that as much as 7 per cent of grocery purchases will be made online by 2005 (Forrester 2000), making this the biggest single market, and the UK the country with the highest Internet penetration of the grocery market in the world.

Table 3.3 UK online shopping forecasts by selected major product categories

| | 1998 | | 2005 | |
	£m	% retail sales	£m	% retail sales
Grocery	165	0.2	4,950	4.9
Clothing	5	0.01	1,843	4.0
Computer software	122	10.0	1,502	51.9
Electricals	18	0.2	993	7.6
Music and video	85	2.9	782	20.4
Books	106	5.2	473	18.3
Health and beauty	1	0.01	355	2.5
Total, all products	581	0.3	12,533	5.0

Source: David Hughes, Professor of Agribusiness and Food Marketing, Wye College, University of London, BOCM Pauls conference, 'Building Relationships in the Food Chain', The Belfry, 28/9 September 2000

A huge range of goods is now available on the Internet, and new Internet businesses spring up every day. Most cannot survive, but it is impossible to tell which will be the lucky ones. Evans and Wurster (2000) propose one model to assess the impact of the Web on a business. They distinguish between the economics of *information* and the economics of *things*. All businesses are a combination of the two, and each business offers a compromise: it is impossible to optimize the economics of information and that of things simultaneously. A retailer, for example, would maximize inventory to provide maximum information, but minimize it to lower the cost. As they point out, this explains why the retailing of some goods, such as books, is more vulnerable to the Internet revolution than that of others, such as food. For books, the value of the product is relatively high, inventory turn low, and the premium on selection is high: the compromise suppresses value, and separating information from the physical product releases value. Amazon can offer a choice of millions of books, because it does not have to provide them on display in hundreds of shops around the country. Food retailers, on the other hand, work with products of low value and high inventory turn; beyond a threshold – say 30,000 SKUs (stock-keeping units) – increased selection does not offer greater value to shoppers. Splitting the information from the product should not, in this analysis, release so much value (though one segment, who value their time very highly, may prefer to order over the Internet and pay for delivery).

Each business, then, can analyse its value chain, and determine what are the relative importance of information and physical product, and what compromises have been made. In some industries – retail banking springs to mind – bricks and mortar premises are an expensive way of delivering an information-based service, and they must feel vulnerable. Others, such as high-fashion clothing, would feel that much of the information inherent in the product is provided by the location, design and ambience of the shop itself (selection, interestingly, is increased by the clustering of rival fashion shops close together).

What each firm must also look at are their consumers. Every market will segment into those who are:

- Interested but unattractive
- Uninterested and attractive
- Interested and attractive

Unattractive customers will be those who buy very little, or are otherwise unprofitable to serve. Some people will remain impervious to the charms of the Internet, and will never shop that way. It remains to identify the interested and attractive group. At present, it is easy to describe them. They are:

- young
- cash-rich, time-poor
- techno-literate
- wired (have access to the Web).

These are the people who buy online, who sign up for Tesco Direct, and at whom Le-Shop aims its Internet grocery service in Switzerland. The question is, how much will that rather small group expand in *your* market?

The answer depends on how access and ease of use develop. Access is growing very fast in Europe, although actual uptake and use will continue to be held back by telephone charges, unless the telecoms suppliers change their tariffs. The spread of affordable 'fat pipes', providing the bandwidth that will enable fast download of sound and video, will also affect the attractiveness of the medium. Ease of use will be helped by interactive TV, and by effective voice recognition. Much Internet access will migrate to handheld communication devices (the next generation of mobile phones), and in the medium term to cars, kiosks and kitchens.

There remains the question of how many people actually want to be interactive. Trials so far suggest strongly that most people, offered the chance, are happy to take control of their evening's TV viewing, but are not very interested beyond that. Internet banking, for example, is growing at only 2 per cent a year in the USA, and it has a very high churn rate (customers leaving). If and when the process itself becomes automated, so that your refrigerator (or dustbin) records when you use food items, and automatically re-orders them, then the need for personal interaction may be by-passed – but that is still an idea for the future. No one has any idea whether such schemes will work, or be economically viable, let alone whether consumers will accept them.

The functions of the Internet

To explore further, let us look at the way the Internet functions: as a channel of communication, as a network, and as a virtual company.

What is different about the Internet?

As a communications channel, the Internet is just another option for companies to use in reaching their customers. It is most similar to the telephone, in that it is instantaneous and two-way. Indeed, much of e-commerce is merely direct marketing with added hype. Consider a company such as Capital One, which offers financial services to tightly targeted segments.

> **When a customer contacts Capital One, his or her identity is established, and file details are called up, including the last twenty transactions; intelligent software calculates from these the probable nature of the query, and routes the call to the staff member best qualified to help – all this automatically, before the call is answered. This is a highly sophisticated service, but it is based on the telephone, not the Internet.**

Many Internet retailers, or e-tailers, will offer nothing more than this, and often rather less. In this sense, e-tailing will become just another aspect of direct marketing. What the Internet can add is interactivity, connectivity to other sites, comparison information, and the potential to create a community. The telephone offers some interactivity, but it is limited. Interaction with a Website can be a much richer, broader experience than a phone conversation. The customer can do everything that the telephone conversation can offer, but much more: they can explore a huge range of web pages, with pictures, sound and movement; download information; linger at what is interesting; return any number of times to previous pages; choose items to buy, and change the decision easily; and even configure the experience to their own preferences.

Interconnectivity offers further enhancements: from an outdoor clothing site, an Internet shopper can hop to check the weather in holiday destinations, or the snow conditions in chosen resorts, and move on to a travel site to book a holiday before returning to the original site to order appropriate clothes and equipment.

Before (or indeed after) visiting an online shop, the customer can use intelligent agents to compare prices and services – in theory at least. At present, while big claims are made for intelligent agents, or bots, their performance is not always impressive. One test found that 'Not one of the shopping services came close to running up all the items I sought. And none offered the best prices' (Wildstrom 1998). No doubt they will improve, and the possibility that consumers will be able to check a wide range of prices in seconds, from their desk (or wireless phone connection to the Web), is a prospect that some will find encouraging, others threatening (the emergence of buying groups is discussed below). At present, there is ample evidence that the price dispersion (between highest and lowest) on the Internet is just as high as between terrestrial shops. Moreover, online shoppers do not necessarily buy from the cheapest site: a well-known and trusted brand (such as Amazon) can charge a premium (*The Economist* 1999).

Finally, and perhaps the one area that truly distinguishes the Internet from other channels, is the potential to form online communities. Such communities are a feature of the Internet landscape as a whole; the chance to join, and play a part in, a community seems to be a benefit that millions find attractive. Shoppers, too, can and do form communities in which they register their opinions and experiences of the product or service, without the intervention of the shop. Communities are more likely to form around high-involvement products, such as major durables, than low-involvement items such as groceries. Where they do spring up, they will be something quite new, and it is not yet clear whether they will be an opportunity or a threat for the retailer and suppliers. In theory, any brand owner ought to welcome the chance to learn more about consumers' likes and dislikes, and the richness of unmediated communication will be fascinating. But such communities may also bring pressure, particularly on pricing, that companies may not find comfortable.

The other way that the Internet changes business models is the combination of richness and reach. Evans and Wurster (2000) point out that, traditionally, there is a trade-off between richness and reach. A personal sales call offers great richness, for example, but poor reach; a TV advertisement, on the other hand, gives huge reach, but little richness. Sophisticated direct marketing techniques can add richness to a mailshot, but it is still limited by the medium's possibilities. The Internet, because of the size of the network and its infinite connectivity, can combine great richness with huge reach. While there will still be some compromises, companies such as Amazon can offer millions of customers a much richer experience than the most targeted mailshot.

What even Amazon cannot offer is the physical and sensual experience of a real bookshop, which suggests the limitations of the medium. Internet shopping will not completely replace ordinary shops, because, for many people, there are rewards such as the sight, feel and smell of goods, or the contact with other people, that the Internet cannot provide. Ironically, the very people who are the most likely to use the Internet may also be those who most want to get away from it. 'After staring at a screen all day, the last thing I want is to spend another hour shopping at one', may be the response of many.

The effects on marketing

The coming dominance of the Internet may have all sorts of effects on marketing. It may:

- transform marketing
- destroy existing retail models
- cause disintermediation
- modify existing models
- create new models, and
- increase confusion.

Let us look at each in turn.

Transform marketing

The Internet is part of – and the result of – the broader revolution brought about by the whole set of technological changes in electronics, computing and telecommunications.

Some think that the revolution will transform marketing. If change is discontinuous and unexpected, but constant, then old models of strategy will no longer cope. According to this argument, the old model is *make-and-sell*: even though, in enlightened firms, marketing guides what is made, it is still a top-down model. Where change is unpredictable, the new organization must *sense-and-respond*, becoming an adaptive enterprise (Haeckel 1999).

The cat and the supertanker

In an illuminating metaphor, Alan Mitchell calls the old way the supertanker, and the new way, the cat. Today's large corporation is a supertanker, with a pre-planned destination and route; it collects data on its position, and on weather, tides, and the movements of other ships; it has a large database, and sophisticated communications; it is very slow to change course if conditions alter suddenly. A cat, on the other hand, does not collect data on the mouse it is stalking: it waits, senses when the mouse moves, and pounces. If conditions alter suddenly, it can respond, even in mid-air. Tomorrow's markets will demand the responses of a cat, not a supertanker (Mitchell 1999).

If these commentators are right, then large areas of business will indeed be transformed. Concentrating on our own field, we may see new entities emerge as *demand aggregators*, leading to the disintermediation of existing businesses. We have seen such processes before, in financial services, where large companies now by-pass previous intermediaries, and go straight to the providers of finance. The large supermarket groups have taken over the role of wholesalers, causing many to go out of business. Indeed, we might regard supermarkets as demand aggregators themselves: instead of acting merely as channels through which dominant manufacturers distributed their brands, they decide what consumers want, and commission manufacturers to supply them.

The Internet now allows new groups to aggregate demand. Buying co-operatives exist in many areas, but the Internet allows consumers to set up their own. In a well-known example, a woman in America was trying to get a better discount on a car, but the dealer was resisting. Eventually, through the Internet, she recruited twenty-seven people who wanted the same model, and went back to the dealer. She got the discount (and indeed, by-passed the dealer to a higher level in the chain). If not too many consumers are willing to go to these lengths, then Websites will do it for them. Mercata, with its PowerBuy is a current example of such services (www.mercata.com). If they became widespread, they could transform some product fields (and their distribution chains).

As we noted above, there are also the effects of consumer communities, and of price comparison agents. These will tend to make information more widely available, particularly information on prices. Bill Gates has argued that this will lead to 'frictionless capitalism', and that many businesses have relied on the friction for their profit margin. Another way of putting it is that information has been asymmetric: the supplier knows more than the buyer, and exploits that to charge a premium. Information, widely available over the Internet, will destroy that asymmetry, and restore some balance to the relationship.

Certainly, the one group that is sure to gain from the Internet is consumers. Some manufacturers hope that they may regain some of the power that they have lost to retailers (see below), but that seems wishful thinking. If greater consumer knowledge produces price pressure on retailers, they will surely transmit that to their suppliers. Only if manufacturers succeed in building a genuine new relationship with consumers will they win; we return to this later. Consumers have everything to gain, and nothing to lose.

Destroy existing retail models

The most lurid forecasts – such as that all supermarkets will be abandoned hulks around our cities – are not credible. Some sectors will be hit hard, the travel and music businesses being prime examples. Others will be affected, as some buying shifts to the Internet. The danger in such cases is not so much the size of the online segment, as its nature. If a range of e-tailers manage to attract the most profitable customers in a sector – those who buy most, or tend to buy the products with the higher margins – then such cherry-picking will have a more than proportionate effect on the bricks-and-mortar retailers' profits.

For retailers, this poses a dilemma. If they react by starting their own Internet offer, to what extent will it interfere with their existing business? It is now clear that Internet business is completely different from the traditional form: it demands a different mindset, different skills, and much faster reaction times – a whole new culture. How will the traditional retailer manage this switch? From a branding point of view, how will the Website affect brand perceptions? For Tesco, this may not be a problem (as long as the Internet offer works well); but for Harrods, it is a real challenge. A comparative report rated Iceland's site above Harrods', which it described as 'surprisingly average for what is probably the most famous store in the world' (*Financial Times*, 1 December 1999). The response of Wal-Mart has been to say it will split off its Internet business, and set it up with separate offices away from the Arkansas headquarters (as Procter and Gamble are doing). While 'clicks-and-mortar' operations (a combination of online shopping and actual shops) may be the best solution for many retailers, managing two very different cultures may be difficult.

Cause disintermediation

The most threatening models are Dell in direct sales of computers, and Charles Schwab in share trading. Both exemplify the ability of online businesses to combine richness and reach, and the savings they gain by cutting out the retail stage of the chain mean that they can offer very competitive prices. As buyers in each market become more expert, they will feel more able to do without the help and personal contact they get from face-to-face retailers. A segment of personal shoppers will remain, but it may shrink to a minority. On the other hand, even here some firms are finding that a combination of bricks and clicks works best. Charles Schwab now does 80 per cent of its business online, but seven out of ten of its customers are recruited through the physical premises of its branches; both Merrill Lynch and HSBC are to build a branch network to support their Internet bank aimed at wealthy investors (*Financial Times*, 9 October 2000).

Direct and indirect effects

Direct effects are easy to spot (though not necessarily to deal with). The fact that buyers can download music directly, or travellers book flights and hotels online, are direct effects, and already visible. Indirect effects could be the migration of classified advertising to the Web. If a substantial proportion of advertising for jobs, cars and houses, for example, transfer to the Internet (which is particularly suited to scanning and searching such material), the indirect effect on the profitability of newspapers could be profound. Many papers rely on classified advertising for a large part of their profit, and they have not had to work too hard for it in the past – especially when they had a local monopoly. Losing a chunk of that revenue could take them towards the vicious downward spiral of shrinking advertising – fewer editorial pages – fewer readers – shrinking advertising (Evans and Wurster 2000).

Modify existing models

Many markets may see some modification of existing shopping patterns, without a total transformation. We have mentioned grocery, where the economics – at least in current models – do not offer huge benefits for Internet versions, and fashion, where the in-store shopping experience will remain a dominant attraction. Many other fields will be influenced by the Internet, but not transformed.

One variant is that some visionary retailers will use the Web to enhance the service they offer, and develop a competitive advantage. Home Depot in the USA, for example, allows trades people (small builders etc.) to access the Website and get advice on a particular job; the software will then estimate the materials needed, assemble the order and dispatch it. Lively competitors will be constantly looking for imaginative ways of differentiating themselves.

Create new models

We noted the potential rise of buying groups earlier. The other new phenomenon is the auction, and its cousin the reverse auction, discussed earlier. In both cases, it seems that only a certain sort of person will regularly buy in this way. Those who enjoy the thrill of the hunt, or are willing to take risks, will take part. Others may do so occasionally, for certain types of goods, but not as a habit. Both are businesses that could not exist without the Internet. No doubt wholly new ideas will spring up in future.

More generally, the Internet will allow more flexible pricing than in most conventional businesses. The danger is that firms may lose control of the price level, finding their achievable prices forced downwards by auctions, exchanges, buying groups and so on. This is in no one's long-term interest, as the earlier experience of deregulated airlines in the USA showed. Initially, a rash of new companies appeared, offering significantly lower air fares; People Express was the best-known example. It was not long, however, before most of the upstarts failed, as the price level that fierce competition produced simply did not allow sustainable profits. Now, only South West Airlines remains as a successful operator. Companies using the Internet must bear in mind that a realistic business model must underpin their pricing strategy.

Increase confusion

The Web is already a confusing place, and the number of sites continues to grow at an astonishing pace. Anyone who has used several search engines will know that they vary enormously in the number of sites they find when looking for a specific word or phrase. The Internet has an unparalleled richness, but the other side of the coin is total confusion. If a search for 'books' can produce a list of several thousand sites, then the temptation is to go straight to Amazon.co.uk, even if you know that their prices are not the lowest available.

In this confusion, consumers still want to trust their supplier, and so, paradoxically at first sight, the Internet brand becomes all-important. This is the reason that e-tailers are spending vast sums on advertising in conventional media (see below). Trusted brands, whether portals, navigators, agents, or e-tailers, will win; but the corollary is that many thousands of hopefuls will lose.

What should existing brands do?

The ways different brand owners have reacted to this new, frightening, confusing world range from the clear-sighted and proactive, through the cautiously experimental, to rabbit-in-the-headlights catatonic. How should you proceed? The only certainty is that there is no certainty: there are no general, one-size-fits-all answers. Wise firms will take stock, then act.

Analyse the situation

As marketing people, we should start with our consumers. Who are they, what do they want from us, what do they buy, when, how? All the information that should inform our marketing actions becomes even more important. We have to look at our customers from a different angle, or shine a different kind of light on them. Where does buying and using our brand fit into their lives? What are the problems with buying and using our brand, how could we (or someone else) make it easier, more enjoyable, richer? Is the shopping or buying experience enjoyable in itself, or part of something enjoyable, or a chore? What are their attitudes to technology, and how are they changing? This is a tricky area, since we cannot just ask consumers. People do not know in advance how they will react to new technology. It is already clear that access to the Web will be available not only through interactive TV (possibly voice-activated), but also hand-held devices (mobile phones, palm computers, and hybrids), and even the refrigerator and microwave oven. We also know that children growing up now are much more comfortable with computer technology than previous generations, and we can assume that this will stay with them. What we do not know is how interactive the mass of consumers will want to be. All that firms can do is watch, and be prepared.

Then we must think how our intermediaries may be affected. Using analytical ideas such as the economics of information versus that of things, and richness and reach (Evans and Wurster 2000), we can try to work out how the structure of the industry value chain may change, and what the effect would be on our business. Such is the level of uncertainty that brainstorming and scenario analysis may be necessary to help cope with what otherwise may appear chaotic.

Decide broad strategy

If it is possible – and we must accept that, in some cases, it will be extremely difficult – we should decide on the broad strategy to adopt towards the Internet challenge. The basic responses include:

- carry on as at present
- dip a toe in the water
- develop customer service
- develop new services
- start a new business
- radical transformation.

Carry on as at present

If the analysis suggest that the changes in your market, and in the structure of the industry, will be incremental and slow, then it makes sense not to panic. Most companies have a Website, and they can watch developments and react as and when they need to. To feel secure in this strategy, you also have to be very confident that no radical shocks can upset your course, whether from inside the industry or from outside.

Toe in the water

What many companies are doing now is allocating some resources to e-business, and seeing what happens. The Website is probably interactive, and the firm will monitor customer reactions. You should also be monitoring what competitors are doing, and what is happening in other, similar, markets. It is frightening that some 50 per cent of British company directors have received *no* briefing on the Internet: that suggests complacency (or fear) at the highest levels. The great majority of companies ought to be at least at this stage of development, and the top managers must lead.

Customer service

Using the Internet to enhance customer service is an obvious development. Best known of the early ideas was FedEx's allowing customers to access their site to check on the exact whereabouts of their parcel. Similarly, many companies have developed extranets, and allow clients to access them for information or for transactions. For many, the extranets will replace EDI (electronic data interchange), which was much more expensive and restrictive. In business-to-business markets, this pattern is pervasive.

A choice that has to be made is whether or not to allow or encourage online purchasing. Much will depend on the nature of the product, and the associated economics of transport and delivery: for small, low-ticket items like many fmcg (fast-moving consumer goods) brands, online buying is unlikely to be attractive. The other – and major – consideration is the relationship with existing intermediaries. Developing a new channel while maintaining the old is always a tricky business, and some way has to be found to retain the support of current retailers. In this sense, the Internet does not present a new challenge, just a different and dramatic form of an old one.

The other possibility is to encourage the development of a community of customers. As we noted above, the Internet gives users a unique opportunity to exchange information and views. The company can actively participate in this, as long as it does not appear dominating or manipulative. Others could perhaps learn from the experience of companies in the computer industry, where user groups predate the Internet, and have been very influential.

New services

We described the Home Depot idea above, and this is typical of the way that the Internet provides new opportunities for differentiation. The radically different culture of most Internet businesses suggest that traditional firms may have to find new ways of stimulating 'out of the box' thinking – new people, new organizational structures, new incentives.

Radical transformation

It takes a great deal of courage to set out on this path. Although Jack Welch called on his managers to destroy their businesses, few have done so. The difficulty, and the danger of being half-hearted, is shown by the experience of Barnes & Noble, the US booksellers. Starting some way behind Amazon.com (who of course began with a clean sheet of paper), Barnes & Noble have spent millions on their Internet book operation, but are still a very poor second to Amazon. Perhaps only Charles Schwab has been radical, and has accepted that they have to completely cannibalize their old business to build their new, online share-trading model. They have been notably successful, and even the mighty Merrill Lynch, having been slow to respond, is now playing catch-up.

New business

Recognizing that the mindset and skills needed to run an Internet business are totally different from those required in normal mode, some companies are setting up a separate firm. Notably, Procter and Gamble have set up reflect.com as an independent entity, in San Francisco, to offer a personalized cosmetic service. This avoids the tensions and stresses of trying to run two different – and antipathetic – cultures within one company. It is suitable where it seems probable that the original business will continue in a reasonably healthy way, and can learn from the new operation without being disrupted by it.

Building a brand on the Web

For those who do develop a significant Web presence, the challenges of brand building are in some ways remarkably similar to those in normal markets. The first problem is that of creating awareness, and this is getting exponentially more difficult. In the early days of the Internet, when it was still the preserve of enthusiasts, a brand could be built by 'word-of-mouse'; as the Web became newsworthy, some start-ups benefited from widespread media comment. Later, banner advertising on search engines and what became portals worked (though at dramatically increasing cost). Now, start-ups that need to gain customers rapidly have to contemplate spending huge sums on advertising.

In late 1998, it was estimated that Internet companies were spending at an annual rate of some $200–250 million. A year later, the figure was $7.5 *billion* (*Financial Times*, 1 December 1999). This rate of growth is unprecedented.

The problem the dot.coms face is that the stock market at one period made millionaires and billionaires overnight, but only for start-ups that demonstrated rapid growth in customer numbers. Profits seemed irrelevant, but the ability to attract customers and keep them coming back was – almost literally – priceless. In the increasing clutter – an inadequate word for the situation on the Web today – making yourself heard is an expensive task. According to one expert, it is now impossible to build an Internet brand for less than $100 million (Patrick Keane, quoted in *Financial Times*, 1 December 1999). This has now changed, and venture capital for B2C start-ups has dried up; even already-established businesses are finding it harder and harder to win additional rounds of funding, and many are going under. A real prospect of profitability is now a major criterion.

The advantage of being first, and early, may prove to be decisive for those firms that play their cards right. Those arriving later, such as Barnes & Noble, face an uphill struggle. And when you find competitors such as Pets.com, Petstore.com, Petopia.com and Petsmart.com, all fighting for the same limited number of consumer dollars, then deep pockets and strong nerves are needed. The consolidation that has already happened is sure to continue.

Yet, as we saw, consumer trust and brand awareness may be even more important on the Web than in earth-bound markets. When we do not even know for sure that a business exists, and have no way of checking (we can't look them up in the phone book, or go round to examine their premises), then trust becomes paramount – and that is without the fear of giving away a credit card number, or having one's privacy invaded. If huge advertising budgets can build awareness, only superb service, consistently delivered, can build trust. Jeff Bezos, the founder of Amazon, says that it is pre-eminently a customer service company, and he has worked hard to make sure that the site is easy to use, and the delivery service efficient. Even so, the experience of Amazon.com at the end of the 1999 holiday season was instructive. Its sales rose dramatically, but it admitted that it had over-stocked to make sure that it could deliver gifts in time for Christmas; its losses also increased. Even with a brand name, the old retailing skills are still needed.

Conclusions

To quote one consultant involved in this new, strange world:

It's not easy, it's not cheap, and it's not optional.

(John Dickie, Insight Technology)

The Internet presents wholly new challenges, and managers will need to find new ways of meeting them. It is, above all, a top management responsibility. Companies in Europe have been slow to recognize this, perhaps because many senior managers have been personally technophobe. They may have a PC on their desk, but often it is only for show. Recently, there have been encouraging signs of change, but the change will have to be fast, and the new strategies determined, to catch up with our American rivals.

If your brand is Mars, or Persil, the Internet will certainly change your business, but it may have little effect on your brand. You will use the Web to open up a new channel of communication with your consumers, and the task of integrating all your marketing communications will become that much more complicated. The companies most likely to see an impact on their brands *qua* brands are those in financial services and business-to-business, where the Internet may produce radical re-structuring.

As with any strategic issue, adapting to the new Internet age is a top management responsibility. The board cannot delegate this to the techies (nor to the marketing people alone). Top management must lead, and – as we have argued throughout this book – all functions must be involved in building a business fit for the next century.

Key learning points

- The Internet, and other technologies such as wireless communications and interactive digital TV, are transforming many industries.
- The business environment is turbulent, and it is extremely difficult to forecast exactly what will happen.
- All organizations need to analyse their own situation and monitor it constantly.
- B2B is, and will remain, the biggest e-commerce sector.
- The impact of e-commerce on marketing will vary. For some, it will offer a new channel of communication, for others, a complete transformation. Basic rules of business and of marketing will continue to apply.

Further reading

Evans, P. and Wurster, T.S. (2000) *Blown to Bits: how the new economics of information transforms strategy*, Boston, MA: Harvard Business School Press.
Ries, A. and Ries, L. (2000) *11 Immutable Laws of Internet Branding*, New York: HarperCollins.

Most books will date rapidly: keep up to date with Websites such as:

www.clickz.com

www.Nua.ie (good for stats and surveys)

www.Emarketer.com

www.Wdfm.com

www.Crmguru.com (Customer Relationship Management)

www.MarketingSherpa.com

www.B2bmarketingbiz.com

www.i-advertising.com

cyberatlas.internet.com (not www.).

Case study

You are the third generation to work in your family firm of wholesale and retail butchers. Through long-term relationships with livestock producers, the firm has built up a reputation for quality, and it supplies many hotels and restaurants. It also makes products such as black pudding, sausages and pies; at present, these are sold only through its own outlets, but you feel that they could find a wider market.

The firm has a Website, but it is static, and provides only contact information. You feel that this new technology holds great potential for you.

Questions

1 List all the ways you could use the Internet for the firm's various activities.

2 Which ones would you recommend pursuing first, and why?

3 Critically examine your own organization's use of the Internet. How could it be improved?

Chapter 4

Understanding environments and markets

In recent years 'the environment' has taken on the particular meaning of the physical environment. That is not the meaning used here. We use the term in the systems sense of the entire environment within which an organization exists and with which it interacts. The physical world is part of that, but more important to a business are the other aspects: political/legal, economic, social, and technological (the term PEST analysis is often used to summarize these). Every organization exists within this environment and may be vitally affected by it, but on the whole it can do little to control it.

Scanning the environment and assessing its impact lies at the overlap between marketing and the broader issues of business strategy. As marketing must always look outside the business, the environment must be one of its concerns.

In this section we shall look briefly at the main potential impact of environmental change from a marketing point of view – that is, how the changes may affect markets, customers, consumers and competitors. There are, of course, other potential impacts of environmental change on the firm, for example on human resources or financing policy;

they are ignored for the purposes of this book, though in real life they may be vitally important.

1 Economic change

It is for the managers of each organization to assess which aspects of the environment are most important to them. All aspects should be examined initially, as it is not always easy to know in advance what changes may occur and how they may affect you. Later, it may be possible to concentrate on those which are likely to have most effect. To take the economy, for example, some industries are very closely connected to changing economic trends – machine tools or the construction industry, for instance. Others, such as cosmetics, are much less affected and can concentrate on other factors. Some industries are counter-cyclical, that is, their sales tend to go up in hard times and decline when the economy as a whole is booming; some cheaper foods have this tendency. If one or more of your products is very sensitive to the economic cycle, this may have implications for the overall product portfolio, though it is not always easy to find suitable counter-cyclical products to balance the existing ones.

Every marketing person should be aware of the relationship between their market and the various economic indicators, so that at least they can forecast the possible effect, even if they cannot avoid it. Operating on an international scale makes this more complicated, but may have advantages in that when one market is in recession others may still be growing.

2 Social change

Markets may be affected profoundly by social changes. Demographic change is easy to predict for most markets, since we know the size of the various age cohorts and can see how the population profile will change in the future. The declining birth rate in the UK meant that the late 1980s and early 1990s saw a sharp drop in the 18–24-year-old age-group – a prime market, for many companies. The Burton Group, seeing this, adjusted the ranges on offer in its different shops to compensate. Food manufacturers and retailers have acknowledged the change in household structure (a significant increase in one- and two-person households, and a corresponding decline in traditional two-adult-two-children homes) by offering smaller pack sizes. The growing size of the fifty-plus age group (combined with their greater wealth) means that in many countries new opportunities are opening up for marketers.

Other forms of social change are less tangible and can be tracked but not always predicted. On the topic of food, it is known that family eating occasions have become fragmented; formal occasions when all the family sit down to a meal together are less common. There is also greater interest in healthy eating. Such trends can and must be responded to by manufacturers, but forecasting the next trend is less easy. Will people become more and more health conscious, or will there be a reaction, towards indulgence and luxury? There are companies which produce forecasts of social trends – necessarily mainly extrapolations from existing patterns. These can be useful in gathering data from a variety of sources and in providing a stimulus to thought, and for companies whose markets are sensitive to social change, they may be worth investing in. Such outside views can also be a valuable corrective to the tunnel vision to which we are all liable when we are immersed in day-to-day detail.

3   Technological change

This is sometimes ignored by marketing people as not being their concern, but such change can create and destroy markets.

The Swiss watch industry held a dominant share of the world market for mechanical movements, but failed to appreciate the significance of the threat from electronic watches; the industry was almost wiped out, and though it managed to survive and adapt, it has never recovered its previous position.

This is a good example of technological change in many ways. The innovation came from outside the traditional industry. Early electronic models were not functionally perfect; their displays were poor, for example, and needed both hands to operate. The digital display was strange to many people used mainly to analogue faces. Electronic watches were expensive compared to average mechanical watches, and appealed initially to buyers interested in gimmicks. Nonetheless, as we now know, they have virtually taken over the market. All these features can occur with technological change, but unfortunately they cannot be predicted with consistency.

A major factor is timing (no pun intended). Some innovations which we now take for granted were resisted for reasons we find difficult to understand. Frozen foods and zips, for instance, both took decades to achieve market acceptance. In the case of frozen foods, one can perhaps appreciate that changes in long-held attitudes to fresh food were necessary; but zips? The Xerox plain-paper copier was widely predicted by experts to have no future; other seemingly promising technologies have never found a market. To some extent it is up to the marketing person to try to understand the fundamental motivations at work in order to predict the impact of possible new technology; the issue of acceptance of innovation, for example, has some theory to guide us (and is dealt with later in the next chapter), but our knowledge is imperfect and judgement will remain the key. The impact of information and communications technology is of major importance for many industries, while bio-technology will affect others.

4   Political and legal change

Political and legal changes can also affect markets, sometimes dramatically. Hoffmann La Roche lost half its sales in the UK when the government dropped some of its major brands from the list of drugs allowed to be prescribed on the National Health Service. Formal tariffs and informal agreements severely limit the markets for many products in certain countries. Legal changes may impinge upon product formulation, packaging design and advertising claims. Some markets – those for food and pharmaceutical products, for example – are far more sensitive to such changes than others, but the general tendency seems to be towards greater regulation. Even as some governments are trying to move away from excessive interference in business, other organizations such as the European Union are increasing their involvement. Awareness of these changes is not something that marketing people can leave to the company chair, the public relations department or the lobbyist.

With all these aspects of the environment, marketing must monitor, think and react. Change may be influenced: it can sometimes be speeded up or slowed down. It cannot in the end be controlled.

Understanding markets

Definitions and structure

It may seem obvious to say that the first step in understanding a market is to define it, but the process is in fact important. The definition adopted affects the total size of the market, number and identity of competitors and your market share – all of which are vital factors in your marketing planning.

Most market definitions are product-based: the company defines its market as the total sales of all similar or directly competing products. This has the advantage of being straightforward, but may obscure certain important aspects, particularly what consumers think. A confectionery manufacturer may define the market as count lines, or filled bars; a consumer may see a purchase as a piece of any confectionery, or as a snack in which nuts and crisps are competing with confectionery. A hi-fi may be competing with other consumer durables, or even a holiday. The quote from the chairman of Carborundum suggested that the market for metal removal is potentially quite different from the market for grinding wheels. Market definition is therefore something to be thought about rather than taken for granted.

Consumer-based definitions can prove fruitful in thinking about strategic decisions: who are our target consumers, what benefits are they seeking, what is the competition, what is the long-term future of this market, what product modifications or new products should we be working on? Narrower product-based definitions may be more useful for short-term control: how are our sales this period against target, and compared with last year? Narrow definitions may be dangerous over the medium and longer term, however. You may be maintaining your share of hi-fi sales, for example, but if that sector is a declining proportion of consumer durable sales, you are at the least missing out on profit opportunities, and may be under threat. It may be, then, that different market definitions are needed for different purposes.

Finally, market definition is vital because of the way it affects your interpretation of market share; this, as we will see below, is a topic of major importance in strategic thinking.

One influential writer (Abell 1980) has suggested that market definition should be seen as three-dimensional: a product is the physical manifestation of a particular technology to the provision of a particular function for a particular customer group.

Buzzell added a further dimension: level of production/distribution. Depending on how many levels competitors operate at in the chain from raw materials to final product, one may decide to include or exclude levels from the market definition.

From a marketing point of view, the function/customer group focus should take precedence, since different technologies could meet the same functional need (as in the Carborundum case). Further, a marketing person ought to look not at the function as such, but at the benefits that the customer is looking for.

One further refinement is needed: the distinction between total market and served market. Some companies (but probably only a few) do in fact aim at the total market produced by the technology/function/customer group definition; others target only a part – their served market.

To take hand power tools, for example: Black and Decker would have a very broad served market, while Wickes aim at only the 'professional' end of the consumer segment, and Snap-on Tools only at professional mechanics. It would not make sense for Snap-on Tools to use the same market definition as Black and Decker (see Day 1990).

Figure 4.1 summarizes the multi-dimensional approach to market analysis, ending with served market (the final stages shown, segmentation and positioning, are dealt with in Chapters 7 and 8).

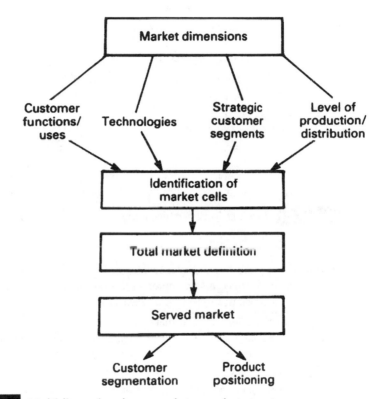

Figure 4.1 Multidimensional approach to market structure

We can distinguish levels of product-industry hierarchy, which may help us to see where to focus attention. Figure 4.2 shows a hierarchy for coffee-makers (Day 1990: 97). A company may want to look at any of these levels, depending on the nature of the firm, and the decision under consideration. A multi-divisional firm with products in many areas of housewares may look at the top level, whereas the brand manager for a percolator may concentrate only on the bottom; managers in between may want to examine the product class, or the specific type. What level in the hierarchy is appropriate depends on what you are using it for.

The other idea we need to absorb is that of the total and served market. Few firms compete in the total market, for various reasons. Figure 4.3 (Randall 1997: 221) shows how potential customers leak away. The main sources of leakage are:

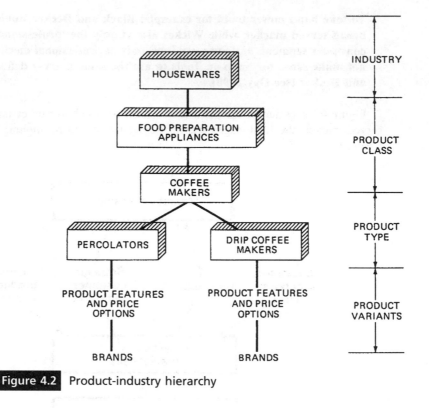

Figure 4.2 Product-industry hierarchy

- *Functions/technologies/price ranges not offered.* Few firms offer products in every possible sector (see also Chapter 7). Boeing does not make small business jets, and Caterpillar does not make small excavators.

- *Customers not served.* The marketing programme may miss out some customers, for example through geographical or channel gaps. This may be deliberate, because the coverage is not profitable, but it is worth checking to see if there are accidental gaps that no one has noticed.

- *Customers competed for and lost.* Not every customer will buy your product or service every time, although much marketing effort is devoted to trying to maximize the proportion of customers who buy frequently.

The company's *served market* consists of all those customers for whom it is competing by offering a product/service range that meets their needs, through a marketing programme that gives them a real opportunity to buy. This is the market definition to use for setting objectives, short-term planning and measuring results. The whole should be reviewed at intervals to make sure that the picture is not out-of-date (for example, because the served market is shrinking as a proportion of the total, or there are more customers uncovered).

As a final point before leaving market definition, it is worth recalling the concern of marketing, stressed in Chapter 1, with matching the firm's resources and capabilities with market opportunities. At the somewhat abstract level of discussion, these two sides – the firm and the market – can produce slightly different uses of market definition. The

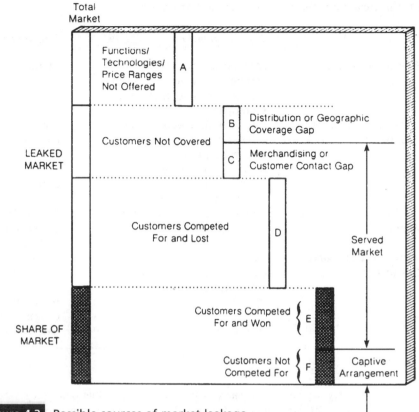

Figure 4.3 Possible sources of market leakage

corporate strategist uses a top-down or supply-side view, while the marketing person tends to take a bottom-up view. The differences between the two perspectives are summarized in Table 4.1.

It is important to grasp the difference between the two perspectives, as otherwise little sensible dialogue is possible when people are coming from different directions.

Market structure

At its simplest this means: 'Who are the competitors in the market, and what are their shares? Kotler suggests that a typical market structure would contain a *marker leader*, a *market challenger*, a *market follower* and a *market nicher*, with shares of 40, 30, 20 and 10 per cent respectively (Kotler 2000: 231). You can identify market leaders in many industries, for instance Tesco in supermarkets, McDonald's in fast food, Nokia in mobile phones; usually, they lead not only in sales, but also in profit, pricing policy and new product introductions. Similarly, the Boston Consultancy Group has suggested a likely structure, and studies of various industries have produced structures shown in Figure 4.4.

These suggest that a common structure may exist, though we must stress that many markets vary from this pattern. Why a particular pattern should be found in a particular industry is not clear. It may reflect outstanding management, or better resources, or past

Table 4.1 The view from the top-down versus bottom-up

Issue	Top-down view	Bottom-up view
1 Definition of market	Markets are arenas of competition where corporate resources can be profitably employed	Markets are shifting patterns of customer requirements and needs which can be served in many ways
2 Orientation to market environment	Strengths and weaknesses relative to competition: ■ cost position ■ ability to transfer experience ■ market coverage	Customer perceptions of competitive alternatives: ■ match of product features and customer needs ■ positioning
3 Identification of market segments	Looks for cost discontinuities	Emphasizes similarity of buyer responses to market efforts
4 Identification of market niches to serve	Exploits new technologies, cost advantages, and competitors' weaknesses	Finds unsatisfied needs, unresolved problems, or changes in customer requirements and capabilities
5 Time frame	Two to five years	One to three years

Source: Day 1981

history, or just luck. There will be random fluctuations every year in every market, so individual firms may experience different growth rates; over time, this will produce a skewed distribution. If scale economies play a part, then any firm gaining an early advantage will stand to gain still more, and increase its lead. Local conditions or regulation may also affect the outcome: the brewing industry is becoming more concentrated in much of Europe and the USA, but is still fragmented in Germany.

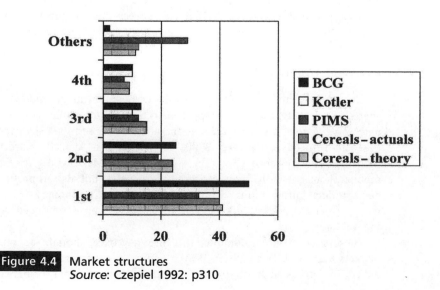

Figure 4.4 Market structures
Source: Czepiel 1992: p310

The current trend is to further concentration in many markets, with take-overs and mergers leading to larger and larger entities. This is related to globalization and the perceived need for global scale (see Chapter 18). Some markets are stable over long periods, others are dynamic and fast changing. We need to understand what sort of market we are in, and how it may change; altering a very stable structure is difficult, but changing share patterns may be easier in a volatile market.

At a rather different level, we need to understand the patterns of production and distribution in the chain: is the pattern the same for all competitors, or do some companies cover more stages than others? What are the relative sizes and strategies of participants at the different stages? How might they affect us?

At a further level of complexity there is a complete industry analysis. The work of Porter has had an extensive influence here (Porter 1980, 1985), and readers will come across his work elsewhere. For the present, we will summarize his views in two main areas. First, he suggests that the competitive structure of an industry is formed by five major factors: barriers to entry, bargaining power of suppliers, bargaining power of distributors, threat of substitutes, and degree of rivalry of the competitors in the industry (see Figure 4.5).

Second, he points out that firms compete in different ways; within an industry there will be strategic groups, with the firms in each group competing in a similar way. For example,

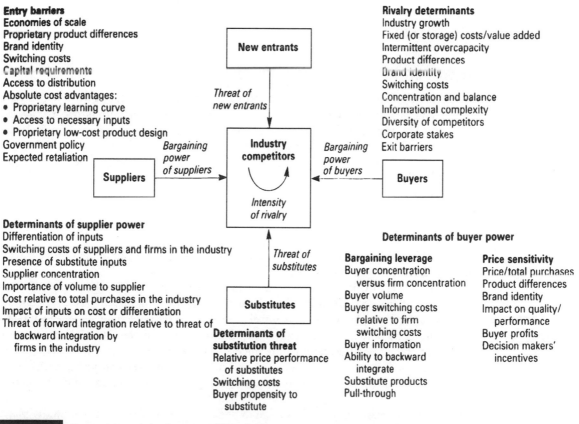

Figure 4.5 Porter's model of competitive forces

in many packaged goods industries there will be a group of competitors making nationally distributed brands supported by heavy advertising, and a group of companies making own-label products, unsupported by advertising and often distributed locally or through only one or two retailers. The profitability of a company is determined not only by the industry in which it operates, but also the strategic group in which it competes.

One of the advantages of Porter's work is that he provides a detailed method of analysis which – with sufficient resources and application – can yield a complete industry structure. Even without the complete analysis, the approach can give useful insights. A brief summary cannot do justice to the richness of the books, and interested readers are referred to them.

Models and analytical tools

Although marketing is not a science, nevertheless there are attempts to measure and to build explanatory models. These are important in our effort to develop understanding, so that decision-making can be based on more than just experience and hunch. In this section we will examine some of the better-known concepts and models which try to explain markets:

1 Product life cycle
2 Market share models:

— experience curve
— PIMS study

Product life cycle

One of the best-known concepts in marketing is that of the Product Life Cycle (PLC). Using the analogy of living organisms, this holds that products are born, grow, mature and eventually die. The most familiar depiction of the PLC is shown in Figure 4.6; the labels indicate the most common terms for the stages:

■ Introduction
■ Growth
■ Maturity
■ Decline

The model is elaborated by describing the conditions likely to prevail in the various stages; one formulation is shown in Table 4.2.

Intuitively, the PLC is attractive. Some products clearly do go through such a cycle, and market conditions do vary according to relative maturity. If one thinks of electronic calculators, for example, we have seen their introduction (bulky, crude, expensive models manufactured by only a few companies), an explosive growth stage (many new competitors, rapid product modification, falling prices), and we are now in a mature phase (many competitors have dropped out, leaving a small number of well-established manufacturers concentrating on segmented strategies and fairly stable technology and marketing policies).

On the other hand, many markets seem to go on for ever in a permanent maturity phase – bread, for instance. To get beyond the superficial idea, one has to introduce a distinction

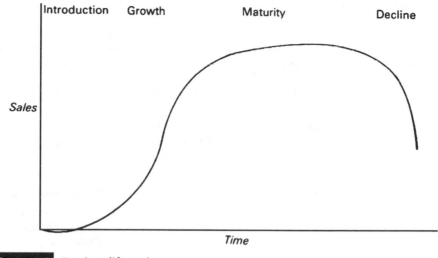

Figure 4.6 Product life cycle

between product class, product form and brand. Product class would be bread in this example, product form wholemeal bread, and brand Hovis. A similar example would have cigarettes as the product class, filter-tip cigarettes as the product form and Silk Cut as a brand. It is easy to see that within the envelope of the product class life cycle, it is possible to have different product form and brand cycles. The life cycle of a particular brand may be the shortest, though this is not necessarily true, as the number of long-lived brands shows.

> **This points up the central difficulty of the PLC concept: the evidence of its existence is contradictory. While some fairly clear life cycles can be seen, there are many markets in which no such pattern emerges.**

Critics of the PLC claim to show that in tests against sales data, 'it has not performed uniformly well against objective standards over a wide range of frequently purchased consumer products' (Dhalla and Yuspeh 1976). Patterns observed may be as much to do with management actions as with any underlying cycle.

> **A serious objection to the PLC is that it may actively mislead. A levelling-off or decline in sales may tempt management to diagnose a PLC effect; they may then withdraw further effort and investment, and the decline becomes a self-fulfilling prophecy.**

Without the PLC blinkers, management might produce a more sensitive diagnosis and some positive corrective action. A favourite example of this Du Pont's strategy for nylon, with continually extended uses for the product beyond its original application in parachutes. This produces the so-called 'scalloped' PLC, shown in Figure 4.7, similar shapes may be seen wherever a brand is successively extended or relaunched.

The real question is, how should a manager use the PLC, if at all? We can conclude from the evidence that it exists sometimes, but not always; that the market conditions

Table 4.2 Conditions through the PLC

Characteristics	Phase			
	Introduction	*Growth*	*Maturity*	*Decline*
Sales	Low sales	Rapidly rising sales	Peak sales	Declining sales
Costs	High cost per customer	Average cost per customer	Low cost per customer	Low cost per customer
Profits	Negative	Rising profits	High profits	Declining profits
Customers	Innovators	Early adopters	Middle majority	Laggards
Competitors	Few	Growing number	Stable number beginning to decline	Declining number
Marketing objectives				
	Create product awareness and trial	Maximize market share	Maximize profit while defending market share	Reduce expenditure and milk the brand
Strategies				
Product	Offer a basic product	Offer product extensions, service, warranty	Diversify brands and models	Phase out weak items
Price	Use cost-plus	Price to penetrate market	Price to match or beat competitors	Cut price
Distribution	Build selective distribution	Build intensive distribution	Build more intensive distribution	Go selective: phase out unprofitable outlets
Advertising	Build product awareness among early adopters and dealers	Build awareness and interest in the mass market	Stress brand differences and benefits	Reduce to level needed to retain hardcore loyals
Sales promotion	Use heavy sales promotion to entice trial	Reduce to take advantage of heavy consumer demand	Increase to encourage brand switching	Reduce to minimal level

Sources: This table was assembled from several sources: Chester R. Wasson (1978) *Dynamic Competitive Strategy and Product Life Cycles* (Austin, Tx: Austin Press 1978); John A. Weber (1976) 'Planning Corportate Growth with Inverted Product Life Cycles', *Long Range Planning*, October pp. 12–29; and Peter Doyle (1976) 'The Realities of the Product Life Cycle', *Quarterly Review of Marketing*, Summer, pp. 1–6. Adapted from Kotler (2000: 316).

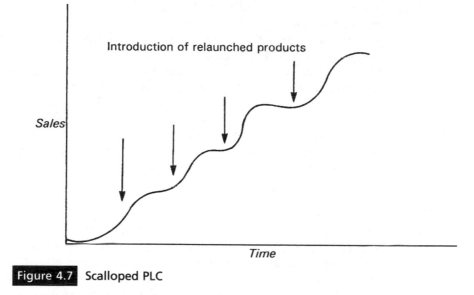

Figure 4.7 Scalloped PLC

predicted do occur, but not always in exactly the order expected; that therefore it can be illuminating, but that it is also potentially misleading.

> **The lesson is that it cannot be applied uncritically, as a complete explanation. The marketing person should go beyond the life cycle stage to examine the underlying causes: what factors in the environment, the market, in the behaviour of buyers, in competitive actions, may be producing the results seen?**

The PLC as an idea does have one important function: it should remind managers that brands are not naturally immortal. Whatever the causes, it is certain that no brand can survive for ever without constant attention and support; most will need periodic rethinking and relaunch. There are markets in which natural cycles do exist for product forms or brands; for example those in which technology is changing (computers) or feature/benefit improvement is the norm (cars). In these cases it is essential to plan product modification and new product development so that the improved or new product is ready to take over in the marketplace before the old one declines.

Market share

Share of the served market is seen as an important strategic objective. It is also seen as a useful control measurement, as it is thought to reflect fairly on the results of marketing effort. Over the last twenty years a number of studies (and other factors) have all pointed towards high market share as a desirable goal promising high profitability. More recently, however, some doubts and dissension have appeared.

▪ **The Experience Curve** The first market-share model was promulgated by the Boston Consulting Group (Boston Consulting Group 1972). Building on the well-known learning curve concept, BCG studied the effect of cumulative experience on cost of manufacture, and found consistent patterns. With a doubling of experience (cumulative volume) came a reduction in average unit cost; the reduction achievable varies considerably, but the figures centre around 15 per cent. The sources of the reduction are usually thought to be learning by doing (and this applies throughout the process, not just in manufacturing itself), technology improvements, and economies of scale (some writers suggest, logically, that scale economies should be treated separately).

The implications of the experience curve are that the market leader potentially has the lowest costs, and therefore the greatest profit (or the margin to allow attacking or defensive marketing effort, further product improvement, etc.). Similarly, small competitors will always be less profitable unless they can find a distinct segment within which they can achieve their own specialized experience savings.

Subsequent work has found all sorts of complexities which throw doubt on these simple statements, however, and some critics have argued that the concept can be misleading (e.g. Porter 1985; Day and Montgomery 1983). At present it is not clear to what extent it applies outside manufacturing industry (evidence on service industries is conflicting). Nevertheless, as a pointer to the need to understand the cost structure and behaviour of your company and your competitors, the concept is still valid.

- **The PIMS study** The PIMS (Profit Impact of Market Strategies) project began at General Electric in the USA in 1960, subsequently being transferred to the Strategic Planning Institute. It consists of a database now containing detailed figures from several thousand 'businesses'; each 'business' is in fact a strategic business unit of a larger company.

The best-known result from PIMS was a regression model using thirty-seven variables to explain ROI (Return On Investment). With a very large database, and an impressive result (the equation explained 80 per cent of the variation in ROI, an extremely high figure in business research), the PIMS results gained a very high profile. From a marketing point of view, the most important result was the weight given to market share: the major article (Buzzell and Sultan 1975) suggested that a 10 percentage point difference in market share is associated with a 5 percentage point difference in ROI. The explanation for this is usually that it is due to two factors: experience/scale effects, and the use of market power. This apparently simple, certainly dramatic finding has had great influence.

The PIMS finding has not gone unchallenged; there are complexities. To follow the debate about market share and profitability needs a good grasp of econometrics, and cannot be covered in detail here (interested readers may follow the argument in the references listed). A few main points should be made:

- Criticisms have been made of the nature of the PIMS database, and of some technicalities of the analysis.

- It is clear that the broad generalizations from the whole sample conceal some variations: for example, there are low-market-share companies which nevertheless make good returns (Woo and Cooper 1982).

- Subsequent analyses have suggested that the influence of market share on ROI is in fact rather less than had been claimed.

- A common view is that high market share and high ROI are possibly both caused by a third factor – good management, or even luck.

This is a slightly depressing conclusion for a scientist looking for enlightenment, and an optimistic one only for successful managers who do not have to explain the secret of their success.

Other evidence (Doyle 1989) has also underlined the value of high market share. Studies have shown that the market leader makes on average over six times the return on sales of the number two brand, while the number three and four brands are totally unprofitable. A further factor, though not one which has been quantified, is that in fast-moving consumer-goods markets, the power of retailers has meant that brands lower than number two are under increasing threat of losing distribution (see Chapter 14). All these factors have tended to put even greater emphasis on market leadership as a strategic objective, and it is common to find companies which explicitly aim to be either number one or two in every market in which they operate.

All one can say at this stage is that this is over-simplifying. It is certainly possible to earn reasonable returns without being number one or two, though it is likely to be true that a small share can be defended only with some specific competence – the sustainable competitive advantage, which is essential.

Careful, thoughtful analysis of the particular market situation and one's own strengths and weaknesses will always be better than applying the latest management panacea.

Key learning points

- **Every organization, whether a business firm or a not-for-profit organization, exists within an environment and interacts with it. Changes in the environment may profoundly affect the company, and it must therefore be aware of what the important influences are and how the environment is changing.**

- **The first step is to identify which parts of the environment are vital to your company, since different firms are susceptible to different aspects.**

- **The environment is often broken down into four main areas, summarized as PEST: Political/legal, Economic, Social (or Socio-cultural), and Technological.**

- **Definitions of a market are important, and not as straightforward as may at first appear. It is valuable to think of the market from the viewpoint of customers.**

- **The structure of markets must also be understood: who are the major competitors, what are their shares; what are the main patterns of production and distribution, how are they changing, who controls them?**

- **Some models are available to help managers understand their markets. The Product Life Cycle is explained, and discussions about the importance of market share summarized.**

Further reading

Czepiel, J.A. (1992) *Competitive Marketing Strategy*, Englewood Cliffs, NJ: Prentice Hall.

Hooley, G.J., Saunders, J.A. and Piercy, N.F. (1998) *Marketing Strategy and Competitive Positioning*, London: Prentice Hall.

Porter, M.: selections from any book on competitive strategy.

Case study: Chemcon

Chemcon is a German-based multinational firm with worldwide sales of over $10 billion. Its business is divided up into these sectors:

- pharmaceuticals
- speciality chemicals
- man-made fibres
- plastics
- consumer products sold through wholesalers and retailers (proprietary medicines, household products)

The spread of sales is approximately:

	%
North America	30
Western Europe	20
East Europe	10
Asia	20
Rest of the world	20

Questions

1 List the environmental factors which you think would be most likely to affect Chemcon's future. Do these vary according to which part of the business is being examined?

2 What information would you want to analyse in order to assess their situation in each of their markets?

3 Apply the exercises in questions 1 and 2 to your own organization. Is this sort of analysis carried out now? If not, should it be?

Chapter 5 | Understanding customers and consumers

Understanding customers

Customers' business and where you fit in

We now move on from understanding markets in a broad sense to understanding the people who make them up, the buyers. First we look at customers, then in the next section at consumers.

In this book the term 'customer' is used always to refer to organizations buying goods or services for their own use or for resale; 'consumers' are final buyers at retail level, purchasing for their private consumption. This section therefore deals with what is usually referred to as industrial or business-to-business marketing. In fact, customers include manufacturers buying raw materials and components, any organization buying supplies for its own use, and governmental and institutional buyers. A major category not always included within the gambit of industrial marketing is that of retailers, but the relationship between them and their suppliers is exactly like that between many manufacturers and the companies they buy from. In other words, virtually every firm has customers, and needs to understand them.

The characteristics of business-to-business marketing are examined in more detail in Chapter 16; here we will concentrate on how one should go about applying the basic marketing principle – first, understand your customer.

Only through a thorough understanding of who your customers are and what they are trying to achieve can you succeed in serving them. This becomes even more important as the relationship between supplier and customer becomes more and more of a partnership, rather than a continuing battle (see Randall 1994).

To begin with, you need to apply the lessons of the previous sections to your customers: what is happening in their environment, and in their market or markets? To understand and anticipate their needs, you have to understand fully what is affecting their business. Their markets may be wider or narrower than your own; in some cases you may even have to understand the end-use consumer market which your customer supplies. As a basis, you need to understand the structure of their industry and the forces driving change within it. A good grasp of the 'Value Chain' (Porter 1985) and where you, your competitors and your customers fit within it is necessary. Perhaps most important is to put together the latter two and to anticipate how the industry may change over the next few years, and how you may profit from that (or avoid possible threats).

Moving to the customers individually (and it is likely that a relatively small number of customers account for a major portion of your business), you need to understand as much as possible about each. Relevant questions are:

- **What is the current competitive position of the firm?** Market share, sales volume and value, profitability and share price are of interest. The views of their customers and of industry experts would be valuable.

- **What is the company strategy?** What are its chosen target markets and segments, what is its overall positioning, how does it try to achieve its objectives in terms of operating policies? A standard SWOT analysis (Strengths, Weaknesses, Opportunities, Threats) is a useful framework.

- **What is the specific role of the product to which your product contributes within the strategy?** How can your products help the customer achieve the strategic objectives? Is your product essential, or peripheral?

- **Who are the people running the business, in the different departments influencing the buying decision?** What sort of people are they, what are their aspirations, what are they trying to achieve, what are their problems and difficulties? What is the company culture: relaxed or formal, flexible or rule-bound?

- **Who really makes what decisions?** Who influences them, who controls the flow of information, how are decisions made, which policies are set in concrete and which can be bent a little?

(adapted from Randall 1994)

As will be discussed in Chapter 16, one of the main features of industrial marketing is this last question of decision-making.

Except for very routine purchases, it is likely that several people will take an interest in buying decisions, and it is vital to identify them and to understand each, as they will have different objectives and motivations.

This is explored fuller in the next section.

The Decision-Making Unit

The idea of the Decision-Making Unit (DMU) is fundamental to business-to-business marketing. There are different roles in the process of making a purchase:

- Initiator
- Influencer
- Gatekeeper
- Decider
- Buyer
- User

The initiator starts the whole process, one or many people both inside and outside the firm may influence the choice. The gatekeeper controls the flow of information to the others, and could be a purchasing manager, or a technical person, or the chief executive's secretary. Usually, one person has responsibility for making the final decision, but it may be a committee, or the whole board. The buyer is the person designated to make the formal purchase, for example by signing and issuing the relevant form. In a large company, many people might play a role, for example as users or influencers. In small firms, one person might play most of them, though there would usually be other influencers and users.

Marketing's job is to identify who plays which role in a particular target organization. Each identified person or group may differ in their:

- Objectives and criteria for the purchase.
- Influences at different times in the process.
- Importance in the overall decision.

The Finance Director, for instance, would look differently at the purchase of new equipment from the Manufacturing Director, and at an advertising campaign differently from the Marketing Director. The Chief Executive may appear in the process much later than the users, but have more importance in the decision. Each organization is unique, and its DMU is likely to be different in make-up and action.

Organizational buying behaviour

Although there is no substitute for the detailed understanding of each customer described above, there are some general principles of buying behaviour which can inform and broaden such understanding. There is a considerable and growing body of literature an the subject, both in the USA and in Europe. Organizations are constantly changing in response to changes in their environments, and over-generalization is therefore dangerous. On the other hand, some patterns of human behaviour stay reasonably constant, so we may draw some conclusions. The first thing to do is to dispel certain myths about industrial or organizational buying behaviour.

Probably the most powerful myth is that industrial buying decisions are 'rational' (as opposed to consumer buying decisions, which are in some way 'irrational'). All the research into how buying decisions are actually made underlines the fact that they are not purely rational economic decisions, although there are rational components. There are also other components, such as emotion, personal goals, or internal politics.

In the classical model of organizational buying behaviour, these components or variables are classed as task (directly related to the buying problem) and non-task (extending beyond the buying problem). Applying these to the four main classes of variable – individual, social, organizational, and environmental – produces the scheme shown in Table 5.1 (Webster and Wind 1973).

The other important concepts in the classical model have been summarized in the following terms:

> Organizational buying behavior is a complex *process* rather than a single, instantaneous act, and involves many persons, multiple goals, and potentially conflicting decision criteria. It often takes place over an extended period of time, requires information from many sources, and encompasses many interorganizational relationships.
>
> The organizational buying process is a form of problem solving, and a *buying situation* is created when someone in the organization perceives a problem . . . that can potentially be solved through some buying action. Organizational buying behavior includes all activities of organizational members as they define a buying situation and identify, evaluate, and choose among alternative brands and suppliers. The *buying center* includes all members of the organization who are involved in that process. The roles involved are those of user, influencer, decider, buyer, and gatekeeper (who controls the flow of information into the buying center).
>
> (Webster and Wind 1973)

The model as a whole is complex, as is shown in the diagrammatic representation in Figure 5.1. How much of the total analysis would be needed in any particular situation will depend on the nature of the buying situation. These vary considerably in complexity, of course. A useful classification is into new task, modified rebuy, and straight rebuy situations, which would generally be expected to decline in complexity. A more complete structure is provided in the so-called 'Buygrid' model shown in Table 5.2.

The most complex buying situations occur in the upper left portion of the Buygrid matrix, and involve the largest number of decision-makers and buying influences.

Table 5.1 Classification and examples of variables influencing organizational buying decisions

	Task	Non-task
Individual	Desire to obtain lowest price	Personal values and needs
Social	Meetings to set specifications	Informal, off-the-job interactions
Organizational	Policy regarding local supplier	Methods of personnel evaluation
Environmental	Anticipated changes in prices	Political climate in election year

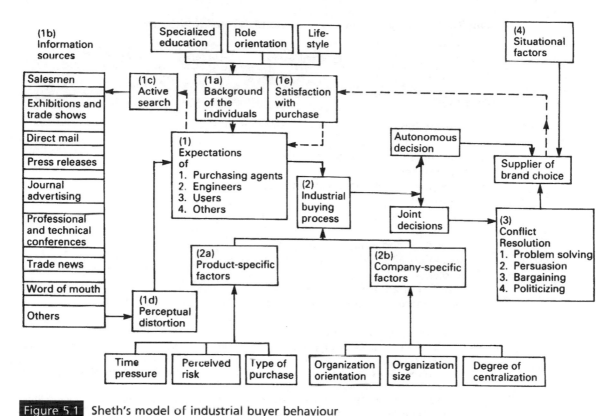

Figure 5.1 Sheth's model of industrial buyer behaviour
Reprinted with permission from *Journal of Marketing*, published by the American
Marketing Association, J.H. Sheth, 1973, vol. 37, no. 4 (p. 50–6).

The value of such frameworks is that they enable one to take a view of the nature and complexity of a particular situation, so that decisions can be taken on how to approach it. The more complex the situation, the more time and effort it will be worth spending on information-gathering and analysis. Disregarding complexity may lead a supplier to ignore important influencing factors and people.

The major change observable in buyer behaviour recently was mentioned briefly above: it is the trend towards partnership and away from adversarial relationships. The old style, still seen in many markets, was for a buyer to buy from a number of suppliers, partly for security, but partly also to play them off against each other. This sort of adversarial relationship tends to concentrate discussion on terms, especially price, and introduces an element of machismo. Changes in manufacturing practice, and the introduction of concepts such as Just-in-Time and total quality, have shown that this may not be the best approach and may lead to inadvertent suboptimization.

Over the last few years, Xerox has slashed its suppliers from 5,000 to about 350, and plans to cut the number further still. Each of the ones left is, or is becoming, Xerox's 'partner', each company aiming to make the other profitable. Paul Lawrence, of Harvard, calls this a value-added partnership (VAP).

(Peters 1989)

Table 5.2 The Buygrid framework for industrial buying situations

	Buyclasses		
Buyphases	*New task*	*Modified rebuy*	*Straight rebuy*
1 Anticipation or recognition of a problem and a general solution			
2 Determination of characteristics and quantity needed of item			
3 Description of characteristics and quantity of needed item			
4 Search for and qualification of potential sources			
5 Acquisition and analysis of proposals			
6 Evaluation of proposals and selection of supplier(s)			
7 Selection of an order routine			
8 Performance feedback and evaluation			

Source: Robinson *et al*. 1967 (p. 14)

Notes: 1 The most complex buying situations occur in the upper left portion of the Buygrid matrix, when the largest number of decision-makers and buying influences are involved. Thus, a new task in its initial phase of problem recognition generally represents the greatest difficulty for management.

2 Clearly, a new task may entail policy questions and special studies, whereas a modified rebuy may be more routine, and a straight rebuy essentially automatic.

3 As buyphases are completed, moving from phase 1 through phase 8, the process of 'creeping commitments' occurs, and there is diminishing likelihood of new vendors gaining access to the buying situation.

Other manufacturers are adopting a similar approach, and suppliers must be ready to adapt to the new style.

The IMP interaction approach

In Europe, a group of researchers decided in the late 1970s that the existing models did not represent the reality of organizational buying. They formed the Industrial Marketing and Purchasing (IMP) Research Group, and started publishing in the early 1980s. Essentially, they believed that much of the current literature concentrated on individual buying transactions, whereas in practice firms in business-to-business markets are involved in a continuing process of *interaction*. Any two partners are involved in a *relationship*; moreover, because of the complexity of many markets, they are probably part of a wider *network* of relationships. Analysis therefore needs to focus on these, rather than on a single decision.

At first sight, this approach seems to mirror those mentioned earlier, of relationship marketing and closer partnership, and indeed the group's work originally adopted this view. Later, it became clear to them that, in fact, the nature of relationships varies enormously. Some are still distant, adversarial and transaction-based, because that is the way that one or both partners prefers it (Ford 1997). Close co-operation and partnership is not always the best option. The electronic exchanges being set up, for example, will encourage price-oriented transactions, not partnership.

Clearly the nature of organizational buying behaviour is enormously complex, and only a flavour can be given here. Interested readers are referred to the texts at the end of the chapter for further information.

Understanding consumers

Bases of consumer behaviour

If industrial buying behaviour is complex, then how much more so is consumer behaviour? The social sciences which could contribute to our understanding include economics, anthropology, sociology, psychology, and perhaps psychiatry and psychoanalysis. None is yet a complete science of human behaviour, yet each has a vast literature. The ability to really understand consumers, and therefore to influence them or at least to predict the effect on them of marketing programmes, is the equivalent of the philosopher's stone which would turn base metal to gold. Over the years, marketing people have raided the social sciences for ideas which offer promise, and have also produced their own models. The problems with most of this work are that it is:

■ **eclectic:** only parts of a body of theory are chosen, with little regard for the overall theoretical framework;

■ **ad hoc:** not programmatic: pieces of research are carried out to tackle particular problems, rather than programmes of work over years to build up generalizable knowledge;

■ **commercial:** that is, kept secret, especially if the results are valuable.

Marketing people – and perhaps managers generally – are also prone to fashion: the latest technique or gimmick is taken up to loud claims, then quickly dropped when difficulties appear (as they inevitably do). All this makes it extremely difficult to present a body of knowledge which is generally accepted, and which is helpful in carrying out the marketing function.

What this section will do is to list briefly the main areas of knowledge which contribute to marketing understanding, looking in particular at those ideas which are commonly used by marketing people or appear in the literature, and examining the models used by practitioners.

One well-known British text on the behavioural aspects of marketing (Chisnall 1975) examines the following areas of knowledge:

■ Cognition

■ Motivation

■ Interpersonal response traits

■ Attitudes

■ Culture

- Social class
- Group influence
- Innovation (and marketing strategy)

It is a formidable list, and clearly cannot be covered in any detail here. We will look at a few relevant examples as illustrations of the way theories are used.

1 Cognition

This covers mental processes such as perception and learning, and as such has been of particular interest in advertising. One concept which enjoyed great favour was cognitive dissonance, associated with Festinger. The aspect of the theory which was used in marketing suggested that when we make a decision, dissonance occurs because we are not certain that we have made the right choice. We indulge in dissonance reduction activity, trying to convince ourselves, as it were, or rationalize. The theory could explain why people who have bought a brand are more likely to pay attention to advertisements for that brand than non-buyers. Other uses of cognition theory have concentrated on learning processes; complex models have not on the whole produced widely used results.

2 Motivation

Motivation is of course fundamental to purchasing behaviour, and at one time motivation research was extremely popular. Unfortunately its success relied mainly on the inspiration of the practitioner concerned, and was not reproducible. The theory which has lasted best, and is still used, is Maslow's hierarchy of needs. Maslow believed that humans are motivated by a series of needs; when a basic need is more or less satisfied, the next level comes into operation. The hierarchy is:

1 **Physiological needs:** hunger, thirst, sex.
2 **Safety needs:** security and order, protection.
3 **Belongingness and love needs:** to love and be loved.
4 **Esteem needs:** prestige, success, status.
5 **Self-actualization need:** personal fulfilment.

(Chisnall 1975)

Maslow's theory has been used in recent years in studies of the differences between European nations; some studies claim to show differing patterns of basic motivation, which could be used in positioning brands and developing advertising strategies, for example. On the whole, motivation remains elusive, though it is borne in mind in a qualitative way.

3 Interpersonal response traits

Personality, as we might more normally express it, has been a rich source of investigation for marketing. There have been many attempts to discover personality types associated with product and brand buying. The typical pattern is for a few studies to claim success, and many to be partially or totally unsuccessful. This topic will be returned to in the discussion on segmentation.

4   Attitude

Of all the fields listed, attitude research has been adopted more than any other in marketing. This seems to be mainly an intuitive reaction: marketing people measure attitudes to their brands anyway, and communications strategies are often couched in attitudinal terms. Unfortunately, even in the psychological literature, the concept of attitude is the subject of disagreement, and most marketing measurement is rather loose. The main problem, however, is the connection between attitude and behaviour.

We are interested only in people's behaviour, in particular whether they buy our brand or not. Attitudes are only a convenient intermediary, but the assumption is too easily made that the connection between favourable attitude and behaviour exists and is proven, it is not. There is no evidence of a direct, causal link between attitude and behaviour.

The fact that people have a favourable attitude towards our brand, or that we can change their attitude in a favourable direction, does not mean that their behaviour will change and that they will necessarily buy our brand. It is worth spending a little time on this because it is one of the fundamental misconceptions held about marketing. It seems intuitively right that attitudes and behaviour are linked, and we feel more comfortable when our brand is looked on favourably than unfavourably. But it must be stressed that, at least in the way that attitudes to brands are usually measured, attitudes cannot be used to predict behaviour.

Particularly in Britain, attitude research has been popular with practitioners, and many quite complex models have been developed. In the common form, a large number of attitude scales are generated (fifty to a hundred or more) using a repertory or 'Kelly' grid technique; these are reduced to a manageable but still large number by a statistical technique such as factor analysis, applied to a sample of consumers, and the results again factor analysed. Because of the statistics used, the results appear complex and impressive; but there is really no underlying theory, there can be considerable subjectivity in the use of the analysis, and the results are not normally generalizable. Potential buyers and users of such models should beware.

The only approach to the attitude–behaviour problem to show any real promise has been that of Fishbein, an American psychologist. He introduced a number of new ideas. First, it is the attitude to the act (e.g. buying, using the brand) which should be measured, not to the object (the brand itself). Second, the number of attitudes to be elicited is quite small, say six or seven. Then, the link between attitudes and behaviour is mediated by normative beliefs ('what other people important to me think is right'). Fishbein's approach has had some impressive successes, but not many applications have been reported in marketing. (For a clear explanation and some illustrations, see Tuck 1976.)

5   Culture

'Culture' means the whole complex of traditions, myths, beliefs and values which form a society. The notion has become more important in marketing as its international dimension has grown. It has become clear that although in some ways people in western countries are becoming more similar to each other, they are still different in ways which cannot be explained in terms of superficial variations. The chapter on international marketing will return to this theme.

6   Social class

This factor has been used in Britain for many years (much more so than in the USA) to measure and explain consumer behaviour. It has become progressively less useful, however, and there are now few markets in which it is a valid discriminator. The terminology is still with us, however, and should be explained. The British classification (not used elsewhere, and not normally outside marketing) is briefly:

AB: senior management, professionals, etc.

C1:   lower management, clerical, white collar

C2:   skilled manual workers

D: unskilled manual workers

E: unemployed, pensioners, etc.

The British government uses a different social (or socio-economic) classification, as do other governments. All are based on the occupation of the head of household. Other methods of classification are now much more useful, such as those based on residential neighbourhood (see Chapter 7).

7   Group influence

The use of theories about group influence falls under three main headings:

- **The reference group** is that group of people to whom we consciously or unconsciously refer in our actions and thoughts. There may be a number of such groups – friends, work-mates, groups to which we aspire (including heroes and idols). Some purchases are influenced by group thinking, and it can be seen that many advertising campaigns play on this.

- **Opinion leadership** is a seductive idea: that within all groups there is a small number of people whose opinions are important and influential. If these people could be identified and reached by marketing effort, it would make campaigns much more efficient. Unfortunately, the task has proved difficult in practice.

- **The family** is clearly a special sort of group, and is highly influential in many situations (though perhaps becoming less so). Interestingly, industrial marketing ideas on buying centres and the roles of influencer, decider, etc. can be applied to the family. The housewife may make the actual purchase, but is often acting as the agent for other family members. As roles within the family change, research will need to keep our views of family behaviour up to date. The various stages of the family life cycle and their influence on buying patterns are referred to in Chapter 7.

8 Innovation

Theories on how innovation spreads are of enormous interest in marketing, both consumer and industrial. If we could explain and predict how new products and new ideas would be adopted, many mistakes could be avoided. The main theoretical work was done by Everett Rogers (Rogers 1962). He split the population into five categories, according to the speed with which they adopted an innovation:

1	Innovators	2.5 per cent
2	Early adopters	13.5 per cent
3	Early majority	34 per cent
4	Late majority	34 per cent
5	Laggards	16 per cent

These categories form a normal distribution. There is a link with the idea of opinion leaders: if innovators are also opinion leaders, for example, they would be prime targets for marketing activity. Again, however, life is not so simple. There appears to be no general category of innovators: people who innovate in one field may be conservative in others. Some studies suggest that it is in fact the early adopters who are opinion leaders; innovators will try anything new, but will move on to the next novelty quickly. Chapter 10, on new product development, examines in more detail the theme of innovation.

Finally, we should mention the main attempts to produce an integrated model of consumer behaviour. The names of Nicosia, Engel Kollat and Blackwell, and Howard and Sheth occur in all the texts on the subject; theirs represent the three major integrated models. The Howard and Sheth model is shown diagrammatically in Figure 5.2; it is similar in content to the others, and can be taken to be representative of the general approach. It can be seen that it is, to say the least, complicated. Only one partial test has been reported, with mixed results (Farley and Ring 1970). The lack of substantive development since then suggests that these enormous, complicated constructions are a blind alley, and it is not clear why they are given so much prominence in the literature.

How can one try to sum up such a welter of detail?

1 It is important to try to understand the springs of human behaviour in order to understand and predict how consumers will behave.

2 The progress towards this goal has been disappointing, mainly because research in marketing tends to the *ad hoc*, and is commercially sensitive (if there are huge successes, we don't know about them). There are some insights, and relevant theory can be applied, but great care is needed.

3 Marketing people should try to build knowledge about their particular markets and the behaviour underlying them over time and in a systematic way. One example of this is given in the next section.

Buying patterns

Apart from trying to understand *why* people behave as they do, it is important to monitor *what* they do, in particular what they buy, how often, where, and so on. Huge amounts of

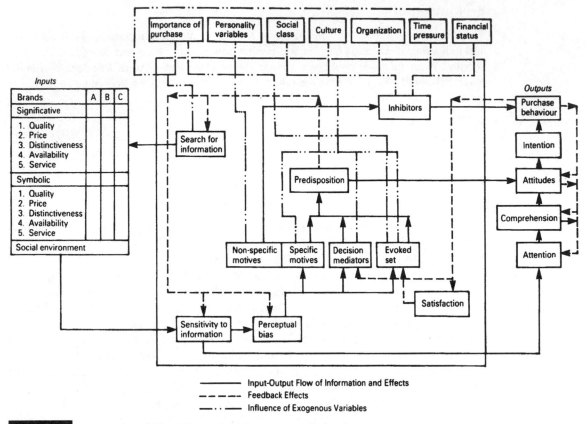

| Figure 5.2 | Howard and Sheth's model of consumer behaviour |

data are collected on purchasing, but little of it is analysed systematically. An exception, however, is the work of Ehrenberg and his colleagues, who over many years have been analysing buying patterns in many different markets (Ehrenberg 1972; 1988).

What Ehrenberg found was that in 'stationary' markets, in which sales and brand shares are stable, regular patterns can be discerned, and can be described using the proportion of the population buying in a period and the average number of times they buy. The number of repeat buyers of each brand in the next and subsequent periods can then be predicted. These basic, regular patterns have been found in a very large number of different markets, both consumer and industrial. The same technique has been applied to television viewing, with similar results.

Although Ehrenberg's work can be criticized (mainly on the grounds that it does not explain why the structure appears as it does), it is of the highest importance. The reason for this is that it establishes beyond question *what actually happens*, rather than what people think or hope happens. That Ehrenberg's results disprove some long-held assumptions is in its favour, rather than against. Any model (such as Howard and Sheth's, for example) which sets itself up to explain consumer behaviour can be tested against the Ehrenberg results to see if the patterns predicted match up.

As an example, ideas about brand-switching often rely on the notion, either explicit or implicit, that a buyer is loyal to a single brand over some period, and then for some reason (perhaps advertising) switches to another brand, to which they are then loyal. Ehrenberg's results show conclusively that most buyers in most markets normally buy a repertoire of brands; their favourite brand is the one bought most frequently, but it is rarely bought exclusively. Models of how advertising works must take account of this knowledge (see Chapter 12). Most consumer markets are in fact stationary; they are mature, and brand shares do not often change dramatically. If they do, then Ehrenberg's model can be used to see how the new patterns have changed from the old. More programmatic research of this kind would be of great value in increasing our understanding of consumer behaviour.

Key learning points

- **Marketing must proceed from a profound understanding of customers and consumers. In this book, the word customers is used to refer to firms buying for their own use or for resale, while consumers is used to refer to individuals buying for their own or their family's consumption.**

- **To understand your customers, you need to understand their markets and the environment in which they operate. The structure of the industry, and the forces which are driving it, will affect your customers and therefore the way you can best meet their needs.**

- **To understand an individual customer, you need to look at: their current competitive position; their strategy; the specific role of your product within that strategy; the people running the business, and the company culture within which they work; who makes what decisions, who influences them, who controls the flow of information; how decisions are made.**

- **Industrial buying is different from consumer buying (though it may or may not be more 'rational'). Models of organizational buying behaviour may help to understand the complexity of the process.**

- **Consumer behaviour can be enormously complicated, and we know relatively little about what makes human beings act in the way they do. There is a large literature on this subject, briefly summarized in the chapter.**

Further reading

Chisnall, P.M. (1995) *Consumer Behaviour*, 3rd edition, Maidenhead: McGraw Hill.
Ford, D. (ed) (1997) *Understanding Business Markets*, 2nd edition, London: The Dryden Press.

Case study: Chemcon 2

Chemcon was described briefly in the case study at the end of Chapter 4. Here we will look at two of its divisions – man-made fibres and consumer products (proprietary medicines and household products).

The man-made fibres division produces filaments and yarns which are sold to textile manufacturers: the textile manufacturers in turn sell to firms who make clothing and furnishing fabric (some for consumer markets and some for industrial applications).

The consumer products division makes a variety of mainly branded products which they sell through wholesalers and retailers. They also produce some retailers' brands.

Questions

1 For each division, specify the people amongst their customers and consumers whose decisions it would be important to understand and influence.

2 Compare the two divisions: how different will their approaches be to understanding their customers and consumers?

3 Apply question 1 to your organization (or to a manageable part of it). How well do you know your customers and/or consumers? If you have not done so recently, talk to a few and try to understand how your product or service fits into their life.

Chapter 6 | Marketing information

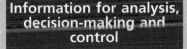
Information for analysis, decision-making and control

Why do we need information? If you have studied statistical decision theory you will know that it is used to reduce uncertainty to risk, that is, to convert a situation in which you do not know the probabilities attached to a set of outcomes to one where you do know the probabilities and can therefore assess the risk.

We will return to that way of looking at it in the next section. For now, let us try to take a broader view.

A manager needs information to help analyse situations, make decisions and control the implementation of plans. In terms of analysis or diagnosis, take a common situation, in which sales of a product are below target. Those of the 'Ready, fire, aim' school will take immediate action ('Reduce the price, put in more sales calls . . .'). The more thoughtful manager will want to ask, 'Why are sales below expectation?' For this, you need information: are sales down in all areas, are total market sales down or just your share, are sales down for all customers or only one, has a competitor made some aggressive move, and so on? At progressive levels of diagnosis, further levels of information will be needed, down perhaps to detailed measures of product performance amongst consumers.

For decision-making, our own experience tells us that we need information to help. When we choose a new car, we will have certain constraints in mind (such as a maximum price) and some explicit or implicit objectives: number of passengers to be carried, ability to carry large loads, fuel economy, performance, appearance and so on. To choose between the hundreds of car models available, we collect information about these criteria. A business decision is essentially similar. As Figure 6.1 shows, a logical procedure for making a decision starts with the definition of objectives, which enables criteria to be set up; you can then see if information is available, and if it is not, set up an information collection procedure. When all the information is available, the options can be evaluated against the criteria, and a decision made.

A central problem with marketing is that many of the decisions to be made concern choices between different courses of action; unfortunately, information on the effects of marketing action is often extremely difficult to collect.

To take the sales example further: let us assume that we have found out that a competitor has launched a new product which has taken sales from us. The possible courses of action are to lower our price, to increase advertising, or to put on a special trade

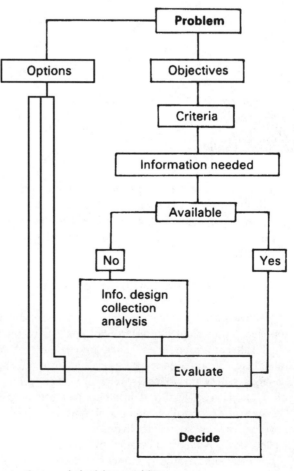

 **Figure 6.1** Information and decision-making

promotion to retailers. How do we evaluate those choices? The information we need would show the likely effect on sales of each option, which we could set against the costs to compare the results with our objectives (profit, market share). We could rely on experience, we could try different actions in different areas and compare results (if the retailers would co-operate!), or we could, in an ideal world, refer to information we had previously collected and stored. This is typical of many marketing problems, and will affect the design of a marketing information system discussed below.

The third way in which we would want to use information is in control. In systems terms, control is provided by feedback. In a central heating system, the thermostat measures the temperature and switches the boiler on or off when the lower and upper limits are reached. Similarly, once we have launched a marketing programme, we need feedback to make sure that it is going according to plan. If it is, no action is needed; if it is not, then we are back to the analysis phase. What sort of information is needed will depend on the objectives and nature of the particular programme, but apart from total sales it might include, for instance, sales in particular target groups, measures of advertising impact, or buying and usage patterns.

It should of course be said that all this is logical and rational, but there are other reasons why information is collected and ways in which it is in fact used in real life. One manager in a large corporation had a file labelled DZB–l; when asked what it was, he said that obviously DZB–l stood for CYA, and the file contained information which he might need to protect himself. Information, including marketing information, is used for political reasons, to justify decisions already taken, and sometimes even for comfort. None of this is wrong, as long as you are clear about the reasons and are aware of the cost – a point we move on to in the next section.

It must be stated that information, however detailed, can only ever *help*; it can never take the place of judgement. There will always be a very high degree of uncertainty in marketing decisions, and managerial judgement and flair will always be at a premium.

Costs and benefits of information

All information has a cost. How can we decide how much it is worth spending on it? The statistical decision theory mentioned earlier has an answer, or at least an approach, which will be very briefly outlined here.

The first step is to calculate the Expected Value of Perfect Information. Of course, perfect information is impossible, as it stands for certainty; we can never know the future with certainty. What the concept can do is set an upper limit on what would be worth spending. An example will help to show what is meant.

A firm has the choice of continuing with its present policies, of expanding cautiously, or of expanding rapidly. Three possible 'states of nature' would reflect low, medium and high market growth; they would result in potential sales to the firm of £5,000, £15,000 and £30,000 respectively. The probability of each is 0.5, 0.3 and 0.2. The outcome for each strategy (say contribution after costs) under each state of nature is calculated and put into the table. The Expected Monetary Value (EMV) is the sum of the outcomes multiplied by the probabilities.

Probability	.5	.3	.2	EMV
Outcomes	5K	15K	30K	
Strategies:				
Present	1,000	1,100	1,200	1,070
Expand slowly	− 500	2,000	2,200	790
Expand rapidly	− 2,000	500	3,000	− 250

If the firm knew with absolute certainty which state of nature would prevail, they would choose the option which would give the best result in those circumstances. The probability of each state of nature is therefore multiplied by the best choice (1,000, 2,000 and 3,000 respectively) to give an Expected Value Under Certainty of 1,700.

The maximum EMV is 1,070, so the value of having perfect information to improve the expected outcome is 1,700 minus 1,070, or 630. That is the Expected Value of Perfect Information.

Thus in this case it would be worth spending an amount of up to 630 on information. We could then go on to calculate the expected value of survey information, building in the possible margin of error inherent in non-perfect information. Using Bayes' theorem we could do some quite sophisticated calculations of the effect that information would have on our decision. Interested readers are referred to the text listed at the end of the chapter.

This is the theoretical approach; if we do not wish to use that technique, how do we decide? Often, the criteria are cost and time; how much is in the budget, and when can we have the information? These are perfectly practical and reasonable considerations in certain circumstances, but ideally one would prefer a more rational approach, certainly to major decisions. The real criterion must be the potential benefit of a better decision, and the possible cost of a wrong one. In the launch of a new product, for example, the difference between a good and bad decision could be millions of pounds; even a hundred thousand pounds in information costs could be cheap. The problem then is, how to estimate these possible benefits and costs. Without using Bayesian techniques, the only answer is judgement. Even a broad guess (hopefully an informed and experienced one) may throw light on the issue; very exact answers cannot be expected.

This leads on to the attempt to plan what information may be needed, and how to obtain it.

Designing an information system

Although information systems have been written about for decades (often in rather grandiose and far-fetched ways) it is only recently that large computer-based systems have become a reality. An information system does not have to be complex and computer-based, of course. The idea of a system is merely to try to look ahead and plan what marketing information you will need, and make sure it is available at the right time in the right form to the right people. The existence of cheap computer power and user-friendly software does offer opportunities for storage and retrieval of large amounts of data, and of performing complex analyses on them, and it would be foolish to ignore that. But even the smallest department or firm can plan its information needs without sophisticated hardware.

We have seen how information is needed for analysis, decision-making and control. In principle, then, we need to think about what sort of analyses we may want to make during the year (or years) ahead, what decisions we will take, and what control measures we will need. It may be, of course, that the marketing information is just part of a wider management information system, and its planning will be affected by that. It is important, however, for the marketing people to make sure that they get what they want out of the company system. As will be seen, this may not happen of its own accord; a system dominated by computer professionals and accountants is often not responsive to marketing needs.

The sorts of information required will come from both inside and outside the company and can be grouped as follows:

1 **Internal:**
   - ▪ Production
     - – production capacity
     - – stock levels
   - ▪ Accounting
     - – product profitability
     - – customer profitability
     - – budgets and reports
     - – forecasts
   - ▪ Sales
     - – booked
     - – shipped
     - – volume and value

2 **External:**
   - ▪ Environment
   - ▪ Markets
   - ▪ Competitors
   - ▪ Customers
   - ▪ Consumers
   - ▪ Effects of marketing action

Internal information

Production information is increasingly important in many marketing situations, as company operations become more integrated. Depending on the industry, you are likely to want access to up-to-date information on production levels, stock and perhaps lead times for new orders.

Accounting information, allied to data from production, is vital for understanding cost–volume–profit relationships, of which all marketing people ought to have a good grasp. A word needs to be said about accounting data, however, which should be treated with care:

- Accountants – rightly – produce data for their own purposes, often for statutory reasons. What they produce may not be suitable for other uses.

- There is also reason for caution in using standard costing data, as many traditional systems produce figures which may be inaccurate at best, and actually misleading at worst. As an example, overheads are often allocated to products on the basis of share of labour costs; but in some cases, labour costs now make up only 5 or 10 per cent of total direct costs. This can lead to serious distortions, and possibly wrong decisions (Johnson and Kaplan 1987). The cost data go into profit calculations, and the results may be the basis for decisions on where to allocate resources.

- Product profitability should be one of marketing's main concerns, and as much detail as is reasonable should be asked for. There are companies with thousands of products, and in this case they must be grouped; but it is vital to know where the profits are being made.

- Customer profitability may also be important when a few customers make up a significant proportion of total sales (as with a manufacturer selling through major retail multiples; see Randall 1994). Such analyses sometimes produce surprising results, showing that some customers are hardly worth supplying, or should be supplied in a different way. Most businesses have a long tail of relatively unprofitable clients, but it is difficult to sort them out without the right information.

- Budgets and reports should be timely and should contain the relevant information, including variation from target and comparison with the previous year. This may sound obvious, but one consultant has built up a world-wide business based on supplying software which produces easy-to-use forecasts and budget reports for sales and marketing managers. The clients are multinational companies whose central accounting and computing experts were apparently unable to provide what was wanted.

- Forecasting is closely connected with budgets, and is therefore included here. One might assume that marketing people are best placed to make market and sales forecasts; surprisingly, they do not always do so. Whoever produces them, they should clearly state the assumptions used; making adjustments becomes much easier, as does the reconciliation of sales to forecasts when what has happened is that one or more of the basic assumptions has been wrong.

Sales

The bridge between internal and external information is sales. It is important that everyone discussing sales figures knows exactly what they mean: it can mean orders booked, ex-factory shipments, invoiced total (gross, or net of discounts or returns), or some estimate of purchases by customers. In many industries it is helpful to have data on both volume and value of sales. From a marketing point of view, it is extremely useful to have total industry data and market share; these can only be provided by an outside source, either a trade association which collects data from members, or a market research company which collects and sells syndicated information.

External information

1   Environment

Other external information can cover a very wide range. If we need to keep abreast of trends in the environment, we need some information; depending on what aspects we have decided are important, this may involve government and international publications, economic reports, commercial reports from 'future' specialists, or a clipping or monitoring service. A huge amount of information is available from government sources at www.statistics.gov.uk. Another government site, www.foresight.gov.uk, brings together expert views on future developments. A good local library is free, and staffed by trained information specialists who may be glad of a new challenge. The Internet now makes vast amounts of information available, so much that practice and skill are needed to find the most relevant, and to sort the good from the bad.

2   Markets

At the level of your own industry and markets, a great deal of information probably already flows into the company, through trade publications, regular market research reports, and feedback from the sales force. It is worth examining the nature of the information now and again, to make sure that what is timely and relevant is reaching the appropriate people. Sales force call reports, in particular, are a potentially rich source of information, but are not always properly filled in, collected and disseminated.

3   Competitors

Related to, and in some sense part of, this is information on competitors. Large or well-staffed companies may attempt a full Porter industry structure analysis, placing competitors in strategic groups. Others will want to collect as much objective intelligence as possible. Major competitors in your strategic group should be identified, and a dossier compiled on each. Much information will already be available, but financial data, for example, can also provide useful insights. It could be a way of bridging the gap that too often exists between marketing staff and accountants to ask your finance people to produce financial analyses of the main competition (and explain to you what the ratios mean in practical terms). Well-prepared companies have rich detail on their competitors, including estimates of their cost structure, management organization and style, strategy and policies, and probable future moves. It is possible to stay well this side of industrial espionage and still collect a great deal of information.

Apart from immediate competitors, there are others of whom we should take account. They may come from several sources.

- Other strategic groups in the industry.
- Segments in which we do not currently compete.
- Other industries.
- Other countries.

The probability that new competitors will enter depends on:

- The attractiveness of the industry and strategic group.
- Any barriers to entry.
- The resources and capabilities of potential new entrants.

The PC market has seen many new entrants, including start-ups such as Dell and Gateway as well as foreign competitors from Asia. The UK financial services industry has witnessed entries from supermarkets and the Virgin group. Many previously domestically controlled markets have been entered by competitors from overseas. These new competitors may have unforeseen strengths, and different strategies.

4 Customers

Customers should be studied in the same way as competitors; in some cases, they are to an extent competitors too. The discussion in the previous chapter on understanding your customers outlined the sort of information you will want to collect and record on a formal basis. It should include information on trends in their industry as well as financial, share and strategic information on each major company. Details on the buying process and who are the influencers, deciders, users and gatekeepers within major customers should be available and kept up to date. If possible, such external data should be linked to internal data on past ordering, any problems experienced, and the general history of your relationship with them. We will return to the issue of customer databases later in this chapter.

5 Consumers

Consumers, if you sell to them, should be at the heart of the information system. It is the job of every marketing person to know as much as possible about consumers, both quantitatively and qualitatively. Much of this will be collected through market research (see next section), but it is valuable also to make some personal contacts. There is no substitute for actually listening to consumers talking about your product, or watching them use it in a natural setting.

> **What you need to understand above all, beyond the basic facts about who they are, is where your product fits into their lives: what they are trying to achieve with it, what the problems and particular satisfactions are, everything, in fact, to do with the product in use.**

The other major focus should be on the brand personality: what makes it a brand, not just a product, how do consumers relate to it, how does it compare with competing brands? Branding (see Chapter 9) is at the centre of the consumer marketing job, and the more relevant information you can collect to help, the better.

6 Effects of marketing action

The final area which you need to build into your information system is also probably the most difficult – measurement of the effects of marketing effort. To make sensible decisions about how much to spend on advertising, or what price to charge, or whether to increase product quality, or when to run a promotion, you ideally need information on what the likely effect of alternative actions will be. Unfortunately this is extremely complex, if not impossible. Take the question of price. Economists will tell you how to set an optimum price – as long as you know the price elasticity of demand. While there are techniques for trying to gauge price sensitivity through survey techniques (Gabor 1977), the only real way is through experimentation; but experimenting with different prices is impossible in some markets, and difficult in most. Neither customers nor your own sales force will be happy, and controlling the experiment is often tricky. Controlling what happens in the market-place, and particularly what competitors do, is impossible. In any attempt to measure the effect of marketing effort, this problem of lack of control is present. The issue is complicated by the dynamic nature of many markets (if you understand it this year, it may have changed by next year), and by interaction between marketing variables (different levels of price have a different effect when combined with different levels of advertising or different distribution patterns). Some effects are also lagged: advertising this period causes some sales next period, and possibly in later periods.

All this may be rather depressing, but it does not mean that the attempt should be abandoned; it means that the aim of understanding should be a long-term one, and information design and collection should be planned to take place over time. It means planning the measurement at the same time as the marketing programme, and also perhaps designing an experiment into the programme itself. Without such determined, long-term effort, plans and decisions will continue to be made on the basis of hunch and experience.

Putting all this together may produce an enormous list of information which would be very costly to collect and store. Apart from the approaches outlined in the previous section, you can sift the 'ideal' list through the following checklist of questions. You should ask yourself:

■ What analyses and decisions will I have to make next year?

■ How will I control my marketing programmes?

■ What would I do differently if I had that information? (If the answer is 'nothing', you don't need it.)

■ How would I actually use it?

■ What information do my competitors use, and for what? (They may not always be right, of course.)

This should cut down the list to a manageable size; if it does not, some judgements on priorities will need to be made.

The final stage is to decide how the information is to be stored, retrieved and disseminated. To repeat, cheap computing power and software should be considered, as they can enormously enhance the accessibility and usefulness of information (the use of major databases and data warehouses is discussed later in this chapter). They are not essential, however. The most important ingredient is careful thought and planning as to who needs what information, when; quite simple systems can provide valuable, timely information.

Market research methods

Clearly the whole subject of market research cannot be covered in any depth here, and readers who wish to learn more are referred to one of the books listed at the end of the chapter. Most managers will sometimes need to use market research, or to commission it; this section will try to give you enough basic understanding to do that sensibly.

Let us start with a definition. Some books try to distinguish between market research and marketing research: market research in this view is research into markets, and is one type of marketing research, along with advertising research, consumer research, and so on. Personally I have never found this distinction helpful, and in this book the two phrases will be used interchangeably, usually in the standard British form of market research. The definition of market research used is:

The collection, analysis and presentation of information to help in marketing decision-making and control.

Secondary data

The first thing to do when information is needed is to see what is available already. Such information is somewhat confusingly referred to as 'secondary data', to distinguish it from primary data – information collected for the first time. In the UK, this first step is usually called desk research. As the previous section outlined, a carefully designed information system should provide much of the data you want.

Further secondary data are usually available too. Large companies may have specialized information units to help find what is needed, but in smaller organizations it is often up to the individual manager. In many markets there are large amounts of data published by the government, by trade associations and by commercial market research companies. A big central library should have a good range. In London in particular there are specialized libraries, such as the City Business Library. If you really know very little about a market, a good place to start is often the relevant trade association or the editor of the trade journal. Finding one good contact frequently leads on to others. The Internet, as we have noted, is now an almost inexhaustible source.

The problem with secondary data is that they are collected for another purpose, are often not detailed enough for what you want, are out of date, or biased. They should be evaluated carefully before being used.

Primary data

Once the possibilities of desk research have been exhausted, new data may need to be collected. There are three main sources: experimentation, observation and respondents.

1 Experimentation

Experimentation has already been mentioned; it is an under-used approach, and for certain types of information is the only one which will provide reliable, valid data (the effect of advertising on sales, for example). The difficulties should not be minimized, but there are occasions when quite simple experiments can yield useful results. Where feasible, different prices could be charged in different areas, for example, or different advertisements placed in different publications and the results measured by coupon returns. Careful and accurate design and analysis of experiments is vital; managers who wish to try them are referred to the book listed under further reading for guidance.

2   Observation

Observation, too, is often forgotten and can also provide valuable insights. It may be unstructured, for instance watching how people shop; or structured, for instance using a physical pantry check to see what brands are actually in the home. Current techniques allow consumers to record their purchases by scanning the bar-codes using a special wand. Watching what people actually do, rather than what they say they do in buying and using products, may provide useful clues, and avoids the problems of memory and bias. Observation may also be carried out by mechanical means such as traffic counters or meters attached to television sets.

3   Respondents

Most market research exercises involve obtaining data from respondents by asking them questions. This may be done by personal (face-to-face) interview, by mail or by telephone.

- Personal interviews are the most flexible, and overall yield the richest data; they are usually the most expensive, however, and may be subject to interviewer bias.

- Mail surveys can be cheap, but suffer from limitations as to what can be covered; it is also difficult to control who fills in the questionnaire. Their main drawback is that the response rate is usually low, and the sample obtained may therefore be unrepresentative; it is dangerous to rely on the results of a mail survey unless some check has been made on non-respondents.

- Telephone interviewing has always been used widely in industrial markets, and in recent years has become very much more common in consumer markets. There are two reasons for this: the spread of domestic telephones to the majority of homes, and the development of computer-assisted telephone interviewing (CATI). The latter can control the interview as the questions are asked from the screen, and enables the responses to be entered directly as they are given, allowing very rapid turnaround times for surveys. Sophisticated systems will redial engaged numbers, or even redial a given number when the interview is interrupted and return the interviewer to the place reached in the questionnaire. Telephone interviewing is relatively cheap, but obviously is limited to topics which can be asked about over the phone. It may of course be used in combination with one or more of the other methods.

Qualitative research

Market research can be either qualitative or quantitative. Qualitative research is often used at the beginning of a project, when we know little about the subject. Individual in-depth interviews or small group discussions are used to explore people's views and attitudes in a fairly unstructured way, allowing respondents to speak for themselves in their own language. This is important, as it is only too easy to assume that we know how people think about products and what words they use. Qualitative methods can produce very rich and fascinating data, and should throw up hypotheses for further investigation. The results should not be relied on for decision-making, however, as normally the sample size is small (probably less than 100) and the sample may not be representative.

Quantitative research

As the name implies, quantitative research tries to measure things, to put numbers to them. A great deal of research is of this type: how many people buy which brand, how often, where, and so on. Even research into attitudes and motivation reaches a quantitative stage when we try to measure how many people hold which attitude.

Choice of methods

To decide which particular methods should be used for a specific project, it is helpful to use a checklist:

- **Define the problem**
  then decide on:
  1 What data.
  2 From which source(s).
  3 How to collect.
  4 How to contact the source.
  5 How to select the units.
  6 What analyses to carry out.
  7 Costs and timing.

- **Communicate the results.**

The first and last stages are emphasized, because they are the ones in which a manager is most likely to be involved, and because, although they are vital to the success of the project, they are often neglected. Defining the real problem is crucial, and needs careful thought. What might appear at first sight to be the problem may be merely a symptom, or part of a wider problem. Further, market research may be able to contribute to some parts of the problem, but not to others. This problem definition stage is therefore the responsibility of the manager who suffers the problem, but demands joint discussions with the market research expert.

The detailed questions of research design are really the province of the expert, but a manager needs to be able to understand enough to judge whether the design will produce the information needed. Do not be afraid to ask questions, and make sure the expert can explain everything in a way you can understand. The process is the same as buying any outside service, whether the provider is actually outside the firm or just in a different department. Good questions to ask are, 'Why use that particular method?', 'What other ways could it be done?', 'What are the advantages and disadvantages of each?'

Sampling

The most technical part of the design, and the most difficult for a non-expert to understand, is the sample. Most non-statisticians do not understand why we can rely on figures from a sample of a few hundred or a few thousand people out of a population of millions, and how much reliance we can place on them. The reasons lie in the field of statistical theory, which you will study elsewhere. Only two things will be said here:

1 Provided that the sample is representative and unbiased, we can rely on the results,

2 The results will always be only an estimate, subject to sampling error.

Statistical theory will tell us that we can and should apply confidence limits to any figure from a sample: we can say with a given level of confidence (say 95 per cent, or twenty to one) that the true figure in the population lies within a certain range. For example, the political polls which measure people's voting intentions may throw up a figure of 39 per cent who say they intend to vote for Party A. What we should really say is that there is a 95 per cent chance that the true figure is between, say, 35 per cent and 44 per cent. How big those confidence limits are depends on a number of factors, particularly the sample size and design, and how much variation there is in the population in the thing being measured.

The importance of taking this probabilistic view cannot be over-emphasized. It is never justifiable to say that a survey shows that exactly 54 per cent of buyers prefer brand X (or even worse, that 54.3 per cent prefer it). In interpreting survey results, you should always see each figure as a range, rather than a specific number, even though for convenience we may quote them as single figures.

As a manager, you need to ask what level of accuracy is needed in this specific case, which goes back to the decision you have to make. It is useful to look at the smallest cells (subdivisions of the sample) which you want to use in making comparisons. For instance, if you want to compare brand usage amongst housewives aged under thirty-five in the north-west with those over thirty five, it is the size of those groups in the sample which need to be examined. As a very rough guide, sample sizes under one hundred will measure only very large differences.

Random samples

The best type of sample design (and, strictly speaking, the only one on which statistical tests may be used) is the random or probability sample. 'Random' in this sense has a technical meaning, that every member of the population being sampled has a known probability (usually, though not always, equal) of being selected. For technical and practical reasons, a random sample is expensive for personal interview surveys, and is used only when a very high-quality sample is needed; the same considerations do not necessarily apply to mail and telephone surveys, so random sampling methods can be used there more easily.

Quota samples

Non-random samples are called quota (or judgement, or purposive) samples. Frequently we know enough about the population to be sampled – housewives, or the general population, or firms in a particular industry – to be able to set quotas for each category which will produce a representative sample. For the general population, these quotas would be set for age within sex, perhaps with social class as well. Thus each interviewer would have a daily quota of so many males and females in each age-group; other controls might be concerned with buying patterns, for example (so many product buyers and non-buyers). When all the quotas are added together, the result reflects the target population. The obvious problem with quota samples is that people who are difficult to find or to interview – working women, people who travel a lot, teenagers, old people, immigrants – will be under-represented. This may or may not matter, depending on the objectives of the survey. The dangers of bias must be weighed against the ease and cheapness of the method.

Market research agencies

Most managers will be buyers and users of market research, rather than practitioners. Most research is carried out by independent agencies, who cover the whole range from large generalists to small specialists; you or your market research specialists may already be familiar with some suppliers. In Great Britain the Market Research Society's annual handbook gives details of firms, from which a selection may be made. The Industrial Market Research Association may also be useful. After preliminary enquiries have produced a short-list, the chosen agencies should be carefully briefed; the brief should set out the background and objectives, relevant data on the market and population, type of research envisaged (if known), timing and any cost limitations, and action standards. It is not appropriate to ask several agencies for elaborate proposals unless the job is a very large one.

In evaluating a research proposal, you should look for and assess the following:

- statement of objectives
- description of research methods
- details of fieldwork, including sample design
- questionnaire
- data handling, including analysis proposed
- reporting method
- timetable
- costs.

As with any proposal, the firm's track record, and the justification and supporting evidence in the proposal, will be important.

Lastly, the vital importance of communicating the results of research to the relevant people must be underlined. British researchers have the reputation of being technically very proficient, but less good at making action recommendations. It is the responsibility of the manager who has commissioned the research to understand it thoroughly (perhaps with help from experts) and to make sure that the key results and their implications are communicated to everyone else concerned. Research which is not used is a waste of money.

Databases, data warehouses and data mining

Databases

Earlier chapters explained how important customers are, and how relationship marketing and customer relationship management are being applied. Here we look a little further at what the data requirements are for these applications. As we noted, it is the availability of cheaper computing power, and relevant software, that have made such developments possible.

The idea of a database is simple, and we saw earlier in this chapter how companies might think about what data to collect about their customers. To formalize it in a database, we may list what we want to know in more detail. We will, where possible, want to record: identity, DMU details, demographics, soft data, buying patterns, history with us, and responses to past marketing (Chapter 12 expands on these in more detail).

The nature of the database should reflect what the user wants from it, from simple listing and mailing to everyone, through selecting only those with certain characteristics, to very complex analyses of buying patterns and responses. It is important to think through what you may need, as you will be able to carry out an analysis only if the relevant data have been recorded, they are recorded in a form that allows the analysis you want, and the software is capable of performing that analysis.

The sources of data will include much internal data, external sources such as directories or business information services (such as ABI Inform), or mailing list houses. One of the main tasks is to prepare data from different sources so that everything is compatible; this will be true even for internal data from different departments. Accuracy and timeliness are important, too, as with any data. As we saw in Chapter 2, getting co-operation from all functions is not always easy. Setting up and running a successful database involves getting and keeping the full support of all the relevant departments.

Data warehouses

The idea of data warehouses arose from the need to use data from a wide range of sources, and the ability of computer technology to store and analyse large amounts. 'Data warehousing is an approach to the capture, storage and management of data' (Herman 2000), and tries to put together data from within and outside the firm that can contribute to management decision-making. Originally, some companies tried to centralize *all* data, but it quickly became clear that the benefits of this extremely difficult task were elusive. More recently, most firms centralize and standardize some data, but only what is necessary. Further, the idea of one, centralized warehouse has been superseded in some organizations by data marts, that is, a series of smaller collections of data each devoted to a specific area or purpose. So-called third-generation warehouses are tailored to corporate Intranets.

The way that firms use data warehouses depends on their size and the nature of their business. Smaller firms focus particularly on customer retention and market segmentation, while larger firms additionally look for applications to utilization and cost reduction (IDC 1997 Technology Implementation Panel Study, quoted in Herman: 2000: 18). The type of business that has had most success with the approach is that which generates large amounts of standard transaction data, such as financial services, retailing and banking.

Data mining

The existence of data marts and warehouses with very large amounts of data threw into relief the need for new methods of analysis. While it is clear what the potential benefits of huge databases might be – sharper focus on customer needs, clearer understanding of shopping patterns, more refined segmentation, more efficient and effective targeting – crystallizing these from millions of bits of data is a challenge. Data mining refers to a set of techniques from statistics, computer science and artificial intelligence. They can be classified as:

Descriptive:
- segmentation
- cluster analysis
- basket analysis

Predictive:
- linear regression
- logistic regression
- discriminant analysis

Data reducing:
- factor analysis
- principal component analysis

CHAID
- Chi-squared Automatic Interaction Detector

(Pearce 2000)

Typically, a practitioner uses a suite of software programs provided by one of the main suppliers in the field, such as SAS Enterprise Miner, SPSS Clementine, or IBM Intelligent Miner (www.sas.com, www.spss.com, and www.IBM.com). The analysis proceeds through the stages of, in SAS terms, SEMMA: Sample, Explore, Modify, Model, Assess (see Figure 6.2).

A newer technique, borrowed from artificial intelligence, is *neural networks*. This searches for patterns in data, with no formal structure or preconceptions. It is often used as an alternative to regression analysis, or as a comparison. Hybrid modelling tries both approaches, and adopts that with the better result. For example, the analyst can compare the response rate to a mailing using several different methods. The overall rate for the whole sample might be 3 per cent; using traditional analysis, segments with response rates of 18 per cent are identified, but with neural networks, an improvement to 27 per cent is possible (Pearce 2000).

All the techniques are sophisticated, and demand a good understanding of statistical theory. The software packages offer speed and ease of use. However, as with all such approaches, they need good data: the old adage, GIGO (Garbage In, Garbage Out) applies. The fact that complex computer technology produces impressive-looking output increases the danger that, in the wrong hands, techniques may be misapplied and results misinterpreted. They will be applied increasingly to large databases, and to click-stream analysis for Websites, and offer rich promise when well used.

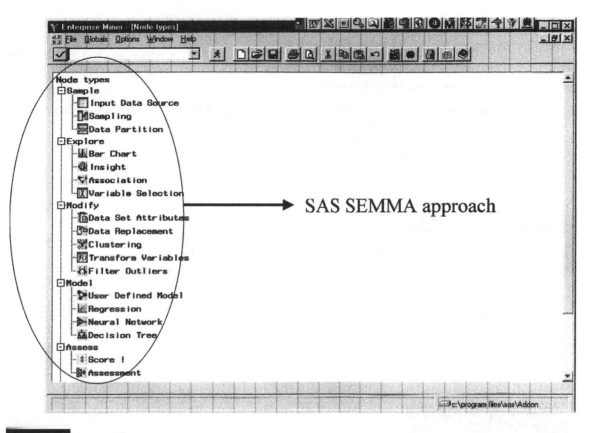

Figure 6.2 Data mining

Key learning points

- We need marketing information for analysis, decision-making and control. In the analysis phase, we need to diagnose what is happening in our markets, and we collect information (total market volume and value, market shares, buying patterns, etc.) to help us.

- The decision-making phase is difficult because we need to choose between courses of action, but precise information on the results of marketing action is hard to obtain.

- Control information is needed in order to monitor whether our programmes are going according to plan or are out of control.

- In collecting information, existing sources should be tapped first (secondary data or desk research). There are probably large amounts of secondary data accessible, but they need to be evaluated for up-to-dateness, relevance, accuracy and bias.

- New information (primary data) can be collected by observation, experiment or from respondents.

- Surveys of respondents may be carried out by mail, telephone or face-to-face interview. Mail surveys are cheap, but usually suffer from low response rates which reduce their validity. Telephone interviewing is increasing, and is cheap and effective for many applications. Face-to-face interviewing is the most flexible and usually the most expensive.

- Newer techniques using databases, data warehouses and data mining offer great promise, but need care and expertise.

Further reading

Chisnall, P.M. (1997) *Marketing Research*, 5th edition, London: McGraw Hill.
Crouch, S. and Housden, M. (1996) *Market Research for Managers*, 2nd edition, Oxford: Butterworth Heinemann.
Fleming, M.C. and Nellis, J.G. (2001) *Principles of Applied Statistics*, 2nd edition, London: Thomson Learning.

Case study: Amalgamated Electrical Plc

Amalgamated Electrical PLC (AE) is a British-based multinational company with annual turnover of just over £2 billion. The result of mergers and acquisitions over sixty years, its operations cover a number of sectors. The turnover is split between the product divisions as follows:

	%
Defence and aerospace	15
Electrical contracting	20
Instrumentation and control	5
Computers and telecommunications	10
Consumer durables	30
Consumer electronics	20

AE sells all over the world, with particular strength in Europe, the Middle East and the old Commonwealth countries. Its market shares vary from dominating positions in some markets (up to 40 per cent in some UK defence sectors) to very small shares of others (especially newer markets in instrumentation and telecoms).

The organization is fairly decentralized, but there is a corporate headquarters which contains, among other functions, a marketing information section.

Questions

1 As head of the central marketing information section, sketch out the headings for a marketing information system which would serve the main board. Specify what regular reports the board should receive, and what else the information system should offer them.

2 Take three of the divisions, at least one of which should serve a consumer market, and list the main components of an information system for each.

3 You are a marketing manager in one of the divisions; write a brief for a piece of market research to determine the acceptability of your products compared with those of competitors. Specify who should be interviewed, and what sort of research method you think would be appropriate. Repeat the exercise for another division, making sure that you cover one industrial division and one consumer.

Chapter 7 | Segmentation and targeting

Do segments exist?

According to the marketing concept, firms should try to produce exactly what their customers and consumers want. We know that no two individuals are exactly alike, so does marketing account for every person wanting something slightly different? There are a few markets where that is true – a bespoke tailor, or a builder of bridges, creates something unique each time – but they are quite rare. Even in those cases, there are some components which are common. At the other extreme, there are few markets in which everyone wants exactly the same thing: commodities such as salt, perhaps (but then some people buy sea salt . . .).

The idea of segmentation is that in any market there will be groups of buyers (segments), those within each group being similar to each other and different from those in other groups. In marketing terms, the differences under consideration should be in what benefits buyers seek from the product, or in how they react to the marketing mix. Manufacturers can then design products and targeted mixes for each segment.

Thus there are two issues for companies:

1 What, if any, segments exist in a market?
2 What should you do about it?

The car market is a good example of the dynamic interaction between these two issues, since markets change over time and also react to the actions manufacturers take. After being the first to introduce mass production methods, Henry Ford had great success for some time with the completely undifferentiated Model T ('Any colour you like so long as it's black'). After a while, Alfred Sloan, running what was to become General Motors, realized that there were opportunities for providing something different; his company began to design different cars for different groups, and overtook Ford. The market today offers a bewildering choice of hundreds of different models and configurations. Two important lessons about segmentation can be drawn from an analysis of this situation:

1   There are broad price segments: buyers usually have a price bracket within which they choose. This may be only loosely connected to their income, however, for two reasons: first, in the UK many people are provided with a car by their employer (who is really the buyer), and second, the importance attached to a car varies, so some people are prepared to spend a higher proportion of their income on a car than others. Of course, people on very low incomes do not buy Rolls-Royces, but on the other hand some quite well-off people choose to buy quite modest cars.

2   Beyond price, there are also groups of functional needs, such as size and space; a large family needs space for many passengers and lots of luggage. whereas a single person does not. As with price, there is no complete and logical correlalion between characteristics and purchase, since some single people choose to buy large cars. Once we begin to look at other variables, such as performance and styling, we are into the realms of personal preferences, and a good example of the problems of segmentation. The old, simple segmentation by price/engine capacity/luxury has broken down – not completely, but in the mass market to a great extent. Within the broad middle market it is possible to buy a small high-performance model or a large economical one, an ecologically sound car (well, relatively), a safe, staid model, a stylish car, and so on and so on. Current flexible manufacturing methods allow the production of an almost infinite variety of configurations, so that one can order a completely individual combination of engine size, body style, trim, colour, etc.

This progression in the market from undifferentiated through clear-cut, orderly segments to the present apparent confusion reflects both real market changes (as people have become better off, more knowledgeable, perhaps more demanding), and the actions of competing manufacturers seeking an advantage by offering something slightly different. The question of whether all the segments actually exist will be answered by the market in the sense that if there are insufficient consumers wanting a particular product, it will fail. That is not much consolation to the manufacturer who has to decide several years ahead what to make.

A comparison with the motorcycle market is interesting in that the (almost entirely Japanese) manufacturers have been competing ever more fiercely, introducing more and more new models, so that every conceivable taste must now be catered for. It seems likely that not all can possibly survive, and that at least one manufacturer will go out of business.

The car market is approaching the same situation; the application of marketing thinking and segmentation are not the only things that a manufacturer who wants to survive will have to get right, but they are necessary conditions.

A somewhat simpler market also illustrates the interaction between manufacturer and consumer. At one time, the aerosol household cleaner market in the UK appeared to be segmented into two: a group of traditional housewives who used a wax-rich aerosol polish on wooden furniture, and a group more interested in speed and convenience who preferred a product with less wax which could be used an a variety of surfaces. If this view of the market were correct, the situation would be that shown in Figure 7.1(a). On the other hand, it might be that in fact the majority of housewives simply did not differentiate between the two types of product, and used either or both indiscriminately. In that case, the market would appear as in Figure 7.1(b). The implications for the manufacturers would be quite different, depending on which interpretation was correct.

Two points may be made here:

1 Manufacturers are much more interested and involved in their products than most consumers, and may therefore exaggerate the importance of small differences.

2 The very extensive research by Ehrenberg and colleagues over many years (Ehrenberg 1972, 1988) demonstrates clearly that in most markets, most buyers buy a repertory of

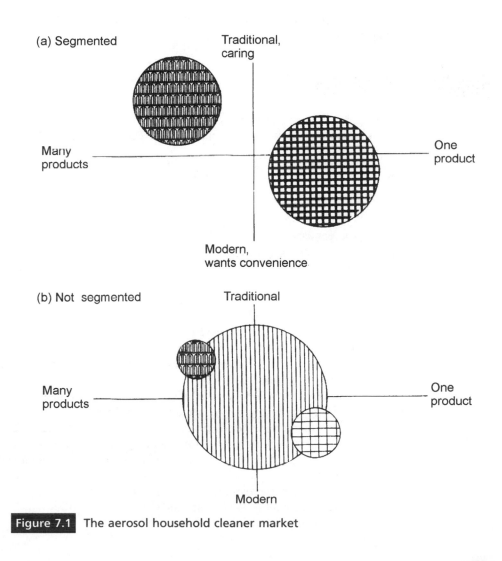

Figure 7.1 The aerosol household cleaner market

brands rather than a single one; in a given product field, they are likely to buy two or three brands with varying frequency. The second interpretation, as depicted in Figure 7.1(b), is therefore more likely to be right, though it would need to be checked for this particular market.

The answer to the question as to whether segments exist, therefore, must be that sometimes they undoubtedly do; in some markets, there are groups of buyers with different needs or preferences, and there are opportunities for manufacturers to cater to those groups. There is a danger, however, that manufacturers can impose their own view of a market on consumers. Market research should be used carefully to examine exactly what consumers use brands for and what they think about them.

The point of thinking about segmentation is to help define, structure and understand your market from the consumers' point of view, so that you can go on to decide on the best strategy for your existing and new brands.

What marketing action is appropriate is discussed below, in the last two sections of this chapter.

Bases of segmentation

The approach to segmenting a particular market will depend on what is already known about it and what structure is thought to exist. The most common bases used in consumer markets are:

- Demographic
- Socio-economic
- Geo-demographic
- Buying patterns
- Personality, attitudes, values
- Life style.

As we shall see, the boundaries between some of these categories are not clear-cut, and sometimes more than one base is used in analysis.

A useful way of looking at these different bases was suggested by Frank, Massy and Wind (1972): they set up a matrix reflecting the fact that we can look at either general or situation-specific consumer characteristics, and that the measures we use may be either objective or inferred (see Table 7.1).

This approach helps us to keep in mind what sort of measures we are using, and how near they are to the reality of our market. Generally, hard, objective measures are to be preferred to soft, inferred ones (they are likely to be more reliable); and specific measures are to be preferred to more general ones, although the common rule of thumb, 'Keep It Simple, Stupid' (KISS), applies in all sorts of situations; here it might lead us to look first at simple measures such as demographic data rather than at more specific but complex buying patterns. (In practice, we would, of course, want to look at demographics in relation to our particular market as well as in general.)

Let us examine each main type of measure.

Table 7.1 Market segmentation measures

Measures:	Customer characteristics	
	General	Situation specific
Objective	Demographic Socio-economic	Consumption patterns Brand loyalty Buying situations
Inferred	Personality traits Life style	Attitudes Perceptions and preferences

Source: Frank *et al.* 1972.

Demographics

The basic demographic measures are:

- age
- sex
- geographical distribution.

Some markets are clearly segmented in these terms: pop records and cinema seats, for instance, are bought mainly by young people: many products are aimed clearly at either men or women (though 70 per cent of disposable razors are bought by women, for example); and there are geographical variations in taste, even within a small country such as the UK.

Even if a certain pattern exists now, marketers should look beyond the static to the dynamics of the situation. Suppose that tea-drinkers, for instance, tend to be concentrated in older age groups, while younger people tend to drink more fruit juices and carbonated drinks. Does this reflect the fact that as people get older their tastes and habits change, and that the young fruit-juice drinker will mature into a middle-aged tea drinker? Or does it reflect a permanent shift, which will lead to an irreversible decline in tea sales? Again, to what extent does the present pattern of consumption merely reflect manufacturers' past and current marketing policies? Products aimed at particular segments through distribution or advertising might appeal equally to other segments if they were made available.

Slightly more complex demographic measures are:

- family size
- family composition
- life cycle stage.

These used to be fairly stable and predictable, but are becoming less so. The old 'average' household of husband, wife and around two children is no longer the norm; single-person households, one-parent families and other structures have become more common. This may, of course, offer more segmentation opportunities rather than fewer.

The traditional life cycle (and one which is still prevalent, if less dominant than before), is the progression through childhood, adolescence, young single adulthood, marriage without children, marriage with young children, marriage with older children, marriage without children at home (the poignantly-named 'empty nest' stage), and single old age. Clearly, different products will be needed at different stages, particularly home-related items such as consumer durables. For our purposes, the important thing is to keep an eye on changes, which are happening faster than they used to; old assumptions about household structure and family life cycles need to be checked to see if they still correspond to current reality.

Other demographic variables which have become more important are:

- ethnic groups
- geographical mobility
- physical characteristics, such as skin and hair type.

Socio-economic

By this term we usually mean two things: social class and income. In the past, social class was one of the basic ways used to classify consumers (in the UK in particular, perhaps reflecting a British preoccupation). This was discussed earlier, in Chapter 5. As was said then, it has become progressively less useful as a segmentation tool, though it is still used in some markets.

Income may be a more direct measure of buying power, though it should be noted that ability to buy has three components:

1 earnings
2 wealth
3 credit potential.

In recent years many individuals have experienced rapid changes in their buying power, both upwards and downwards. Rises (and falls) in house prices have had a dramatic impact, as have economic fluctuations, deregulation and so on. This turbulence may make it more difficult to track and target income segments, and it may make the size and importance of segments change quickly.

Some commentators have suggested that there is a trend towards polarization in buying power which is reflected in a polarization in markets. The growing numbers of the relatively poor will increase the demand for economy products and outlets, and the growing disposable income of one sector of the population will create growing demand for premium brands. In between, the market for standard products may decline, leaving a U-shaped distribution.

Geo-demographic

This name has been given to a relatively recent development which classifies small local areas (usually postcodes) by housing type. The best-known system is ACORN (A Classification Of Residential Neighbourhoods). There are eleven main groups:

A Agricultural areas
B Modem family housing, higher incomes

C Older housing of intermediate status
D Poor quality older terraced housing
E Better-off council estates
F Less well-off council estates
G Poorest council estates
H Multi-racial areas
I High status non-family areas
J Affluent suburban housing
K Better-off retirement areas.

These groups are further broken down into thirty-eight types of neighbourhood, which can be precisely identified, with their population. Market research identifies expenditure patterns for each. The system has been found to discriminate well in many markets; it is also used for sampling frames.

Buying patterns

The first distribution which can be made is to divide consumers and customers into buyers and non-buyers of a product, and of a brand. Such an analysis may be revealing, or may only reflect the obvious (children don't buy petrol, men don't buy sanitary towels). It is, of course, basic knowledge, and if the data have not been collected or analysed before, they certainly should be, as some surprises may come to light (for example, the 70 per cent of disposable razors bought by women, not just on behalf of men, but to use themselves). The division is also the basic unit of analysis for most other segmentation variables.

Since, as Ehrenberg and his colleagues have shown (Ehrenberg 1972; see Chapter 5), most buyers in most markets buy a repertoire of brands with varying frequency, an analysis at brand level of buyers/non-buyers is not straightforward. This usually leads to analysis by buying patterns, particularly frequency of purchase. Ehrenberg's work provides a valuable framework against which to compare one's own market.

Brand loyalty is also a concept that has had to be modified in the light of Ehrenberg's results. Very few people only ever buy one brand in a product field and no other. Loyalty must therefore be defined in terms of relative frequency. Further analyses can be made in terms of combinations of brands bought, and brand switching patterns, although these may become complicated.

Another aspect of buying is the type of retail outlet or the actual store or stores patronized. In some markets there are fairly obvious differences between, say, Harrods and Woolworths, which may be reflected in purchase behaviour. In other markets, differences may be more subtle. Even though the range of grocery products stocked by supermarkets is broadly similar, for example, the shoppers at Co-operatives, Tesco and Waitrose supermarkets may show differing profiles and may be looking for different product offerings. Again, many people shop at more than one store or store type, and segments may not be clear-cut.

In these as in all other analyses, it is vital to make sure that judgements are made on the basis of valid, up-to-date information, not old figures or, still worse, prejudice and guesswork.

Personality, attitudes and values

The earlier discussion of consumer behaviour research (Chapter 5) showed the difficulties and uncertainties that have dogged this field. If it is difficult to produce valid, reliable measures of such constructs as personality or attitude, and even more difficult to show connections between the constructs and behaviour, then it may be asked why attempts are made to base segments on them.

The fact is that many such attempts have been made, for understandable if not good reasons. Many product ftelds are mature and contain brands which are really very similar to each other. Given the typical buying pattems discussed above, it is not surprising that in such markets the straightforward objective measures of buying and buyers do not provide useful discrimination between segments. Managers are – understandably – desperate to differentiate their brand and to find other ways of describing consumers which will be useful bases for positioning the brand and developing communication strategies. Since we know that consumers can describe brand personalities and describe differences between brands (frequently, of course, feeding back previous advertising campaigns), it is tempting to speculate that people buy brands which somehow match their personality, or that in some way different brands appeal to differing personality types.

Two statements may be made with some confidence:

1   Some studies have appeared to show useful results based on personality,

2   No general model which works in all fields has been produced.

Some successes have claimed to show that, for example, 'compliant' personality types were more likely to use mouthwash, while 'aggressive' types were more likely to use cologne and aftershave. A real problem of marketing theory is that many such successful studies are commercially sensitive, and may therefore remain unpublished. The experience of most marketing managers is that there are at least an equal number of failures, though again many are unpublished.

An old but charming study of beer drinking in the UK suggested that there were four basic types:

1   social drinkers – drink to help social interaction

2   reparative drinkers – drink to reward themselves

3   indulgent drinkers – drink to escape

4   oceanic drinkers – crave pleasure and comfort.

Each segment had different drinking habits and pleasures, and different socio-economic, demographic and personality characteristics. Unfortunately the model did not work in the USA. More recent work suggested that heavy beer drinkers were hero-worshipping fantasists; quite how that helped marketing decisions is not clear.

It seems probable, though it cannot be stated as a law, that product- or situation-specific measures are more likely to produce useful results than generalized measures of personality.

Similar statements may be made about attitudes. Particularly given the work of Fishbein outlined in Chapter 5, attitudes to the buying and using situation are likely to be more useful than general attitudes. However, this has not stopped advertising agencies producing studies which describe segments based on general attitudes and which claim to provide the basis for useful segmentation, often internationally. Such proprietary models can provide valuable insights, but should be viewed with some caution.

Life style

The term 'life style' has a very 1980s connotation, but has in fact been used rather longer; in marketing, it is a development from, or relative of, the psycho-graphic approaches described in the previous section. It is measured either through the clusters of products used, or through what are sometimes summarized as AIOV:

- Activities
- Interests
- Opinions
- Values.

As with the general attitude models described above, these are often produced on a proprietary basis by firms such as advertising agencies or media owners, and used as a selling tool.

There is a certain intuitive appeal to the life style approach. There are groups of people who visibly buy certain brands to identify themselves as members of the group, and who may share similar activities, interests, opinions and values. Others may buy the brands to show that they aspire to the desired group. The phenomenon is most obvious in fashion products such as clothes, but has been extended to fields such as beer, restaurants and bicycles. The difficulty with such fashion products is that this year's top Mexican beer may by next year be seen as boring and old-fashioned.

The broader problem is that there is no theory to guide the choice of variables to include in the analysis. Powerful analysis methods (see the section below) allow patterns to be produced from a large data set, and the patterns may be interesting and suggestive. Unfortunately, including different variables will change the patterns, and therefore by implication the appropriate marketing action. Many attempts to find structure in markets have used an eclectic approach, taking variables from a number of fields – demographic, buying, shopping and usage patterns, as well as personality traits. Some such attempts succeed, but there is no generalizable rule that guides us as to the likelihood of success before committing large sums of money.

The rule with all segmentation models must be *caveat emptor* – let the buyer beware. Try the simple approaches first; only if they are not helpful move on to more complex ones.

Stages in segmentation

Our knowledge of markets is built up over time, as experience and information contribute to our picture of customers and consumers. Markets change, too, partly because of changes in the environment, and partly because of marketing actions taken by our competitors and us. The linear sequence set out here should be seen as one part of an iterative process; it is not something that is carried out once and once only.

There are ten stages in a segmentation exercise:

- Summarize existing knowledge
- Agree on focus and objectives
- Carry out exploratory research
- Decide on approach
- Develop measures
- Collect data
- Carry out analyses
- Debate and validate segments
- Decide action
- Monitor and evaluate.

Summarize existing knowledge

We already know quite a lot (unless we are entering a market that is new to us). Like all organizational knowledge, it may be scattered amongst different people, in various forms – including in people's heads – stored in different ways. In a formal process, it is useful to start by summarizing and agreeing what we actually know: what do we believe about the market, what evidence do we have for these beliefs, what trends are evident, what forces are driving change? Actually writing a summary of all this may be valuable, so that we can circulate it to everyone who may be able to contribute. Sometimes, it might be useful to bring in an outsider to add an objective view. The exercise will not take place very often, so it is worth doing it thoroughly.

There are three main types of information we should have:

- *Market data*: size, trends, structure, listing of products and brands.
- *Buyers*: as much detail as possible – who, what, when, where they buy, how they use the product.
- *Segments and descriptors*: what segments do we think exist, and how can we describe the people in each.

Agree on focus and objectives

A segmentation exercise can be expensive and complicated, so everyone involved must agree exactly what the end result should be. Further, we may be basing major strategic decisions on the results; a segmentation strategy is not something to be taken lightly, and changed every year. Finally, because the methods used can be complex, using sophisticated statistical techniques, misunderstanding between researchers and managers is only too likely. Research companies who carry out such projects may over-claim, and managers want certainty – but the techniques necessarily involve subjective judgements and manipulation of data. All parties must be clear from the outset precisely what will be happening, what sort of results may be expected, and how much reliance can be placed on them.

Carry out exploratory research

If we know relatively little about a market, it is normal to start with exploratory, qualitative research – group discussions (focus groups), depth interviews, projective techniques – as in any marketing study. We should remember that the exploratory research will deliver only hypotheses to be tested in later stages, not final answers. It will also provide guidance on what ideas consumers use, and what language they apply to the product field – how they talk about the products, how they think about them, how they use them.

Decide approach

Our knowledge of this market, and perhaps others, may give some help as to what approach will be most fruitful. General guidelines, based on experience, are:

- Start with simple, objective measures (demographics, industry, size of firm etc.) and move on to more complex ones only when the simple measures are not enough.
- Use objective measures (buying patterns) rather than inferred (personality).
- Prefer situation-specific measures to general ones (using this brand for that purpose, rather than general lifestyle or attitudinal patterns).

In many mature markets, simple, objective measures are not helpful in discriminating between segments and brands, and that is why people use variables that are more complicated. There is a temptation to throw everything into the pot, and let the computer program find a pattern. The trouble is, the program and its expert user *will* produce patterns, but they will be artificial constructs with little basis in reality. Given the nature of the program, and the statistical processes used, it is difficult for managers to evaluate the results (see below, 'Debate and validate segments').

Develop measures

This is usually the preserve of experts, either in the market research company or in your own research department. Some measures are fairly simple (demographics, buying patterns), but others such as attitudes or trade-offs, may be more complicated. It is common to use scales, such as Likert or semantic differential scales (see Figure 7.2). Semantic differential scales in particular have been used very widely in marketing. They are easy for respondents to complete, and can be applied to almost any field. When numbers are attached to the positions, they are easy to analyse. There are, however, many complications in their construction and use, so professional knowledge is needed.

Collect data

The most suitable data collection method is the sample survey using personal interviews, as the questionnaire may be long and complicated to administer. Where suitable, telephone interviewing may also be used.

We may also be able to use existing data. As we saw earlier, data warehouses may contain large amounts of data on customers, and much of this can be employed in segmentation analysis.

Semantic differential

Suitable for young people	7.....6.....5.....4.....3.....2.....1.....	Suitable for older people
Strong	7.....6.....5.....4.....3.....2.....1.....	Weak
Good value	7.....6.....5.....4.....3.....2.....1.....	Poor value

Importance rating

(Show card) Extremely important

Very important

Important

Not very important

Not at all important

(Read out, and ask respondent to rate each)

Lowest price

Most reliable

Always in stock

Can get spare parts quickly

Agree/disagree (Likert scales)

Collect a number of statements relevant to the topic. Ask respondents to say how much they agree/disagree:

Strongly agree

Agree

Neither agree nor disagree

Disagree

Strongly disagree

Positions are scored, usually 5,4,3,2,1 from favourable end.

The cheapest available

Service is very quick

You don't have to dress up

It's full of young people

Figure 7.2 Types of scale

Carry out analysis

The simplest analysis is cross-tabulation, for example usage or attitude by age and sex. This may produce results that are enough to define segments. In many markets, where little real differentiation exists between brands, it may be necessary to go further, and adopt techniques that are more complex. The most commonly used are discriminant analysis, CHAID, factor and component analysis, and cluster analysis.

- *Discriminant analysis* is a statistical technique related to regression analysis, and is seen by classical statisticians as the most reliable of the multivariate methods. It tries to find a discriminant function that maximizes the ratio of between-group variation to within-group variation; in other words, it tries to find people who are similar to each other, and different from others. It uses descriptors of individuals, such as age, education, income as predictor variables, and a target variable such as frequency of brand purchase. A good discriminant function will classify all individuals into groups, and show the relative importance of each predictor in the classification. For example, in the beer market, we might use data on buying and consumption, frequency of drinking in different locations (pubs, clubs etc.), demographics, measures of fashion awareness in this market, and attitudes to entertainment and leisure. The discriminant analysis will find the function that divides the respondents into groups (such as heavy drinkers of imported lagers), and give a weighting to the variables – for example, that age and fashion awareness are more important than other variables.

- *CHAID* stands for Chi-squared Automatic Interaction Detector. It was developed to cope with the problem that, in marketing, variables are quite often correlated with each other, so that discriminant analysis cannot be used. CHAID splits the sample into groups in a succession of stages, at each stage trying to maximize the variance between groups. As each group is split further at each stage, the cells can become very small very quickly, and this may be a problem with sample survey data. With data warehouses, where there may be thousands of pieces of data, this is less problematic.

- *Factor and component analysis* are related techniques based on the correlation coefficients of the variables (for example, semantic differential scales). The technique searches for the factors or components that explain the underlying patterns; usually, the first two or three explain most of the variance, and the results can be mapped. The most common use is, in practice, to reduce large numbers of variables to a more manageable size. Batteries of scales may contain sixty or a hundred scales, and factor analysis may be applied to reduce these to say six. These may then be inputs to a discriminant analysis.

  The factors have to be interpreted, and are often rotated if no clear pattern emerges. Both involve subjective judgements, which is why some statisticians are sceptical of the over-use of the technique.

- *Cluster analysis* is a set of techniques that try to define clusters of objects that are like each other within each cluster. Unlike discriminant analysis, it does not make any assumptions about the sample; unlike CHAID, it examines several variables at once rather than singly. It uses as inputs measures of similarity, which may be metric (using scales with numbers attached), or non-metric (using respondents' judgements of the relative similarity or dissimilarity of pairs of stimuli, such as brands).

Computer software is available for all these techniques, but clearly, they need to be used by experts. The role of the manager who will apply the results is to understand the principles of what is being done, to ask questions (for example about the use of subjective judgement), and to insist on clear explanations of how the results should be interpreted. Presentation of results is often accompanied by visuals such as maps: it is essential to make sure that the graphical representation does not distort the true picture (as they often do, in fact).

Debate and validate segments

As this makes clear, segmentation analyses need to be interpreted with care. A useful test is to analyse segment members by variables not used in the segmentation, such as demographics. If the groups are noticeably different, that is evidence for the validity of the analysis – indeed, if they are not very different, the results may be of little practical value. With large databases, the segmentation can be run on a sample, and tested on a matching sample from within the total. The most important test is whether the segmentation makes sense to the managers who know the market. Sometimes, an analysis may produce genuinely new insights, but if it does not convince the managers, they will not base major decisions on it.

Monitor and evaluate

The real test of a segmentation model is whether it produces results in the marketplace. We need to monitor what happens, so that we may first evaluate the success of the segmentation, and then so that we can understand *why* it is working or not working. It is also important to monitor the market over the medium term, as we know that markets change; a segmentation that works this year may be inappropriate in five years' time.

Brand, consumer or benefit segmentation

Most of the preceding discussion has assumed that we are trying to segment consumers, although the maps in fact show brands (but brands as perceived by consumers). We can of course use segmentation techniques to look for patterns amongst consumers, amongst brands, or amongst the benefits sought by consumers. Each has its uses, and which one we choose will depend on what our objectives are in a particular exercise. Segmenting consumers allows us to describe and target chosen groups. Segmenting brands may guide positioning and advertising strategy. Benefit segmentation may be used to direct new product development, as well as positioning and differentiation activity.

A thorough and radical segmentation study of a market may involve several approaches, and several different types of analysis. The manager needs to be absolutely clear about the objectives of the study, and not to lose track of them through what may well be an extremely complex process. As pointed out earlier, the decisions to be made are likely to be very important and difficult to reverse. Apart from seeking expert help, readers are advised to consult the further reading at the end of this chapter.

Segmentation strategies

Assuming that we now have a picture of our market, there are a number of decision stages to go through:

1 Evaluate the segments
2 Choose a segmentation strategy
3 Select the segments to be targeted
4 Develop a targeted marketing mix for each
5 Allocate resources to the segments.

For a segment to be useful, as Kotler has pointed out (Kotler 2000: 274). it must be:

Measurable   The variables that define it must be capable of unambiguous measurement,

Accessible   The segments can be reached and served,

Substantial   Enough to be worth bothering with,

Differentiable   The segments respond differently to marketing mix elements,

Actionable   Suitable for targeting by this particular company.

Substantiable and **Actionable** are both related to the size and nature of the company making the decision. Many large corporations have a minimum size of market, below which they feel it is not profitable for them to participate; a smaller, leaner company may be quite happy to take on a smaller segment. Conversely, a small company may identify large segments, or a large number of segments, which they do not have the resources to tackle.

Again, the potential of each segment may be different for different competitors, depending on their varying strengths and weaknesses. There must be a good match between the segment and the range of products and services that the company can offer for potential to be more than theoretical.

A more structured way of evaluating segments is to apply to each the same sort of analysis one would to a market as a whole. We would then analyse, for each segment, the following.

- *Market factors*
  - Size
  - Growth
  - Predictability
  - Price elasticity
  - Bargaining power of customers
  - Seasonality and cyclicality of demand
- *Economic and technological factors*
  - Barriers to entry
  - Barriers to exit
  - Bargaining power of suppliers

- Level of technology use
- Investment needed
- Margins attainable
■ *Competitive factors*
- Competitive intensity
- Quality of competition
- Threat of substitution
- Degree of differentiation
■ *Environmental factors*
- Exposure to economic fluctuations
- Degree of regulation
- Social acceptability, impact on the environment

The strategies to be adopted are usually characterized as undifferentiated, differentiated, or concentrated (see for example Kotler 2000: 275; compare Porter's generic strategies of cost leadership, differentiation and focus, Porter 1980). The names are fairly self-explanatory.

1　**An undifferentiated strategy** means making a single offering to the whole market; the offering is directed towards what most people want, what is common to the majority.

Henry Ford's first mass-produced car, the Model T, is a famous example; Coca-Cola and Guinness, for much of their histories, are others.

Many major companies adopt such a strategy at certain stages of a market's development, since that is the way to achieve high sales and brand share. The strategy usually demands high investment in manufacturing and marketing support, so may not be an option for smaller competitors.

2　**A differentiated strategy** means that the company offers different things to different segments.

The Ford Motor Company today has a model for almost every segment in the market. Most Japanese car manufacturers have moved from an undifferentiated strategy at the beginning, to compete in more and more segments.

Such an approach can produce higher total sales than an undifferentiated strategy, but there are risks of 'cannibalization' (eating away at your own sales) and of reducing profitability. The management of a line of products is discussed in a later chapter.

3　**Concentrated marketing** obviously focuses on only a part of the total market.

Dunhill operates only at the high-priced, luxury end of its markets; Volvo until recently aimed only at a certain segment of the car market, those who wanted a large, safe, solid family/executive car.

Abell (1980) suggested a slightly more complex classification, based on a matrix of product/market segments:

- *Single segment concentration*
- *Selective specialization*: choosing a few segments unrelated to each other
- *Product specialization*: marketing a particular type of product or service that all segments want
- *Market specialization*: focusing on a segment, and offering all the products/services they require
- *Full market coverage*: offering a product in every segment.

Which strategy a company chooses will depend, as has become clear, partly on its strengths and weaknesses. Smaller competitors are more likely to be able to implement a concentrated strategy. Companies which are flexible and innovative may be better able to cover many segments with a differentiated strategy than more monolithic, rigid competitors.

The nature of the market, too, will affect what is feasible – what stage of the product life cycle has been reached, for example, and the degree of differentiation which is actually possible in the products. Of major importance, of course, will be what competitors are doing or may do in future, and your freedom of action relative to those competitors. A small newcomer to the toilet soap market could not afford to tackle the dominating majors head-on, but could adopt a concentrated strategy and focus on one segment; Simple Soap did just that, concentrating on people who wanted a product with no additives.

That example also suggests that the decision as to which segments to choose is affected by similar considerations, in particular who you are and what your objectives are, compared with other competitors. The large, established company will want to be in the big segments, and will have the resources to cover a number of segments. A small company with limited resources will opt for segments more suited to its size and capabilities, and preferably undefended by the majors.

Having chosen the segments, the company must then develop a marketing mix targeted at each. This process is discussed more fully in a later chapter, but its importance must be underlined here. The whole rationale of segmentation is based on the idea that the segments are different, so at least one element of the mix, and probably several, must also be different. Most obviously, the product will vary in some way, but it is also likely that the pricing and advertising will vary, and quite probably the distribution too.

Resources

Finally, the company must decide on what resources to allocate to each segment. It is true, but not very helpful, to say, 'Allocate so as to make most profit.' If we were able to calculate the elasticity of demand in each segment to product quality, price, promotion, etc. (and the interactions between them), it would be simple to maximize profit – but we cannot. What we must do is at least to make some estimate of the likely profitability of the segments. This will depend on size, of course, but also on the price attainable and the costs involved in reaching the segment (manufacturing costs and all the marketing costs). The biggest segment may not yield the most profit, especially if it is hotly contested by competitors. Given a view of relative profitability, it makes sense to allocate resources to the most profitable segment, and to go on doing so until the likely return declines below the level of the next most profitable (or until available resources run out). Such a procedure ought to meet profitability objectives, but there may be other goals the company is seeking. Competitive strategy plays a major role here, since you may wish to develop a new segment before a competitor, or to attack in an area where they are making comfortable profits. Such considerations may override short-term profit, though it is to be hoped that they would all lead to higher profits in the longer term.

The issues of positioning within the segment and targeting the mix are dealt with in the next chapter.

Key learning points

- **Market segmentation is the process of splitting a total market into a number of smaller sub-markets or segments. Buyers within each segment are similar to each other, and different from those in other segments.**
- **Ideally, a segment will consist of people who are looking for a similar bundle of benefits.**
- **Markets are likely to become more segmented as they progress through the life cycle as manufacturers try to differentiate their products from those of competitors; the car market is a good example.**
- **Consumer markets are segmented on various bases: demographic, socio-economic, buying patterns, personality, attitudes, values, life style, or a combination of several.**
- **Once segments have been defined and measured, there are five decision stages to go through: evaluate the segments; choose a segmentation strategy; select the segments to be targeted; develop a targeted marketing mix for each; allocate resources to the segments.**
- **For a segment to be useful, it needs to be: measurable, accessible, substantial, and actionable.**
- **The strategies available are undifferentiated, differentiated or concentrated; which is chosen will depend on the nature of the market, the company's strengths and weaknesses, and the competitors' strategies.**

Further reading

Hooley, G., Saunders, J. and Piercy, N. (1998) *Marketing Strategy and Competitive Positioning*, London: Prentice Hall.

McDonald, M. and Dunbar, I. (1998) *Market Segmentation*, 2nd edition, London: Palgrave.

Case study

Japanese manufacturers dominate the world motorcycle market. They have models in every part of the market, and are continually bringing out new versions; indeed, some critics think that the rate of new model introduction has become counter-productive, since the market will not be able to absorb them all.

Harley-Davidson, the American manufacturer, has survived and is successfully selling its nostalgically-styled models at high prices in major western markets. The British industry, which once led the world, disappeared completely, although some of the famous marques have been revived.

There are some manufacturers in Europe who tend to specialize, e.g. in high-powered sports models or small mopeds.

Questions

1 How would you go about segmenting the market for motorcycles? (If necessary, talk to some enthusiasts or a dealer, and look at some magazines.)

2 Which segments would you recommend a British manufacturer to tackle in (a) Britain, (b) Europe, and (c) elsewhere in the world? Compare your views with what is actually being done.

3 Look at the market for one of your organization's products or services. Is it segmented? Which segments do you serve? Is this the best strategy?

Chapter 8 | Differentiation and positioning

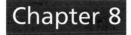

Competitive advantage

Porter famously described (1980) the generic strategies available to firms as:

- Cost leadership
- Differentiation, and
- Focus,

though he later subdivided the last into Cost focus and Differentiation focus. Cost leadership, though an important business strategy, is not a market-oriented one, and here we will concentrate on differentiation. The fundamental question every firm should ask itself is:

Why should any customer buy from me rather from a competitor?

Many people would answer, 'Because we offer a better product/service', but we need to refine that to have a chance of succeeding in today's markets. What we can say is that our differentiation should offer:

- Benefits
- Perceived by a sizeable customer group
- Which they value and are prepared to pay for, and
- That they cannot easily obtain from elsewhere (Day 1984).

129

A real difference in product quality, that is a functional superiority as desired by consumers, is the best way of differentiating, but is extremely difficult to achieve in many markets, and even harder to sustain. The experience of Xerox shows this: their plain-paper copier was clearly superior for many years, and that difference was protected by patents, but eventually their Japanese competitors caught up, and Xerox is now struggling. The whole idea of a sustainable competitive advantage, formerly promoted by many commentators as the aim of all companies, is now regarded as a mirage unless patent protection is available (and even that is short lived). Innovation, if it provides a stream of desirable new benefits, is another way of differentiating, and companies such as Intel adopt this approach as part of their strategy. Finally, marketing tools such as strong distribution, branding or service can provide protection; we return to these in later chapters.

The influential writers on strategy Hamel and Prahalad (1994) argue that, in a future-oriented view, what firms need are distinctive *core competences*. To count as a core competence, the bundle of skills that the firm possesses must meet three criteria:

- *Customer value*: Honda's core competence in making small engines delivers real value to customers for their cars, motor cycles, or lawnmowers.

- *Competitive differentiation*: if the competence is shared by many in the industry, it is not a core competence.

- *Extendibility*: the core competence must be capable of contributing to a wide range of products and services. Canon's competence in imaging will find applications in many of the growing range of products that use a display.

The search for competitive advantage is a complex and difficult task, and one that you will study further in corporate strategy courses (see, for example, Day and Wensley 1983 and Porter 1980, 1985 and 1996).

Differentiation

In marketing terms, Kotler (2000) suggests that firms can differentiate by:

- Product
- Services
- Personnel
- Channel
- Image.

This is geared more to physical products than pure services, but can provide a useful checklist. As we noted, finding real product differences that are valued by consumers is the Holy Grail (and perhaps as difficult to find). Nonetheless, marketing people and their colleagues in operations spend huge amounts of time and effort in searching for ways of offering buyers something different. This may be in features (seen always as benefits from the user's point of view), and an examination of any range of competing products and services will show this. Other ways of distinguishing are in performance, reliability, styling and design. Sometimes they are combined, as in Dyson's bagless vacuum cleaner, which claims to offer superior cleaning power and convenience, but was also styled to look completely different from existing cleaners.

Service and personnel differences should perhaps be combined, as it is the people who deliver the service. We return to this important issue in Chapter 15. Chapter 14 discusses channel differences, such as coverage or expertise, in more detail. In all these cases, what we have to do is to develop a marketing mix that targets our chosen segments.

Positioning within segments against competitors

It has been stressed that segmentation strategies, and segments themselves, need to be chosen with competitors very much in mind. Within a segment, too, the brand must be positioned against competition. The concept of positioning, now common currency in marketing, was promoted by two American consultants, Ries and Trout (1982). The key element, as they expressed it, is that,

> Positioning is not what you do to a product. Positioning is what you do to the mind of the prospect. That is, you position the product in the mind of the prospect.

There are two important facets of the concept:

1　We must always concentrate on the consumer's perceptions of our brand,
2　Those perceptions cover all aspects of the brand – physical, functional attributes, name, packaging, price, advertising, psychological dimensions, everything.

Neither is a new idea, but the usefulness of the concept is that it helps us focus on the way consumers see the totality of our brand against those of competitors. In our constant battle to differentiate our brand in the consumer's mind, that focus is valuable.

The importance of positioning has increased because most markets have become more and more crowded. Most products are not functionally all that different (though a real, salient functional difference remains the best sustainable competitive advantage). In mature markets, small product improvements are usually copied quickly. It remains for the manufacturer to convince consumers that the particular brand is different and preferable in some other way.

In most markets, there is usually one main functional benefit which the products provide; normally the leading brand has, if not ownership of that benefit, at least the strongest identification with it in consumers' minds. Therefore the rival brands must try to convince potential buyers that they should value other characteristics. Positioning then becomes the attempt to shift buyers' views of the relative importance of brand attributes, and to associate our own brand with attributes on which we can claim superiority. Sometimes this is fairly simple, as for example better after-sales service or faster delivery; sometimes it is more intangible, such as younger, more exciting.

Volvo's positioning within its segment has been consistent: this is the manufacturer which takes safety and durability seriously. Waitrose has positioned itself as a slightly superior, middle-class, quality supermarket.

Martini positions itself as the drink for those aspiring to a young, trendy, glamorous lifestyle.

The Volvo example offers two lessons. The first is the value of consistency; Volvo's position has remained the same for many years, and must be firmly established in motorists' minds. Audi, on the other hand, produces high-quality cars in the same segment, but has no clear positioning, in the UK at least. The second lesson is that what has been a solid position can be overtaken. As more manufacturers adopt safety as a priority, Volvo's position may no longer differentiate it.

Choosing a position, then, is a strategic decision in that it cannot be changed quickly and often without confusing consumers. It must on the other hand be kept under review, as consumers and markets change over time. It must be done carefully, to take maximum advantage of any gaps in the market left by competitors. The positioning should be sustainable against competitive reaction, and should be motivating to buyers. This is a tall order, but successful marketing is difficult and challenging.

Developing positioning strategies

The approach advocated by Hooley *et al*. (1998) has four main steps:

- Identify the competitors
- Analyse positions
  - Determine competitors' positions
  - Determine the competitive dimensions
  - Define customers' positions
- Decide amongst positioning alternatives
- Track the positioning.

This may seem an odd order: how can we plot competitors' positions before we have found out what the dimensions are? The answer lies in the type of technique used. This will be made clearer through an extended example (Hooley *et al*. 1998).

Identify competitors

The technique used is a form of cluster analysis (see previous chapter). This needs us to ask respondents to distinguish between pairs of stimuli, such as brands. Since the number of possible pairs of brands is $(n * (n - 1))/2$, the total rises quickly. We need to include all the relevant brands in the consumers' evoked set, but not have too many to be able to use in the analysis. The evoked set contains all the brands that consumers think about when making a choice. One way of defining this is to carry out an item-by-use analysis. For crisps, for example, we would ask for all the occasions when the respondent might eat a bag of crisps (with a packed lunch, at the pub, as a mid-morning snack, and so on). Then, for each occasion, we would ask what other items he or she might have chosen instead of crisps (nuts, an apple, chocolate and so on). This defines the competitive space from the consumer's point of view.

In the Hooley *et al.* example, the evoked set was six leisure attractions in the Midlands of England (interestingly, Kotler (2000: 301) describes a similar example of leisure attractions in America). The British attractions were:

- The American Adventure Park, a modern, purpose-built facility.
- Alton Towers, with large grounds and many 'white-knuckle rides'.
- Belton House, a National Trust country house with an added adventure playground.
- Chatsworth House, one of the grandest of Britain's stately homes.
- Warwick Castle, a medieval castle with added attractions.
- Woburn Abbey, a stately home with a safari park and fairground.

Analyse the positions

The project used similarities-based multidimensional scaling. This entailed asking respondents to rank cards containing all possible pairs of the six attractions, according to how similar they were. A computer program then produced the map shown in Figure 8.1 (the map is in two dimensions, although there were more in the model). We can see that Chatsworth House and Belton House are close to each other, but some way from Woburn, for example.

The dimensions that consumers used were then elicited by asking them to say in what way two attractions were similar to each other. This sort of technique produces a long list of dimensions, which have to be reduced to a manageable number, usually by analysis (many will be highly correlated). The answers here were things like big rides, educational, sophisticated, for teenagers, good food, and so on. Respondents then ranked each attraction on all the dimensions. The dimensions are shown mapped in Figure 8.2.

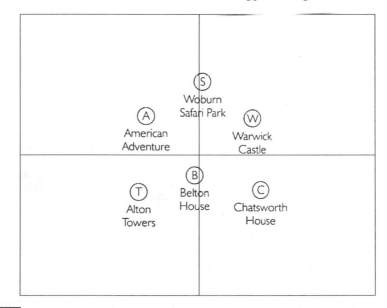

Figure 8.1 Perceptual map of leisure centre
Reproduced with permission, from *Marketing Strategy and Competitive Positioning*, by Hooley, Saunders and Piercy (1998) © Pearson Education Ltd.

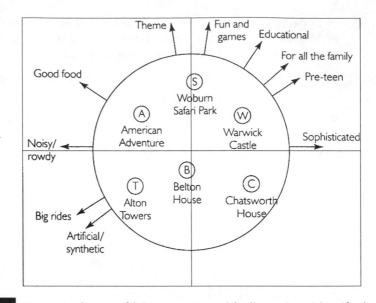

Figure 8.2 Perceptual map of leisure centres with dimensions identified
Reproduced with permission, from *Marketing Strategy and Competitive Positioning*, by Hooley, Saunders and Piercy (1998) © Pearson Education Ltd

Consumers can then be mapped on to the same space, by getting them to rate each attraction in terms of preference, then using cluster analysis. The results are shown in Figure 8.3. From this, it can be seen that Belton House is not well positioned, as it falls between the major groupings, not appealing strongly to any segment, while the others are relatively well positioned.

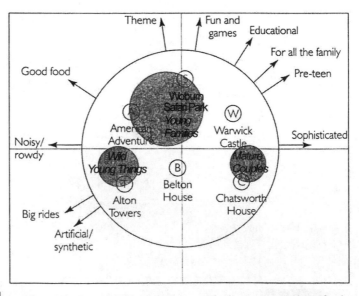

Figure 8.3 Perceptual map of leisure centres with dimensions identified and segment ideal locations
Reproduced with permission, from *Marketing Strategy and Competitive Positioning*, by Hooley, Saunders and Piercy (1998) © Pearson Education Ltd

Decide among positioning alternatives

We look at some possible strategies below, but for the example, it is clear that Belton House needs to choose in what direction to move.

Other techniques that are available for such exercises include conjoint analysis (see for example www.sawtoothsoftware.com), and correspondence analysis (Carroll *et al.* 1986).

Choosing a position

The aim, as we noted earlier, is to match the company's skills and resources with the needs of the consumers in the target segment. Wind (1982) suggested the following possible positioning strategies:

- By specific product features (Volvo stresses the early introduction of side air bags to reinforce its safety position).
- By associating benefits with problems or needs (seen in many insurance company campaigns, or the classic Hamlet cigar advertising).
- For specific usage occasions (After Eight Mints).
- For a user category (Saga Holidays for older people).
- Against another product (Avis 'We're number two – we try harder').
- Product class disassociation (7-Up, 'the un-cola').
- Hybrid (many brands, e.g. BMW using status, performance and features).

As the products in many markets are now so similar, and deliver an expected level of quality – as in the car market – the positioning takes on greater importance. It may also become more challenging, as consumers are sophisticated in understanding marketing programmes, and will not be fooled by mere empty claims. A winning position must always centre around a product or service that delivers what the target segment wants. BMW has done this superbly for its relatively expensive cars, but so has McDonald's for its inexpensive fast-food restaurants, which deliver the speed, convenience, quality and entertainment that its consumers prefer. The position may be communicated by any or all elements of the marketing mix; let us now go on to look at that in more detail.

Definition of the marketing mix

So far in this book we have concentrated on a vital aspect of the marketing job – looking *outside* the firm: at the environment, markets, the trade, consumers and competitors. The other part of the marketing task is to find a best fit between what the firm can offer and that outside world. The tools at our disposal are called the 'marketing mix': the mixture of the marketing variables which we can control, and more precisely the amount of each which we choose for a particular situation. This chapter therefore serves as an introduction to the main variables, each of which will be treated in more depth in later chapters, and also addresses the issue of interaction between and integration of the elements. This theme of interaction and integration should never be forgotten; when we concentrate, as we must at times, on an individual element such as advertising or price, we must always remember that each element never acts alone, but always as part of the overall mix.

The best-known definition of the marketing mix, attributed to McCarthy (McCarthy 1975: 75), is the 'Four Ps':

- Product
- Place
- Promotion
- Price

Current usage is more likely to be in the order product, price, promotion. place.

The Four Ps definition has been criticized, on the grounds that 'place' should be 'channels of distribution', and 'promotion' should be 'communications'; others have produced their own acronyms (usually longer) or definitions. The great merit of the Four Ps is that it is simple and memorable; its widespread use today, over thirty years after the concept was first introduced, testifies to its value, and it will be used here (as we shall see in Chapter 15, we need to add further Ps for services).

Obviously, the Four Ps formulation simplifies; as we shall see in looking at each in turn, there are many facets to the main elements.

Product

Product must be taken to refer also to services, and to the combination of physical product and service which is found in many if not most fields. Many services use large amounts of hardware (transport, fast food, banks), while many products provide service as part of the package. Product means the total offering which the firm makes to the target market. It can be broken down in many ways:

- Physical attributes
- Psychological attributes
- Quality
- Styling, features
- Branding, including name
- Packaging
- Assortment (sizes, colours, flavours, etc.)
- Product range and line
- Service, before and after sales
- Guarantee and returns policy.

Each firm will need to develop an analysis of its product relevant to its particular industry. As we shall see in Chapter 9, we also need to distinguish between the core product, and successive layers of basic, expected, augmented and potential product.

The important point, which can be endlessly repeated, is that it is the marketing function to see all these attributes from the consumer's or customer's point of view.

Place

This refers to channels of distribution. Must products need to be distributed in some way, though the system may be simple or extremely complex. Elements of distribution are:

- Choice of channels
- Depth and breadth of distribution
- Service levels
- Physical distribution
- Relationship management.

Although distribution has in the past been the Cinderella of marketing elements, the huge growth of retailer power has meant that, for consumer goods manufacturers at least, it has become more and more important (Randall 1994).

Promotion

Promotion covers all the means used to communicate with the target market. It includes all the most visible aspects of marketing, as well as some that are less obvious:

- Advertising
- Internet
- Sales promotion (trade and consumer)
- Personal selling
- Exhibitions
- Other publicity (sponsorship, events, gifts, etc.)
- Public relations

There are some boundary disputes, especially around public relations, which can be and are used for objectives broader than product marketing. For our purposes, it matters only that all communications should be consistent and coherent, whatever the medium.

Price

Price is self-explanatory. It can be further broken down into:

- List price
- Discount structure
- Trade pricing
- Variable pricing (e.g. off-peak)
- Credit.

Marketing people will always argue that they have an important, if not decisive, input to pricing decisions, but in practice their influence varies. In fast-moving consumer goods companies, marketing people often have the final decision; in high technology or heavy industry, they often have little or no say. From a marketing point of view, price must be seen as part of the total offering; it tells the customer something, and should be looked at from that aspect as well as from a financial one.

Role of each element in different situations

It is clear that the marketing mix adopted by different firms varies enormously according to the market, segment and situation they are in. Boeing does not use the same mix to sell airliners as Procter and Gamble use to sell toothpaste. A small manufacturer of own-label dishwashing liquid does not use the same mix as Procter and Gamble use to sell Fairy Liquid in the same market. Apart from statements of the blindingly obvious, can we say anything useful of the role of each of the elements of the mix?

The one thing which must be repeated is that the elements cannot be considered entirely separately. An improvement in product quality will need to be communicated to customers, and may involve a change in price; a change in distribution pattern will mean reallocation of the sales force. The impact of a given price will be different at different levels of promotional support ... and soon. With that caveat in mind, let us look at the elements individually.

Product

The product must always be central. No amount of clever advertising, or eye-catching promotions, or brilliant selling, or saturation distribution, will persuade people to buy a poor product – or at least, to buy it more than once. This is not to say that the product must be of the highest possible quality, but it must be of the right quality for what buyers in the target segment want. This immediately raises the interaction with price, since what people are looking for is value for money – a good enough product at an acceptable price. The other major point is that it helps to think of the product in the context of how it is used, so that we can envisage the total product package as experienced by the user. This way of thinking about the product has been called various things: the augmented product, the benefit bundle, for example. In industrial marketing, the approach has been termed 'systems selling'. Taking as broad a view as possible of the interface between your firm and the customers and consumers may lead you to a new way of seeing your total product offering and how it may be improved. In terms of the mix, expenditure on improving the product should be compared with other ways of spending the money: quite how this might be done is discussed later in the chapter. The product should be seen as the fixed point around which move the other elements of the mix.

Distribution

Distribution may be looked at in two ways:

1 From the point of view of the end user, it is a channel, merely a conduit through which your goods pass. From this angle, the important considerations are such things as speed and efficiency of deliveries, service level (proportion of time that the item should be in stock, minimum time for delivery, etc.), coverage of the target population.

2 From another angle, the channel members are themselves customers, and then you must look to how you can improve your service to them: ease of ordering, efficiency of delivery to the channel, invoicing procedures, promotional backup, query-solving, and so on.

As part of the marketing mix, it should reach the target market, by making the product available in outlets used by members of that segment. It should reflect the brand positioning; a premium, exclusive brand should appear only in a small number of exclusive outlets, for example.

Advertising

Of the promotional tools, advertising is the most visible, but it is a major weapon for only some manufacturers. Mass brand manufacturers such as Unilever or Mars use heavy advertising campaigns to build and support their brands. Increasingly, others who cater to a mass market, such as retailers and financial services, also use advertising as an important tool to inform and persuade. For most other firms, advertising is a fairly minor part of the mix. For many industrial marketing companies, advertising is used to make potential customers aware of their name and product range, but really as a platform for the sales people. For firms marketing to other organizations, personal selling is usually the most important tool, together with exhibitions and perhaps direct mail. With such a huge variety of situations and promotional tools available, it is difficult to generalize, but it can be said that the more complex the product, the longer the decision time, the more service and support are needed, then the more likely personal selling is to be the main promotional weapon.

Price

The importance of price varies enormously in both consumer and industrial markets. The less functional or brand positioning differences there are between rival offerings, the more price will play its part. The more real or perceived differences there are, the less important will price be. At the extreme, when performance is absolutely vital, then price may be of no concern at all to the buyer.

Price will always be an indicator of relative quality, so buyers will normally look at the value-for-money equation, expecting better quality for a higher price and vice versa. At another extreme, only a very high price will be acceptable: many luxury brands have a price which bears little relationship to any intrinsic cost of materials: a price which very few people can afford is itself part of the appeal of the brand.

Targeting the mix

Marketing aspires to the objectivity of engineering, but is in many ways still an art. The marketing manager knows certain basic rules which have been passed on and adapted over time. He or she will have been trained to combine certain ingredients to produce (usually) the desired effect, and will also have experimented with new and different combinations, with varying success.

Quantitative targeting

Would we not rather be like an engineer, with theories and models for guidance, so that we could work out in advance, on paper (or in the computer), what effects a particular recipe would produce?

To achieve this, we would need to know the sales response curve for each element of the mix separately, and the effects of interactions within the mix. A possible sales response curve for advertising is shown in Figure 8.4. It represents what most people believe about advertising: there would be some sales without advertising (because of the product's existence, and word-of-mouth); with small amounts of advertising, there would be little effect; as the amount of advertising increases, sales response would increase, and at an increasing rate; at some point, diminishing returns would set in as it became harder and harder to convert buyers: eventually, sales would reach a ceiling and would rise no further no matter how much more money was spent on advertising. A similar response curve must exist for product quality, for distribution, and for price. The price response curve is more familiar from economics as the price-elasticity of demand, and indeed sales response is just another name for elasticity.

The problem, as we have discussed elsewhere, is that it is extremely difficult in practice to measure sales response. If we could (and it is possible in some circumstances), we would optimize the price, advertising, etc. mathematically. Theoretically, it is even possible to optimize the mix, though as far as is known, no one has ever actually done it, the practical difficulties being insuperable. On the other hand, managers make decisions about the mix. They do so on the basis of experience and judgement. They have internal, perhaps unconscious, models of the sales response curves. They are also, of course, normally working within a limited budget, so are implicitly or explicitly trading off elements of the mix against each other. Ideally, each element would receive the amount of money which its potential response justified, as in the case of allocation to segments discussed in the previous chapter. At any level of allocation, the next chunk of money should be allocated to the element which would give most return; the positions on the sales response curves would be re-calculated, and the next iteration would proceed; this would continue until either the returns were less than the investment, or the budget ran out. This is illustrated in Figure 8.5.

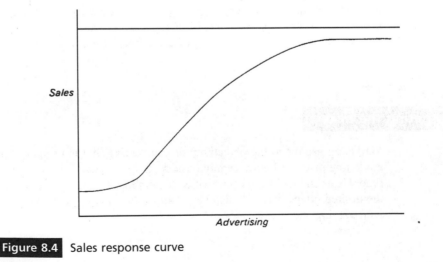

Figure 8.4 Sales response curve

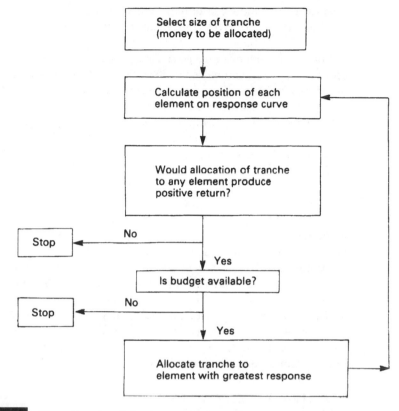

Figure 8.5 Allocating funds in the marketing mix

Qualitative targeting

The nature of the target segment should be taken into account in deciding what mix is most suitable. Some segments may respond better to product quality, others to heavy advertising, others to sales promotion. This is partly a question of coherence: each part of the mix should be sending the same message. A product which appears to be of high quality but which is priced cheaply, or which is distributed in cheap outlets, will confuse buyers. Frequent money-off promotions and gimmicky offers are not suitable for a brand which is positioned as good, old-fashioned quality. The tone of the advertising, the name and packaging – everything – need to be matched to the target segment, and to be coherent with the other elements.

Matching the competitors

So far we have focused on the target segment, but in finalizing the marketing mix we need also to think about competitors. How will our mix fit with what our main competitors are likely to be doing?

Ideally, we would like to both match the competitors in terms of impact, and differentiate ourselves from them in terms of appeal.

Some commentators even go so far as to argue that 'Your tactic should not be customer-oriented . . . [it] should be competitor-oriented' (Ries and Trout 1989). This is exaggerating to make a point, since the consumers must never be forgotten; but in many markets today, the need to differentiate, to stand out from the crowd, means that designing the mix with an eye on the competition is more and more necessary.

Second-guessing the competitors is part of the marketing game; managers make assumptions about what the competition will do, how they will react to a given move. This can be made explicit through a device called the' 'Competitive Response Matrix' (Lambin, quoted in Shapiro *et al.* 1985). The matrix, shown in Figure 8.6, sets out how the major competitor is expected to react to a given action by our company. We are Company A, and the vertical columns represent actions taken by us. The Cs are probabilities attached to the responses of our competitor, Company B. Thus Cp.p is the probability that B will respond to our price change with a price change of their own. Ca.q represents the probability that B will respond to our advertising initiative with a quality improvement, and so on. Such an approach introduces an element of discipline into the decision-making process, and allows a number of possible situations to be thought through and evaluated.

The final matching that needs to be done is between the marketing mix and the company itself, in particular its history and resources. History is important because customers and consumers learn and remember; over time, they come to know what to expect from a company and a brand. Consistency in the mix can be a great strength, reinforcing the effect of all that has gone before. On the other hand, in this as in other areas, 'That's the way we always do it' can be a dead hand. There are times when a fresh approach is needed, and something new and unexpected can have enormous impact. There are no rules for making this sort of decision; is is a matter of flair and judgement. Much will depend on the market situation and competitor activity: if they are doing new and interesting things and you are losing share, then the case for change may be powerful. If,

Our action	Competitor action			
Aq	Cq.q	Cq.p	Cq.a	Cq.d
Ap	Cp.q	Cp.p	Cp.a	Cp.d
Aa	Ca.q	Ca.p	Ca.a	Ca.d
Ad	Cd.q	Cd.p	Cd.a	Cd.d

Figure 8.6 Competitive response

on the other hand, you are in control, holding or gaining share, then the sensible course is to maintain the current policy. The balance between consistency and complacency is a difficult one.

Evaluating the mix

This is really a summary of points made in the preceding sections. It is useful to have a checklist against which to compare one's chosen mix before finalizing the decision. The central concepts are efficiency, leverage and fit. Leverage refers to the fact that in a particular market situation, a market segment may respond much more to one element of the marketing mix than another. One segment may respond much more to price, for example, and another to advertising. Fit, as we have seen, should be sought between the mix and the segment, competitors and the company. A fuller checklist (Shapiro *et al.* 1985) is:

- Are the elements consistent with one another?
- Beyond being consistent, do they add up to form a harmonious, integrated whole?
- Is each element being given its best leverage?
- Are the target market segments precisely and explicitly defined?
- Does the total programme, as well as each element, meet the needs of the precisely defined market segment?
- Does the marketing mix build on the organization's cultural and tangible strengths, and does it imply a programme to correct weaknesses, if any?
- Does the marketing mix create a distinctive personality in the competitive marketplace and protect the company from the most obvious competitive threats?

Key learning points

- **Every firm must ask – and answer – the question: why should any customer buy from me rather than a competitor?**
- **Marketing must seek to differentiate its offering in ways that are important to consumers.**
- **Companies should aim to position themselves and their brands in the minds of consumers.**
- **In developing a positioning strategy, the firm should identify competitors, analyse the positions of competitors and customers, decide among positioning alternatives, and track the positioning.**
- **To target consumers in a chosen segment, firms use the marketing mix: product, price, promotion, place.**
- **The mix must be coherent, consistent, and leveraged.**

■ **It should differentiate the brand, offer total benefits superior to competitors', and match the company's resources and competences.**

Further reading

Hooley, G., Saunders, J. and Piercy, N. (1998) *Marketing Strategy and Competition Positioning*, London: Prentice Hall.

Kotler, P. (2000) *Marketing Management*. Millennium edition, Englewood Cliffs, NJ: Prentice Hall.

Case study

A conglomerate has a number of divisions which operate independently:

■ Building materials,

■ Architectural fittings and supplies (doors, light fittings, etc.),

■ Electrical equipment (small motors),

■ Measuring instrumentation (sold to industry and to hospitals and laboratories),

■ Paint,

■ Security locks.

It has recently taken over a manufacturer of branded grocery products.

Questions

1 What marketing mix would you expect in each division?

2 At what audience(s) would each mix be targeted?

3 Take one product line, either in your own organization or in another to which you have access: find out how the marketing mix is currently targeted. Could the allocation process be improved?

Chapter 9 | Product policy and branding

It has already been stressed that the product is at the heart of marketing, indeed of the company. Although from one angle it could be argued that the company is the sum of its culture and values, from the outside it is perceived in terms of its products and services, and the way it delivers them.

The management of its products must therefore be central to the overall running of the firm. The role of marketing is to make sure that the company offers the right products, that they are correctly positioned for the chosen target segments, and supported by the best marketing mix.

This chapter will look briefly at classifications of products, then summarize and evaluate methods of analysing the product portfolio, before going on to cover the main aspects of product management and branding.

Classification of products

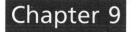

For many years, writers on marketing tried to classify products – or goods, as they were often called. The most obvious divide is into consumer and industrial products; even though there is some fuzziness, where products are sold to both consumers and to organizations (cars, for example), generally the distinction is clear. Consumer products have been classified in a number of ways, the earliest being into convenience, shopping and specialty goods:

- Convenience goods are bought often and with minimum effort.
- Shopping goods are those in which consumers normally make some effort to compare quality, price, style, etc.; these would include clothes, furniture and most durables.
- Specialty goods are those for which a significant effort is needed or given; buyers will spend considerable time and may travel some distance to shop. For example, for most people postage stamps are a convenience good; for a stamp collector, they are a specialty.

Other classification systems are more complex, but in all honesty they are of more interest to academics than to practitioners, since they have no obvious bearing on what managers should actually do.

In industrial marketing, products are sorted by government statistics both in the UK and the USA into Standard Industrial Classifications (SIC). This starts with major categories, such as Manufacturing or Retail Trade, and goes down to increasingly detailed categories. Each category has a code, the more digits in a code indicating the increasingly fine detail; thus a four-digit SIC code indicates a fairly tightly defined industry, such as manufacture of switchgear and switchboard apparatus. As many government statistics are published with this analysis, it can be useful, though the growth of conglomerates makes classification difficult. It is often used as a first stage in a segmentation exercise.

From a marketing point of view, there are more useful ways of classifying products; these will be examined in the next section.

Portfolio analysis

Few firms make only one product; even those which do probably produce several models or variants. Most companies have many products; some many hundreds, or even thousands. The range of products is referred to as the product portfolio, and an essential start to the process of managing our products is to diagnose the strengths and weaknesses of the current portfolio. What we should be interested in initially is how much each contributes to overhead and profit. This seems basic, but many firms do not have an accounting system which provides the information. A further problem is that some costing systems are out of date, and provide information which is positively misleading as to true product cost. Allocation of overheads is another tricky area; arbitrary allocation may obscure the real pattern of profitability.

Marketing managers must make sure that they have access to up-to-date, accurate information which they can understand.

This static diagnosis is only a beginning, as we really need to take account of where our portfolio is going to be in the future. We cannot know the future, of course, but we must take a view of the dynamics of our market: we must identify the forces which are shaping it, and try to anticipate how they will act over the next few years. This involves a number of interacting variables – economic, technological, social, structural, competitive – and the exercise could easily become overpowering. Fortunately, there are some frameworks to help us. The more important of these are described below.

Drucker's categories

Peter Drucker is one of the authentic gurus of management thought. Some years ago, he suggested that managers should examine their products carefully, putting them into the following categories (Drucker 1967).

- **Today's breadwinners.** Substantial volume, adequate contribution; at or near their zenith.
- **Tomorrow's breadwinners.** Show promise and reality; consumer and trade acceptance; high contribution.
- **Product specialities.** Having a limited and distinct market.
- **Development products.**
- **Failures.**
- **Yesterday's breadwinners.** Still high volume, but low net revenue.
- **Repair jobs.** Must have all the following characteristics:
  - substantial volume
  - considerable growth opportunities
  - a significant leadership position
  - high probability of exceptional results if successful
  - one major defect only.
- **Unnecessary specialities.**
- **Unjustified specialities.**
- **Investments in managerial ego.**
- **Cinderellas.** Sleepers who may one day awake.

Drucker's categories are partly qualitative, but they are simple and mainly clear; his insistence that useless products should be cut out so that management time and effort can be spent on tomorrow's breadwinners is still valid. Too many managers are tempted to spend time on products they grew up with, or made their names on, or which are prestige projects. Often these products are yesterday's breadwinners or worse. The scarce resource of top management time must be spent on securing the company's future.

Drucker's classification contains elements of the segmentation and positioning analysis discussed above. It also bears a remarkably prescient similarity to the next model, the Boston Matrix.

The Boston Matrix

Developed by the Boston Consulting Group, the model has been one of the most popular and widely adopted of recent decades. It was developed to help top corporate managers decide how to allocate resources between businesses, but the principles can be applied to products within a single business. Each business or product is positioned within the matrix according to two measurements – market growth and relative market share (see Figure

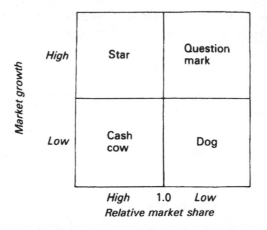

Figure 9.1 Boston Consulting Group product – market matrix. Reprinted with permission from *Long Range Planning*, February 1977, Boston Consulting Group, p. 12, © 1977, with permission from Elsevier Science

9.1). Much of the popularity of the technique stems from this apparent simplicity and from the imaginative naming of the quadrants. Businesses (products) are classified as:

- **Cash cows** – high share of low-growth market.
- **Stars** – high share of high-growth market.
- **Question marks** – low share of high-growth market.
- **Dogs** – low share of low-growth market.

Two points may be made:

1 The market share is always relative to the market leader, or next biggest competitor if you are the leader, with a mid-point of 1.0. This is to distinguish between a situation in which a brand has, say, a 10 per cent share against a leader who has 14 per cent and that in which the brand has 10 per cent against the leader's 50 per cent. In the latter case, the small brand is in a much weaker position than in the former.

2 A high-growth market is often taken as more than 10 per cent a year; this figure is not fixed, but should be chosen so that the diagram is enlightening to users.

The Boston Box, as it is sometimes called, has been severely criticized, but it has its uses as long as it is not over-interpreted. Its main message is that companies need a balanced portfolio. They need one or more 'cash cows' to generate cash today (cf. Drucker's 'today's breadwinners'), but cash cows are probably in mature markets which will eventually decline. Some 'stars' are necessary, because although not all will succeed, and they need considerable investment, it is from among their ranks that future cash cows will come (cf. 'tomorrow's breadwinners'). A few 'question marks' are acceptable, since some of them might turn into 'stars'. 'Dogs' are candidates for deletion, though some might make a positive contribution or be an essential part of a range, and therefore worth keeping. (For criticisms of the model, see Wensley 1981.)

Shell Directional Policy Matrix

A more complex analysis is the Directional Policy Matrix developed by Shell (see Figure 9.2). This sets the company's competitive capabilities against the prospects for sector

Prospects for sector profitability

	Unattractive	Average	Attractive
Weak	Disinvest	Phased withdrawal	Double or quit
		Custodial	
Average	Phased withdrawal	Custodial (proceed with care)	Try harder
		Growth	
Strong	Cash generation	Growth	Leader
		Leader	

Company's competitive capabilities (vertical axis label)

Figure 9.2 Shell directional policy matrix

profitability in a three-by-three table; each of the nine cells contains a recommended strategy, such as 'Phased Withdrawal', or 'Double or Quit'. Like the Boston model, it was designed to assess businesses or strategic business units, but it can be applied to products too. It, too, has been criticized for the assumptions it makes (Wensley 1981).

Other models

Several other techniques are described in the literature. Amongst the better-known are the McKinsey/GE Business Assessment Array, which is similar to the Shell model, and the AD Little Business Profile Matrix, which uses market position and industry maturity as its axes. There are further, more complex models, and a range of techniques which can be adapted to the needs of the individual company. For further details the reader is referred to a major text such as Wind (1982).

Software is easily available for many of these models (and others), for example at www.market-modelling.co.uk. As with all such software, you need to understand what the model is doing in order to interpret its output.

Benefits and weaknesses of models

The whole point of these models is to give managers a picture of where their company is now, and some guidance as to future action. If no analysis has been carried out before, even the simplest technique can be enlightening – even experienced managers can be surprised to find out just where the profit is coming from. One senior manager, completing a Boston Matrix for the first time, was dismayed to find that the company had a large number of dogs, one or two cash cows, several question marks and no stars.

The benefit, therefore, is an objective representation of the current state of the business and a prognosis of where it is going if nothing is done. The analysis should spotlight the areas on which attention and resources should be focused, and encourage management to face up to hard decisions.

All the models have some weaknesses, which users should be aware of. The more complicated the model, the more important it is that the manager understands the underlying assumptions and the implications of the technique.

Models will not make a decision, but should be treated as one source of help. Most have at least some subjective inputs, and these should be checked for bias and wishful thinking. No strategy prescription should be accepted at face value, but should be checked against the specific set of circumstances and the manager's knowledge and experience.

In this as in other similar cases of important strategic analysis, some modified form of Delphi technique can be useful. In the original Delphi approach, a group of experts is recruited to analyse a problem. In this case, different managers within the firm could be used; one or more outside consultants could be added for objectivity. The procedure is for each member to form an opinion independently; these are then summarized and circulated to all participants, who can revise their opinion if they wish on the basis of others' views; the revised opinions are again summarized and circulated. The process can be repeated until some sort of consensus emerges. Given the importance of the decisions which will be made about the company's product portfolio, it is worth making sure that the analysis is as soundly based as possible.

Managing multiple products and lines

Few companies have only one product. There are some famous examples, of course: Coca-Cola for much of its history, and perhaps Guinness, though both eventually broadened their line. Volkswagen was for many years an example of the dangers as well as the advantages of one very strong product. Its 'Beetle' car was tremendously successful, but the company could not launch other models, partly because of the sheer strength of the Beetle image – Volkswagen *was* the Beetle.

While having one product, or a very small range, allows a firm to concentrate all its efforts, it is vulnerable to any change in markets or tastes, which could destroy it. Most firms, then, have several products, and it is the job of product policy to manage them.

Conventionally, we distinguish between the product mix, which refers to the number and range of different types of product offered by a firm, and the product line, which refers to the number of variations offered within one product type. General Electric (GE, the US company) has an enormously broad product mix; it operates in aircraft engines, broadcasting, defence electronics, electric motors, factory automation, lighting, locomotives, domestic appliances, diagnostic imaging and financial services, amongst other products. Nestlé, although it has thousands of products world-wide, is mainly in various food businesses and therefore has a relatively narrow product mix. Within a particular product field, a firm is said to have a long or deep product line if it offers a large number of different brands or models.

As products proliferate within a firm, they are usually divided up into convenient groups, either by market or by technology, often with a geographical overlay. Such questions are really beyond the scope of this book; we assume that managers are dealing with a reasonably homogeneous range of products, organized on some rational principle. From a marketing point of view, we should prefer that the organization was based on groups of buyers having similar needs, but other considerations may override that.

Product policy falls into two major areas: the allocation of resources, and decisions as to product modification, addition and deletion.

Allocating resources to products

In the delightfully simple world of theory, the allocation of resources is easy: you maximize profit by putting resources where they will earn most return, just as with market segments or elements of the marketing mix. Readers who have come this far will not be surprised that the reality is less straightforward. As we have seen earlier, the main problem with the theoretical approach is the near-impossibility of actually measuring the likely response to marketing effort. We would of course argue that managers are making implicit judgements about market response when they make decisions about where to allocate resources, and that it is preferable to make such judgements explicit as far as possible.

Beyond that, there are reasons why straight profit maximization is not always easy:

■ the need to balance short- and long-term profit;

■ the fact that some products may be wanted by buyers as part of a line, even though they are not very profitable. Dropping such a product might lose further business from other parts of the range;

■ the need to keep providing parts and/or service for products which are no longer made; although attempts can be made to make this activity profitable in its own right, customer goodwill considerations may dictate that spares and service are provided at around cost.

The short/long-term profit argument is a perennial one, and we are all familiar with the stereotypes of Anglo-Saxon short-termism against Japanese long-sightedness. Whatever the reasons, marketing people, along with R&D, are most likely to be arguing for investment which may not show a return in the immediate future, but which is essential for longer-term prosperity. Techniques such as discounted cash flow can help, but the uncertainty involved in forecasting several years ahead will be significant. Nevertheless, it is worth carrying out such exercises, at least now and then, so that you can rebut the bean-counters' arguments (or, more sneakily, win resources for your brand rather than another in the company). Most of the models described above (Boston matrix, Shell matrix, etc.) have strategy implications or explicit recommendations – invest, harvest, divest, and so on. These may also help, but may need to be backed up with financial data.

Another view of product line management, typically thought-provoking, is:

Every marketer has three kinds of products:

- **one to advertise;**
- **one to sell; and**
- **one to make money on.**

A burger chain advertises the burger, sells the french fries along with the burger, and makes money on the soft drinks (Ries and Trout 1986).

This is a more positive way of putting the point made earlier about the different products in the line. It is important to know where the profit is being made, but also what is pulling in the customers.

Modification, addition and deletion of products

A product line should be under constant review, to try to optimize the fit between the line and the company, the customers and consumers, and competitors.

The major lesson to be learned from the Japanese, in this author's opinion, is their total commitment to constant improvement – in the manufacturing process, in product quality, and in customer service. Whereas at least some western manufacturers seem to heave a sigh of relief once a product is launched, and look for a breathing space, the Japanese start to make modifications and improvements immediately, and go on doing so throughout the product's life.

The scope for cost reduction in procurement and manufacturing is beyond the scope of this book, but it is of concern to marketers, since it may have an impact on the quality of the delivered product. Procter and Gamble are reputed to have called the marketing executive 'the housewife's representative in the company'. In other words, it is marketing's job to scrutinize any change in raw materials, components, manufacturing process or service delivery, to make sure that it does not detract from performance as perceived by the consumer. How often such changes are actually made will vary widely, depending on the volatility of raw material prices, the state of manufacturing technology and the competitive pressure on price levels. A particular problem in an industry where changes are fairly frequent is that while each change separately will have no discernible impact, over time a gap may develop between the original product and the current formulation or model. In these circumstances there is no substitute for regular testing of consumer reaction to the product in use.

A more proactive aspect of changes in the company is the need to look for ways of serving customers and consumers better. Companies serving organizational customers should be looking at all aspects of the relationship between the firm and the clients; as we shall see in Chapter 14, this is a new and challenging task for many consumer-goods companies, though industrial marketers have been doing it for some time. Recent developments such as Just-in-Time (JIT), Electronic Data Interchange (EDI) and the use of the Internet turn attention to the need for all departments to co-operate in delivering service.

Modification

Marketing's proactive task in product modification is of course to search for ways of improving the product's performance. Harnessing R&D and manufacturing is one aspect of this, as are creativity and careful interpretation of market research.

> **As the marketing manager is always looking for something to differentiate the product from competition, there is a fine line between a modification which is successful – different from competitors, salient to consumers, and more profitable – and one which fails (not different enough, or easy to copy, not important to consumers, and less profitable).**

There is also the question of timing: too frequent changes may alienate customers, particularly if compatibility is an issue, or if consumers feel they have bought an old model.

If your brand is positioned as exciting, innovative, leading-edge, then modification will need to be more frequent than for a brand positioned as traditional and reliable. The nature of the major competitors' strategies will have a strong influence, too. In highly competitive markets, the search for new features and benefits, even if only for advertising claims, is constant, and it is usually impossible to stand aside even if one wanted to.

> **For the dynamic company, the challenge is always to have the best products, and ones which are different from competitive offerings – both these as judged by the buyers and users.**

Addition

Apart from modification, decisions about adding products to the line are probably the most frequent. Two strategies are known as 'stretching' and 'filling'.

1 Stretching

From an original successful position, a product may be stretched by the addition of new models, sizes, variants, etc. The stretching may be upwards (higher price, better quality) or downwards, or even (though our topography may be getting confused) sideways into new niches. Over the years, Ford have stretched their product line upwards, to include larger, more luxurious saloons, downwards, to the supermini class, and sideways, to more sporting niches.

2 Filling

Filling, as the name implies, means adding a product to fill a gap in the existing line. This is likely to happen as a market matures and becomes increasingly segmented.

Both stretching and filling are clearly tied very closely to segmentation and to competitors' actions. Ideally, we should like our product line to include an entry in each segment in which we can make a good profit, and which we can dominate. How we go about this depends a good deal on our existing position *vis-à-vis* the competition. A firm attacking a strong competitor who dominates a central position in the market will try to fill gaps in segments in which the competitor is not active. A market leader may try to stretch its line to reach new segments and to pre-empt or fight off competitive entries. Some competitors will have a full-line strategy, with an entry in all or most segments, while others will cherry-pick only certain segments.

Sales and marketing people are sometimes accused – particularly by manufacturing and finance managers – of wanting too many models and variants in the line, and it must be recognized that proliferation of unnecessary or unjustified specialities (to use Drucker's terms) is a danger. Flexible manufacturing technology has made it much easier and more economical to make different models without costly machine down-time, but every addition to a product line probably has some extra cost, whether in procurement, inventory, manufacturing, or sales and servicing; these extras must be balanced against net additional revenue from the proposed additions.

A further argument for care in extending a successful brand is that, although it may appear a relatively low-risk strategy compared with launching a completely new product (see next chapter), there are possible dangers. Apart from extra costs, particularly unforeseen ones, there are two main problems: the danger of cannibalization and the possibility of weakening the parent brand. Cannibalization means that the new product takes sales from the firm's existing brands. This may or may not be acceptable. If the brand which loses sales is the dominant market leader, then cannibalization will be acceptable only if the new brand is more profitable and the overall competitive position is improved. If the brand being cannibalized is small or less profitable, that may be easier to accept. What is certain is that the cannibalization effect must be thought through; it is extremely rare for a line extension to produce only net new sales (either from new buyers or from competitors), without affecting the parent brand.

The possibility of weakening the parent brand is more difficult to quantify. At the extreme, some would argue that if you have a very strong brand, no extensions at all should be permitted, as they will inevitably weaken the position, either by confusing consumers or by distracting management from concentrating on the main brand at all times. Few brands are in this position, and for those that are, the temptation to extend must be enormously powerful. Some very famous brands have resisted for many years, only to succumb in the end – Coca-Cola now has half a dozen extensions (Cherry Coke, Diet Coke, Tab and caffeine-free versions). (See Ries and Trout (1986: 117 – 36) for a discussion of the 'Cola war'.) Some critics think that this will weaken the main brand in the long term. The Mars Bar remained the Mars Bar for decades, with other Mars brands having different names (Bounty, etc.). The launch of the Mars Bar ice cream was seen by some as a triumph, but by others as the first sign of weakness and confusion. At present it is too early to say whether Coca-Cola and Mars are right, or their critics.

A further risk is that a line extension will fail, directly affecting the reputation of its parent. Again, such results are virtually impossible to predict accurately in advance, but the risk must be taken into account.

Deletion

Deletion of products from a line seems to be as much an emotional problem as a managerial one. Any product which has existed for many years carries all sorts of emotional baggage; both managers in the firm and some customers will be loyal to it. Nevertheless, it will be using up valuable resources, particularly management time, which perhaps ought to be devoted to tomorrow's products rather than yesterday's. A decision to delete must of course weigh every consideration: contribution to overhead, use of capacity and labour, place in the product line as seen by customers, and alternative use of the resources freed.

Once again the Japanese seem to have a solution to the problem, but it is one which is peculiar to their unique industry structure. Once a product reaches a point in the life cycle at which it is no longer growing and at which the technology is mature, the company passes it on to one of its affiliates lower down the technology ladder. This structure makes exit barriers considerably more flexible than is common in the West, and allows the major firms in Japan to concentrate their resources on emerging technologies and products.

To sum up, there are few rules for managing a product line, except to review frequently and to be committed to constant improvement. One slogan is:

Minimize cannibalization – maximize synergy.

Putting this into practice takes flair, objectivity and dedication.

Branding: building and maintaining strong brands

A brand is different from a product. Brands are normally associated with fast-moving consumer goods. They can, however, exist in services and industrial markets: British Airways and Singapore Airlines, for example, are strongly branded, as is JCB earth-moving equipment; IBM, as we shall see below, is one of the world's best-known brands. Managers who work in industries where branding is not common are invited to read the following discussion of the pros and cons of branding, and to consider how branding might affect their organization.

The essence of any brand is that it is more than an undifferentiated, commodity product. In the perception of buyers, it has a unique identity.

It has a unique name, and it may have its own logo, design and packaging, although these are not essential; it is probably supported by advertising, though even that is not necessary in special cases such as Marks & Spencer (though even M&S has now adopted advertising to support its weakened brand). A brand should wherever possible be legally protected, that is the brand name and identity should be registered as a trade mark and the design elements copyrighted. For international brands this is a large and important task, too complex to be dealt with here.

What a brand emphatically is not is just an image created by a jazzy name and clever promotion. The brand image is in fact extremely complex, as it is formed by all the inputs received by the consumer over time: from experience in use,

from word of mouth and display, for example, as well as from all the communications elements (name, packaging, advertising).

This reminds us of key issues in branding, which underlie much of what follows but are easy to forget.

1   Branding is a fundamental strategic process that involves all parts of the firm in its delivery. It is about marketing, but is not confined to the marketing department.

2   The brand must always deliver value, and the value must be defined in consumer terms.

3   The brand has a continuing relationship with its buyers and users; this may change over time, but the firm must always work to maintain it.

4   Because competition is getting fiercer all the time, and because structural changes undermine the *status quo*, branding must be continuously adapted so that it is both effective and efficient.

What is a brand?

As Stephen King put it, 'A product is something that is made in a factory; a brand is something that is bought by a consumer' (King 1973). Charles Revson, the founder of Revlon, made a similar point when he said that in the factory, he made cosmetics; in the store, his customers bought hope.

As Jeremy Bullmore has pointed out,

It is in every human being's nature to invent and build brand values inside each individual head. We do it with people, we do it with animals – and we do it with inanimate objects. The skill of brand management is to see that each consumer is offered the right raw materials from which he or she will build the brand as the brand owner would prefer. A brand is not an objective fact; it is made up of a million or more individual and subjective assessments – a consensus of subjectivity. (Bullmore 1999: 1).

The test must surely lie, not in the views of individual commentators, but in the collective opinion of the target customers and consumers. If they can perceive that a product has a unique identity that differentiates it from other similar products, and they can describe it and the unique set of benefits it offers, then it is a brand.

Certainly it is not the manufacturer or supplier who decides whether it is a brand or not. Some attempts to create brands have manifestly not succeeded. It is tempting to see the early attempts by the British clearing banks to create brands, for instance, as failures.

To an outsider, the failure seems to have been due to their inability to persuade consumers that what they were offering really was unique and different. It seems likely that at the time, the reality of bank services had not changed very much in practice, and that of course was how consumers perceived matters. The 'branding' was just an expensive advertising campaign, making claims that no one believed. This underlines the point made at the beginning of the chapter, that branding is a matter for the whole firm, not just for the marketing department (particularly a weak and semidetached marketing department with no real influence on the firm's products and services).

What we can conclude is that there are strong, successful brands at one end of a spectrum; at the other are failed attempts at branding, where consumers perceive no unique characteristics distinguishing the product from others; and in between are brands of varying strengths and weaknesses. To analyse them more fully, we need to look at the dimensions that describe brands.

Dimensions of brands

As suggested earlier, there are many models of brands. There is no one correct model, which everyone accepts (as is so often the case in marketing). Here we will look at two which are representative. First, let us distinguish between *brand image* and *brand identity*.

Brand image is a phrase used rather loosely, particularly by people outside marketing ('Let's change the image', they say hopefully of a brand in trouble). In fact, the image of a brand is what exists in the minds of consumers. It is the total of all the information they have received about the brand, from experience, word of mouth, advertising, packaging, service and so on; the information is modified by selective perception, previous beliefs, social norms, forgetting. It may be messy and untidy, not what we would prefer; but it is what exists, and what we must work on and from.

Brand identity is what we transmit to the marketplace; it is what is under our control, provided that we understand the essence and expression of our brand. It is here that models can be useful. The first, shown in Figure 9.3, is from the Leo Burnett Brand Consultancy, and uses the dimensions:

■ Functions

■ Personality/image

■ Source

■ Differences.

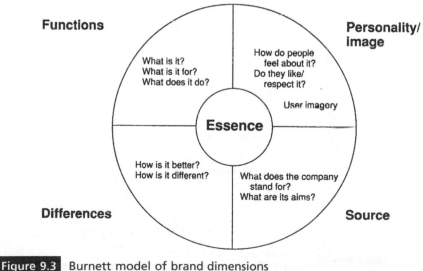

Figure 9.3 Burnett model of brand dimensions
Source: Leo Burnett Brand Consultancy

The dimensions form the Essence at the centre, and the brand identity will be strong when there is consistency between the quadrants, and they are supporting each other. If any quadrant is weak, or sending conflicting messages, then the resulting image in consumers' minds will be confused.

The second model, shown in Figure 9.4 is from Kapferer (1997). His dimensions are:

- Physique
- Personality
- Culture
- Relationship
- Reflection
- Self-image.

By *physique* Kapferer means what others refer to as function, and is wider than the literally physical characteristics of the brand. It is the central purpose of the brand, the 'What does it do?' of the Leo Burnett model.

Personality is straightforward, and has been widely used as a main dimension in fmcg markets for decades. Consumers can describe brands' personalities, and are asked to do so through the sort of projective techniques described in Chapter 6.

Culture can belong to the brand itself, or to the parent company. Mercedes Benz cars have a strong cultural dimension: in their world, engineering excellence and solidity rank high, whereas more modish ideas about styling and features are seen as fripperies. Nike projects a culture of individual effort and commitment to success.

Because in most product markets people buy repeatedly, they can have *relationships* with brands over time. This is an important idea, since many views of markets seem to be based on a view that they are made up of unrelated *transactions*. While the move from

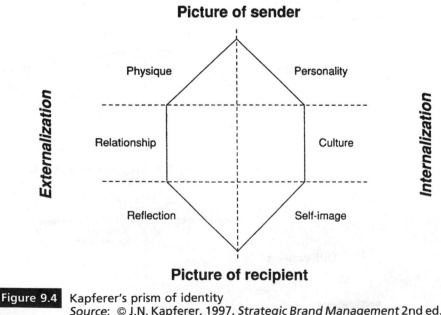

Figure 9.4 Kapferer's prism of identity
Source: © J.N. Kapferer, 1997, *Strategic Brand Management* 2nd ed., Kogan Page

transaction to relationship is talked about in, for example, banking, it is found in most markets. Establishing a relationship between brand and user is healthy and positive (provided that the relationship is itself positive).

By *reflection*, we mean the type of user that the brand appears to be aimed at. This is not necessarily the same as the brand's target market as described in its marketing plan, since many reflections are aspirational: they show the sort of person that the user would like to be, or aspires to be like. Most women know that they do not look like the photographs in cosmetic advertising, but they would prefer to be more like them. Men buying Marlboro are not going to be cowboys, but would like to think of themselves as sharing some of the figure's characteristics.

The *self-image* is the internal version of the reflection. We are familiar with the idea that we are what we eat, and perhaps also with the idea that we are what we buy. The brands we buy represent, at least to some extent, our view of ourselves. Even someone who rejects brands by buying own label is saying something: 'I am the sort of person who is rational and buys on value-for-money, not meaningless advertising'.

To repeat, a strong brand is one that has a consistent, coherent identity. There is interaction between the different dimensions, and the company must

- work out what the detailed identity of the brand is
- ensure that it is coherent across all the dimensions, and
- communicate the identity to the target audience.

Types and levels of brand

Branding can be applied at different levels of the firm. Unfortunately, there is little agreement about the exact terms to be used for the levels, and there can be some confusion, particularly around such words as umbrella or pillar brands. There can also be overlap between categories, or changes over time in the way a brand name is used. What matters is the extent to which a particular analysis helps our understanding of a particular situation, but remember that different people may mean different things by the same word.

- *Product brand or standalone brand.* In its basic form, the brand is identical with a single product or service: Mars bars, for example. Many leading companies use this approach; there is no Procter and Gamble brand, even though P&G is probably the leading branding company in the world. Its brands are all individually named – Ariel, Fairy, Crest, Pampers. There may of course be sub-products of each brand, such as Boy and Girl Pampers, or different types of toothpaste – so there is some overlap with
- *Line brands.* Here a group of products are given a name, such as L'Oréal StudioLine. All the products in the line will be in a similar field, and will be positioned at the same quality/value level.
- *Range brands.* A slightly wider grouping may be called a range, though it must be said that this is a subjective decision. Weight Watchers from Heinz is a range, but whether Vidal Sassoon (from Procter and Gamble) is a line or a range is an open question.

- *Umbrella or pillar brands.* An umbrella, as the name suggests, gives protection to several sub-brands. One example, called pillar branding by its owners Birds Eye Foods, is:

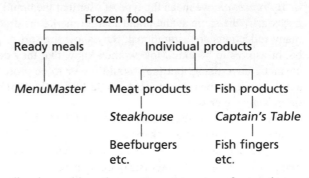

Umbrella branding is used by other commentators to refer to what we have termed line or range brands, or to the next level up when a company name identifies the brand.

- *Company, family or source brands.* Examples of this are common: Sony, Ford, IBM, Cadbury.

- *Endorsing company, corporate or banner brand.* Here the company name appears, but less prominently than the main brand; it acts as an endorsement or guarantee. An example is the brand Kit Kat, with Nestlé as the endorsing company (formerly, of course, the endorsing company was Rowntree). The level of identification and endorsement varies from prominent to understated.

Apart from these levels, we may add that there are other types of brand:

- *Designer labels* such as Armani, or Porsche Design.

- *Griffes, or haute couture brands*: *griffe*, apart from meaning claw, also refers to the signature and thence the brand of fashion houses such as Christian Dior. There is clearly some overlap with designer labels.

- *Licensed names* of which Disney is the best-known example.

- *Retailers' brands* are, in fmcg markets, the most important. They include store name brands, lines or sub-brands, and generics; they will be discussed in more detail in Chapter 14.

Out there in the real world, there is a mixture of styles of branding. The questions we should ask ourselves are, 'What are we communicating to our target customers and consumers?' and, 'What is the best way of communicating what we want to?'

To the obvious question, 'What is the one best way of doing it?' there is unfortunately but unsurprisingly no answer. Kellogg's brands all its products with the company name, Procter and Gamble uses standalone brands. Both have been supremely successful (though both are struggling somewhat now, that is unrelated to their branding approach). It may be argued that the range of P&G's products is much broader, and therefore it makes less sense to try to impose a single brand, whereas Kellogg's produces only breakfast cereals, and even Nestlé, with a huge number of products, is still a food company. There is a discernible trend towards the use of the company name, especially amongst companies seeking to establish global brands. For now, we will continue our exploration of branding by looking at the functions carried out by brands.

Functions of the brand

For customers and consumers, the brand has four main functions:

1 **Identity**   The brand must identify itself clearly and unambiguously; name, legal protection and design elements are paramount here.

2 **Shorthand summary**   The brand identity should act as a summary of all the information held about it. Memory seems to act by storing packets of information in networks, and the brand should provide access to this network, triggering information and associations.

3 **Security**   Buying a familiar brand should be reassuring, as it should guarantee to provide the benefits which are expected.

4 **Differentiation**   The brand must clearly differentiate itself from competitors, and show consumers that it is unique.

5 **Added value**   A brand must offer more than the generic product. Although the security mentioned above is in itself of value, a brand should normally offer additional benefits; it should be better quality, or better value for money, or have features and benefits not provided by the generic product. Although the benefits may be either functional or non-functional, they must be of value to consumers; preferably they should be unique to the brand.

Many brands offer more than one benefit. Indeed, it could be argued that in most of today's highly competitive markets, a level of functionality is taken for granted, and the general price level is also dictated by competition. Brands will then be trying, sometimes desperately, to find ways of differentiating themselves from other brands offering almost the same things at more or less the same price. Whether or not this is a sensible business strategy is a fundamental question. Nevertheless, an identifying difference is central to the brand. This difference may be built up over a long time, and can give products meaning and direction (Kapferer 1997). For example, Citroën cars, going back to the pre-war Traction Avant models, and through later classics such as the 2CV and DS, are definitely different in their engineering design, and sometimes in their styling. The *heritage* of Citroën is clear, and it may be argued that in a market in which most cars are becoming more and more alike, it is this heritage that alone will guarantee the company a future (functionality and quality being taken for granted in cars now).

The value of brands

So far, we have taken for granted that strong brands were worth having. In this section we will examine the evidence for this, since building and maintaining a brand necessarily involve large expenditures. Are we sure that it is worth it, assuming of course that the effort is successful? The evidence falls into a number of categories: that from the longevity of some brands, from various sorts of market data and from take-overs. We will then look at some of the issues arising from the attempt to place monetary value on brands, and at the whole concept of brand equity.

Long-lived brands

Some brands have very long lives. A few, such as Coca-Cola or Gillette, date from the nineteenth century. In both the USA and the UK, many brands have led their category for sixty years or more.

Table 9.1 Leading brands in the USA and UK since 1933

US Brands		UK Brands	
Brand	Market	Brand	Market
Eastman Kodak	Cameras/film	Hovis	Bread
Del Monte	Canned fruit	Kellogg's	Cornflakes
Wrigley	Chewing gum	Gillette	Razors
Nabisco	Biscuits	Schweppes	Mixers
Gillette	Razors	Colgate	Toothpaste
Campbells	Soups	Kodak	Film
Ivory	Soap	Hoover	Vacuum cleaners
Coca-Cola	Soft drinks	Brooke Bond	Tea
Goodyear	Tyres		

Source: Interbrand

The longevity of these brands, and the profits they have earned over their lifetimes, are not accidental (the fact that both Kellogg's and Hoover have lost share to competitors shows that even great brands are not fireproof). They are all leaders because

- they have offered consistent, high quality, equal to or better than any competitor;
- they have been supported by heavy investment in manufacturing and marketing (advertising and distribution);
- they have adapted to changes in consumer tastes, either through research and development and/or through changes in product formulation, packaging or positioning.

It seems certain that the managers of the producing firms have seen the maintenance of their brand's leading position as a major strategic objective, and they have kept their eye on the ball.

Evidence from the Profit Impact of Market Strategy (PIMS) study, the largest database of business results in the world, shows that market leadership is highly related to *perceived quality*, and these long-lived brands are testimony to that.

Market leadership and profitability

Several pieces of evidence as to the profitability of strong brands were gathered together by Peter Doyle (Doyle 1989).

- Brands with a market share of 40 per cent generate three times the return on investment of those with a share of only 10 per cent.
- For UK grocery brands, the number one brand generates over six times the return on sales of the number two brand, while the number three and four brands are unprofitable.
- For US consumer goods, the number one brand earned a 20 per cent return, the number two earned around 5 per cent and the rest lost money.
- Small brands can be profitable: a strong brand in a niche market earns a higher return than a strong brand in a big market. In large markets, competitive threats and retailer pressure can hold back profits even for the top brand.

- Premium brands earn 20 per cent more than discount brands.

- It can cost six times as much to win new customers as to retain current ones.

- The best feasible strategy to achieve profitability and growth is to focus on brand differentiation, rather than cost and price. Although the best strategy in theory is both low cost and high differentiation, it is worth paying some cost penalty to achieve strong differentiation.

These are enormously powerful lessons. They should be engraved in large letters and framed above the desks of marketing directors and, perhaps more importantly, finance directors in every company which has, or thinks it ought to have, brands. The results relate only to fmcg brands, but the evidence from the PIMS study shows that, across a wide range of industries, the biggest factor related to high profitability is market share.

If it is argued that the findings are only about market leaders, and strong brands, then that underlines the message of this book:

Firms should aim for strong brands that dominate their market segment.

Companies that want to be leaders must strive to dominate the large, central segments that account for most volume; but niche brands can also be profitable, as long as they are strong in their chosen target area.

Another study showed that, over a twenty-year period, companies relying mainly on heavily branded goods with those that derive their value independently from brands: the branded firms consistently outperformed the others on the FTSE 350 stock exchange index (Ward and Perrier 1998).

In an especially intriguing comparison, Almquist *et al.* (1998) showed what happened when General Motors and Toyota both marketed a car produced by them both in a joint venture. The cars were functionally identical, but branded as Geo Prizm and Toyota respectively. Between 1990 and 1994, Toyota sold 200,000 Corollas at $11,000 each, while GM could sell no more than 80,000 – and at a lower price of $10,700. Toyota made over $100 million more than GM, and its dealers made a further $128 million. The difference can be attributed only to the greater power of the Toyota brand over GM's. That may well be related to perceptions of greater product quality, based on experience, reports and word of mouth, but, however it arose, it clearly demonstrates the financial value of a superior brand.

Take-overs

The first time that brands became headline news in the UK was when Nestlé made a takeover bid for Rowntree's, the well-known confectionery manufacturer. The amount Nestlé was willing to pay pushed the Rowntree share price from 475p to 1075p. The total paid meant that assets as valued in the company's accounts amounted to only 17 per cent of the price – so it was clear that Nestlé was paying a huge premium for the value of Rowntree's brands. Other take-overs in Europe and the USA gave a similar message.

What were these sophisticated buyers paying such enormous sums *for*? There are three underlying reasons:

- the buyers were paying, not for the current performance of the brands, but for their **future potential**; Nestlé has made Kit Kat into a truly European brand, with greatly improved sales and still some potential for future expansion

- there are very few possible take-over targets in these crowded but lucrative markets: the acquirers were paying a premium **to prevent competitors from getting the brands**.
- It is easier to buy successful brands than to build them from scratch.

In some cases, it seems likely that a considerable degree of overbidding was present, but only time will tell whether the assets acquired were a bargain or an expensive white elephant.

Brands and the balance sheet

Results such as those quoted, and the take-overs described, suggested to many that, if brands really are so valuable, they should be shown on the balance sheet. This idea was particularly attractive to some British companies who perhaps felt vulnerable to take-over attempts themselves, and who wanted to strengthen their balance sheets. Others, who had spent the vast sums on acquisitions, wanted to make the best of presenting the results.

In the UK, Rank Hovis McDougall were the first to try to extend this idea from brands for which a price had been paid to those which they already owned, that is those they had developed themselves. The logic is appealing: if brands have real value, and obviously they do since companies are willing to pay very large sums for them, then they have that value all the time, not just when a firm is taken over. Moreover, the addition of new assets in the form of brands will strengthen the balance sheet, which has other attractive results (including making the firm look much more expensive to a predator). However, the concept gives rise to many problems, not least the valuation method.

In the UK, the Accounting Standards Board published a new standard in 1997, FRS 10, which allowed acquired brands to be capitalized on a fair value basis, as long as sufficient goodwill is available. Such brand valuations must be checked annually for impairment. The Board also stated that home-grown brands *cannot* be capitalized, since in their view, 'It is not possible to determine a market value for unique intangible assets such as brands...' (paragraph 12).

Whether or not brands will be shown on the balance sheet, it seems entirely reasonable to want to know what they are worth. Only then can sensible judgements be made as to how much it is worth investing in them, and how well the investment is being managed. Brand valuation is playing an increasing role in attempts to measure the effectiveness of marketing expenditure; there are, however, many problems.

Methods of valuing brands

The American magazine *Financial World* has a paid circulation of over 500,000 readers. On 2 August 1994 it reported results of a brand valuation survey carried out by FW staff.

> Here's a shock: The IBM brand name is now worthless. That's just one thing we discovered in valuing 290 of the world's most popular brands. Of the 290 brands we surveyed, 14 had negative or zero value... In such cases, a competing generic product could have generated high profits on the same level of sales.
>
> (Macrae 1996: 213)

This finding, nonsensical as it may appear, shows the problems in valuing brands. The method used in the *Financial World* survey is not clear, but it seems to hinge on analysts' views about the strategic competence of firms' managements. IBM has certainly had its problems, but to say that its brand name is now worth nothing seems to fly in the face of common sense. As we now know, IBM has made a successful recovery from its crisis, and is once again a powerful and profitable brand.

How then can we go about valuing brands? There are two classes of approach: the accounting/economic method, and other methods.

Accounting/economic methods

The value of an asset is that it can provide a stream of future earnings. Because accounting rules stress conservatism and factual accuracy, the traditional way of valuing assets has been the historic cost: you know exactly what you paid for an asset, and there can be no doubts about it. Assets that lose their value over time are depreciated, that is their cost is amortized over what is thought to be their useful life. It is this approach that has been used in take-overs to value brands. An alternative approach is to estimate not the actual historic cost of an asset, but its replacement cost; this became popular during periods of high inflation when historic costs were thought to be misleading. It is readily apparent that applying this method to brands also introduces a large subjective element. We know so little about market behaviour, except that it is dynamic, that estimating the cost of building a new brand from scratch would produce very wide margins of error indeed.

A final problem is that known as *separability*, and refers to the difficulty of knowing exactly what belongs to the brand and what to other parts of the company. Finally, it could be argued that if the value of a brand is its stream of potential future earnings, then the way to estimate its value is to calculate those earnings directly (suitably deflated to a net present value). By now it should be clear that, however sophisticated the models used to do this, some subjectivity and uncertainty will necessarily be present. The estimates produced may be mathematically impressive, but the range of uncertainty built into them is just as wide.

Other methods

Any attempt to model future sales and market share will recognize that many factors are involved. Many approaches therefore explicitly list the factors assumed to cause sales and market share, and quantify them. The technique has been widely used, especially in the UK and increasingly the USA. Some models will be described briefly in the next section on brand equity; Interbrand used such an approach for many years.

Other methods include the use of consumer attitudes, the premium price that a brand can charge, estimated royalty income, and momentum accounting. Brand valuation is such a growth industry that all the big five accountants, and other consultants, have their own models (Ambler and Barwise 1998).

Brand equity

In recent years, the debate about the value of brands has been crystallized in the phrase *brand equity* – except that crystallized is probably the wrong word since the concept is anything but sharp and crystal-clear. The phrase is used in varying ways, and seldom precisely.

Let us start then with one attempt to be clear. Aaker defines brand equity as:

a set of assets and liabilities linked to a brand, its name and symbol, that add value or subtract from the value provided by a product or service to a firm and/or to that firm's customers (Aaker 1991: 15).

He goes on to say that these assets and liabilities can be grouped under five categories:

1   brand loyalty
2   name awareness
3   perceived quality
4   brand associations in addition to perceived quality
5   other proprietary brand assets – patents, trademarks, channel relationships, etc.

The difficulty that many people – including this author – have with Aaker's model is the same as we have with many similar marketing models.

No one would disagree that the factors listed – brand loyalty and so on – are in themselves *good things*. We would rather have them than be without them. The difficulty is that there is absolutely no evidence that they are related systematically to brand equity, whatever that is.

We can, using market research, measure the factors listed and obtain ratings of how consumers view a brand. What we do not know is what to do with them then. Are the factors weighted differently, and if so how? Do the weights vary between different product fields, and even different brands? How exactly do the ratings translate into 'confidence in the purchase decision' or 'use satisfaction'?

Ambler and Barwise (1998) define brand equity as 'the marketing asset that exists in customers' minds and is of continuing value to the brand owner because it influences future purchases by the buyer and the buyer's social network through word of mouth'. The other attempts to measure brand equity take a generally similar approach to Aaker's. Some take relatively 'hard' measures such as market share and relative price, while others use 'softer' units such as liking or perceived quality. The test for all of them will be to show over time that they can produce valuable data that managers can use. All are subject to the criticism levelled above at Aaker's model.

How can we helpfully sum up this complicated and messy area?

■   brands clearly have a value, since some companies are prepared to pay large sums for the privilege of acquiring them;

■   all the methods of trying to estimate the value of an individual brand are fraught with difficulties;

■   the concept of brand equity is used, in different ways, to try to capture the idea that a brand has a value;

■   however, no valid, reliable way of measuring brand equity has yet emerged: that is, no one method is guaranteed to produce a valid result for a particular case.

This does not imply that the methods proposed are without merit, nor that managers should not try to measure the value of their brands. As suggested above, it seems eminently sensible to do just that. Rather than arguing vaguely about the long-term value of a strong brand, or the need to treat brand advertising as an investment, surely it would be better to have at least some idea of what value we have built up already; then we can begin to measure the effect of our actions on maintaining or increasing that value.

This is not to underestimate the problems of such measurement; these have been noted above. However, unless we start somewhere, we will never be any the wiser. Systematic collection and analysis of data over many years may bring enlightenment. Some of the uncertainties will remain, as that is the nature of marketing – but an explicit model of exactly how we believe we are adding value will help us think, and argue marketing's case with the accountants, and perhaps even strengthen our reputation in the City. At the very least, it will get people from different functions in the firm talking about the same thing, and developing a common language. If, as this book argues, strong brands are central to companies' survival and growth, then that alone would be worth the candle.

Building and maintaining brands

The critical success factors in building and maintaining a brand are quality, differentiation, consistency, evolution and support.

- **Quality** is fundamental. Two familiar points must be reiterated: quality must be defined from the consumer's point of view, and it is the quality of the total offering that is important. The quality is defined by what the target segment wants, so McDonald's is outstanding at delivering quality to its consumers, even though middle-class critics may sneer at its products. What IBM has delivered over the years when it has led the world computer market is the quality of its hardware, software and service support; the fact that it has not necessarily been at the leading edge of technology has been less important.

- **Differentiation** is self-explanatory but difficult to achieve. Whether expressed in the old phrase 'a Unique Selling Proposition' (USP), or in the more modern terminology of 'sustainable competitive advantage', the brand must have something which differentiates it from its competitors. Moreover, that something must be salient to the target consumers – it must motivate them to buy; even if the difference is small, it must be relevant. It may be intangible, as in the quality of service or the psychological benefits delivered, but it must be perceptible. It can be pre-emptive, in the sense that other products may also have the characteristic, but the first one to claim it keeps it. It should, ideally, be difficult to copy.

- **Consistency** is a hallmark of great brands. Chopping and changing from year to year (or from brand manager to brand manager) may be exciting, but it risks confusing and alienating consumers. The value of a successful brand is so great that a sensible company makes changes only after the most thorough consideration. This does not mean that no change is desirable, however – quite the contrary.

- **Evolution** is essential, since the environment and the market are always changing. Fairy Liquid remained the leading washing-up liquid in the UK for many years, on a platform of softness and kindness to the hands. Without abandoning that claim, it then moved on to a longer-lasting, value-for-money position; it has now been relaunched on a grease-dissolving differentiation. All relate to overall product quality. Guinness has been famous for the consistency of its branding, although the actual campaigns have changed substantially over the years in response to changing social and market influences.

- **Support** may mean different things in different contexts, but always involves substantial investment. For fast-moving consumer goods, it usually means heavy expenditure on above-the-line advertising; not even the strongest brand can rely on its past reputation for long. For industrial brands, it may involve serious commitment to after-sales service, or high R&D costs. For service companies, the need may be for very large expenditure on staff training. An unfortunate effect of identifying some brands as cash cows is that the management tries to siphon off funds from successful brands to invest elsewhere, without realizing that a leading brand will not stay in that position without continuing substantial support. Any signs of this tendency must be resisted, though scarce resources often make the dilemma acute.

Threats to brands

It is obvious that successful brands are always under threat, particularly from competitors. Management complacency or neglect are probably the greatest threats, since an alert management will recognize (or foresee) challenges from competitors and from market and environmental change, and will take appropriate action.

In recent years, other threats have appeared, especially in consumer markets:

- **Fragmentation of markets** is a reflection of changing technology (ability to manufacture variations economically), and of competitive action to segment markets.

- **Repertoire buying** means that in some markets consumers buy several brands, each for a different purpose: cheap instant coffee powder, a premium brand of granules, ground coffee and a decaffeinated brand, for example.

- **Media cost inflation** has affected many countries as some costs, particularly television time, have risen faster than inflation.

- **Media fragmentation** has been caused by technological developments in satellites, cable, pay-as-you-view, video-recorders and the Internet. Some commentators believe that such developments will make it difficult to produce traditional heavy, mass-market campaigns, though the evidence so far is inconclusive.

- **Changing lifestyles**, with more leisure and a wider range of activities to fill it, may make some key target groups more difficult to reach.

Alert management will have recognized these and other threats. For consumer brands, the biggest threat is retailer power, which may see many well-known brands de-listed and the share of others eroded. This vital topic is returned to in Chapter 14.

Making other people's brands

In industrial markets, it is common for companies to make not only components but complete products for other manufacturers, who then 'badge' them with their own name or brand. The firm whose name appears on the product is known as an 'Original Equipment Manufacturer' (OEM). Sometimes the actual manufacturer is not identified at all; in other cases, where the component is important or visible and there is a substantial after-market, as with car tyres, the actual manufacturer's name appears, but is much less important than the OEM's.

The parallel in consumer markets is retailers' brands (own-brand, own-label, private label, distributor's own brand, retailer-originated brand). In some markets such as clothing, retailers' brands account for the majority of sales; in others, for much less. In supermarkets in the UK, own-label sales have settled down at around 40 per cent of total packaged grocery sales, though this covers a wide range in different product categories and different companies.

Retailers' brands fall into five main types:

1 Store name brands – Sainsbury, Aldi.

2 Retailer-controlled brands – Dixons', Saisho.

3 Designer labels – owned by manufacturer or retailer.

4 Licensed names – a real or imaginary character.

5 Generics – absolutely basic products at very low prices.

The decision for both industrial and consumer manufacturers is whether to make brands for other people, either other manufacturers or retailers. Many companies do so, and have made a successful business out of it. The only drawback is a possible loss of control, in that one is essentially a supplier of what someone else decides is needed; if the OEM or retailer decides to drop the product or change to another supplier, you lose the business. In practice, most relationships between suppliers and OEMs are stable and long term; increasingly they are working together as partners to achieve mutually profitable goals.

In the case of retailers' brands, the manufacturer should approach the decision through a number of questions (Randall 1994):

1 **Do I have the choice?** If many brands are de-listed or become uncompetitive, will it become necessary to fill the gap with retailers' brands?

2 **What is the capacity situation?** If there is industry over-capacity either locally (UK) or regionally (Europe), there will be pressure to produce own-label.

3 **What is the company mission and culture?** Some senior managers see themselves as brand manufacturers or marketers, and would see any derogation from that as the betrayal of a trust.

4 **Do we have the skills to make retailers' brands?** Making brands for other people demands different skills and priorities from those needed in marketing manufacturers' brands – perhaps a different culture and different managers.

5 **If we do, what and for whom should we make?** There are several choices, including manufacturing for selected clients only, making products similar to or different from your existing brands, and developing new brands in co-operation with the customer.

From a marketing point of view, it could be argued that meeting customers' needs may involve making their brands, and that this is an acceptable and necessary service. Manufacturers with very strong brands often resist this argument, feeling that their only salvation lies in devoting themselves single-mindedly to their current and future proprietary brands, as for example do Kelloggs and Heinz. Others may not be able to take this stance.

All should at least look into the future and take a strategic view of how they are going to build their relationships with customers – by supplying only proprietary brands, or only customers' brands, or a mixture of the two.

Key learning points

- Most firms have more than one product, some have many hundreds or even thousands. This is referred to as their product portfolio, and the first step in managing products is to diagnose the strengths and weaknesses of the current portfolio.

- Knowing the profitability of each product is the basic first stage.

- In trying to gauge the position of our portfolio now and in the future, some frameworks are available. Those of Drucker, the Boston Matrix and the Shell matrix are described.

- All models can provide a useful framework, but cannot be over-interpreted; they should be used as guidance only, and the specific situation examined carefully to reach specific conclusions.

- The company's product mix and line should be under constant review to optimize the fit between the line and the company, the customers and consumers, and competitors.

- A brand is different from a product; it has a unique identity. The brand has four main functions: identity, shorthand summary, security, added value. Building and maintaining the brand is a central function of marketing.

Further reading

Randall, G. (2000) *Branding*, 2nd edition, London: Kogan Page.
Keller, K.L. (1998) *Strategic Brand Management*, Upper Saddle River, NJ: Prentice Hall.

Case study: Jennifer Rose

Jennifer Rose has been appointed Marketing Manager in the consumer electronics division of IBL, a British company. The division embraces sound reproduction systems sold to both organizational buyers (public address systems, etc.) and to consumers, as well as personal computers and games.

The relative sales and profits are:

Division	Sales %	Profits %
PA systems	10	20
Stereo systems	30	30
Personal computers	45	35
Games	15	15

The company buys in many of the components and sub-assemblies from South-East Asia, though it has its own R&D section, which concentrates mainly on the top end of the audio market. It has a reputation for quality and reliability in the professional sector. The personal computers, which are sold through dealers to consumers and to small businesses, compete mainly on price; an attempt to sell a package adapted to a particular end-market (solicitors) has produced promising results.

Jennifer has been asked to produce a new product strategy for the division within the next three months.

Questions

1 What information would you advise Jennifer to collect in order to develop the new strategy?

2 Making any assumptions you wish (but make them reasonable ones), put forward your own recommendations for the division's product policy. Justify your decisions.

Chapter 10 | New product development

Need for new brands

Although the philosophy of this book should dictate that this chapter is called new *brand* development, the usage 'New Product Development' (NPD) is so well established that it will be adopted here. NPD is strictly part of product policy, dealt with in the previous chapter, but it is so important that it is treated separately. It should, however, be seen very much within the context of the firm's overall product strategy.

It is also worth underlining the point that NPD is about innovation, but that innovation can and should occur throughout the value chain, not just in those activities closely related to product design and manufacture (or their service equivalent). Innovative companies find new and better ways of doing things in the manufacturing process, in procurement, distribution, promotions, personnel policies – everywhere.

Even within the sphere of NPD, it is clear that innovation is a relative term. There is a spectrum of 'new products':

- Totally new inventions (television, contraceptive pill).
- New technology applied to an existing product (electronic calculator, watch).
- New form of an existing product (Sony Walkman).
- Improved technology or combination of technologies (computer-controlled machine tools).
- New model.

- Product new to this market but existing elsewhere.
- Product new to this company.

All these innovations are termed NPD by the companies concerned, but the lengths of time, amounts of capital investment, and levels of risk involved are very different; generally speaking, all three are greatest at the head of the list, and least at the end.

New brands are needed either because old brands die, or because the firm wants more growth than the existing product portfolio can produce. It is generally accepted that product life cycles are shortening in many markets, and that competition – especially international competition – is increasing. NPD, therefore, becomes more and more central to firms' success.

There is, however, a great deal of lip service paid to the idea. Many if not most companies would claim to place great stress on successful NPD, but few actually have a good record in the field. The company must ask itself *why* it is getting into NPD, and what exactly it expects to achieve. Is it trying to develop a whole new business, or to replace an important brand which is in terminal decline, or to use some spare capacity in the factory, or to give someone a job during a career gap? All these and others have been the real if sometimes unacknowledged reasons for NPD programmes. More commonly, a company will have a stated commitment to NPD, but will put few real resources behind the programme; responsibility will be assigned to managers of existing brands as part of their duties; there will be little co-ordination of different functions, and a lack of support from the top. In these circumstances, it is not surprising that success is rare.

It is vital that each company should think through its NPD strategy, taking a realistic view of its resources, strengths and weaknesses. The NPD programme adopted should fit the company's abilities, overall strategy and attitude to risk. It should be clear whether it is trying to be a technological leader, or a fast follower. Above all, it must provide the resources and organizational structure to implement the programme.

In the following sections, we will look at reasons for failure in NPD and try to find some pointers towards success.

Reasons for failure

It is accepted that failure rates for new products are high. Various rates are quoted, ranging from 50 per cent to 90 per cent plus. The reason for these differences is that different definitions of new product are used (from ideas to products actually launched), as well as different market definitions and different measures of failure. Since the rate of new product launch and the incidence of failure vary from market to market, what is important is to have a good idea of what applies in your own market, and then to understand why products fail.

There are of course organizational barriers to successful innovation, especially in large companies. One authority has found the following constraints on innovation:

- top management isolation
- intolerance of fanatics
- short time horizons
- accounting practices
- excessive rationalism
- excessive bureaucracy
- inappropriate incentives.

(Quinn 1985)

If these are general problems, there are also specific difficulties. There have been many studies of new product failure; their conclusions can be summarized as follows.

Reasons for new product failure:

1 Lack of meaningful product uniqueness.
2 Poor price/value performance:
   – three out of four successful products are better than competition in some way;
   – four out of five failures are the same as or worse than competition.
3 Poor planning, including positioning, segmentation, budgeting, market understanding, poor research, over-enthusiasm.
4 Wrong timing.
5 Action by competitors.
6 Product performance – technical or cost.
7 Lack of product champion/internal politics.

The majority of these reasons can be counted as failures of marketing. Although it is the responsibility of others to ensure major elements of the satisfactory delivery of the product offering, it is marketing's job to ensure that any new product launched has real and differentiating consumer benefits which are attractive to a particular market segment, and that the whole mix is correctly targeted. Too often, it seems, these apparently simple – if demanding – requirements are not met.

The huge waste of resources involved in new product failure, together with the concomitant effects on the firm's reputation with customers and consumers, mean that huge efforts ought to be devoted to cutting the failure rate. That this is not always so is a reflection of that potent cocktail of lack of top management will, organizational politics, and managerial incompetence. The situation is often exacerbated by the very limited time which many marketing people spend in one job.

Improving the strike rate in NPD

It follows that a company which wants to improve will show the converse of many of the characteristics discussed above. It will have:

- strong need orientation (towards customers and consumers)
- toleration of experts and fanatics
- long time horizons
- low early costs
- multiple approaches
- flexibility and quickness
- incentives for successful innovators
- availability of capital.

(Quinn 1985)

It will work out and communicate to all staff its strategy for NPD. For example, does it want to:

- Develop one major new business, or lots of small brands?
- Be a technology leader, or a follower?
- Be usually first in the market, or a fast second?
- Maximize the value of a few brands, or accept proliferation?
- Go for high-quality, high-price, or cheap and cheerful products?

There are many other possible aspects to the strategy, but above all it must be market-directed, clear and focused. It must also demonstrate the fit discussed above and in previous chapters: the strategy must fit the opportunities and threats offered by the market (customers and consumers) with the firm's strengths and weaknesses, bearing in mind what competitors can and will do.

Beyond that, research suggests that companies with a successful record in NPD tend to:

- introduce a unique, superior product;
- have market knowledge and marketing proficiency;
- have technical and production synergy and proficiency;
- avoid dynamic markets with many new product introductions;
- be in large, high-need growth markets;
- avoid introducing a high-priced product with no economic advantage;
- have a good product/company fit with respect to managerial and marketing resources;
- avoid competitive markets with satisfied customers;
- avoid products new to the firm;
- have a strong marketing communications and launch effort;
- have a market-derived idea with considerable investment behind it.

(Cooper, reported in Baker 1983)

While we may agree with all this, it must be admitted that there are examples of opportunistic NPD which break many of those rules – and indeed that almost every supposed rule for successful NPD can be shown to have been broken. The process is essentially unpredictable and complex; it may be that the best a firm can do is to create a culture that encourages innovation, choose the right people for particular tasks, and let them get on with it with minimal interference, but subject to real review and accountability.

As many companies will find this cold comfort, the following sections will look at more conventional recipes for successful NPD. If a company is seriously worried about its past NPD performance and wishes to make a clean start, it could carry out an innovation/NPD audit. This would apply the concepts summarized above, and try by a rational approach to develop a new strategy and focus; the process is shown diagrammatically in Figure 10.1.

Most models of NPD set up a stage-by-stage process and recommend ways of proceeding at each. They have their merits, and will be examined here, always with the proviso that real life is likely to be less linear and more messy.

Most models have a series of stages such as this:

1　Idea generation

2　Screening

3　Physical development

4　Communications development

5　Market testing

6　Final checks

7　Launch.

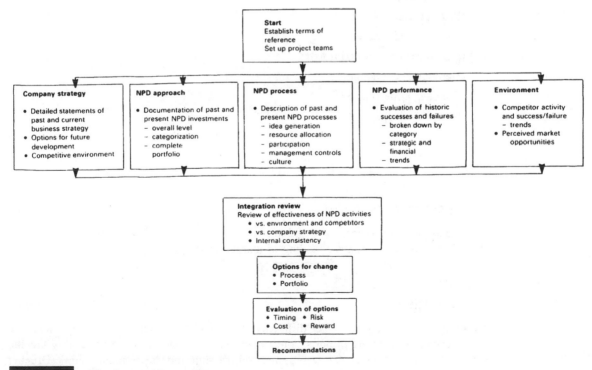

Figure 10.1　The innovation audit

These will be examined in turn, but again with two provisos:

- several stages may proceed simultaneously;
- the process is likely to be iterative, circling back on itself and repeating stages as internal or external circumstances dictate.

Idea generation

There is some disagreement in the marketing and NPD community as to whether or not the availability of ideas is a problem. Some take the view that there are always plenty of ideas, indeed more than can usually be followed up. Others feel that most so-called new product ideas are extremely weak, and that what is wanted is the one really good idea, rather than lots of me-too or marginal concepts. Whichever position one takes, it is sensible to be serious about new ideas, and to be as open to sources of new products as possible. The real receptivity of the company culture to ideas will dramatically affect the flow. One Japanese company received 6.4 million ideas in a year, an average of eighty per employee, and 70 per cent of these ideas were implemented; a similar American company had five ideas per employee, of which 30 per cent were implemented.

Drucker suggested that there are a number of general sources of new opportunities:

- **Within the company/industry**
  - Unexpected occurrences
  - Incongruities
  - Process needs
  - Industry and market changes.
- **Outside the company/industry**
  - Demographic changes
  - Changes in perception
  - New knowledge.

(Drucker 1985)

Unexpected occurrences

These may be either successes or failures; the important thing is that the unexpectedness should lead to a deeper understanding of market needs.

Incongruities

These are such things as the difference between the efficiency of ships and the inefficiencies of handling at ports; 'once managers understood where costs truly lay, the innovations were obvious: the roll-on and roll-off ship and the container ship' (Drucker 1985).

Process needs

Process changes are exemplified by AT&T's calculation at the turn of the twentieth century that, with technology as it then was, by 1920 every single female in the USA would have to work as a switchboard operator; AT&T developed the automatic switchboard.

The other sources of new opportunities are perhaps more straightforward, although as always, the successful identification of a new opportunity looks obvious to most people only *after* the event.

At a more detailed level, new ideas may be sought from the following sources:

■ Employees

■ Inventors (direct and through brokers and patents)

■ Trade publications

■ Gurus/industry experts

■ Social trends

■ Other countries

■ Consumers and customers

■ Market research

■ Specialist agencies/consultants.

With several of these sources (employees, consumers, experts), you can either wait for ideas or try to force them through various creative thinking techniques. The best-known of these is brainstorming, but there are many others, such as synectics, attribute listing, forced relationships, morphological analysis, and lateral thinking. For a fuller description of these, readers are referred to a suitable book from the list at the end of the chapter.

Screening

If there are only a few ideas, then screening is hardly necessary; the more ideas, however, the more essential some screening is before resources are committed to development. The main criteria for screening may be grouped under the following headings:

1 Management objectives, strategies and policies

2 Technical feasibility

3 Market feasibility

4 Preliminary business analysis

5 Legal/governmental/societal constraints.

The screening may be qualitative or quantitative. There will necessarily be a high degree of uncertainty involved, but if hard choices have to be made between projects to back and ideas to ignore, then it is preferable to make the basis for decisions explicit rather than implicit. The newer and more original the idea, the greater will be the uncertainty in the feasibility and business analysis; both technical and market feasibility are almost impossible to quantify in many cases, and when that is so the business analysis may not be worth doing. In such circumstances, managerial judgement (or hunch) will be the only basis for the decision, and rightly so. There are many examples, of which Xerox plain-paper copiers are perhaps the best known, of experts recommending against a product which subsequently proved enormously successful. There are also examples, of course, of managements persevering with products which never succeeded. Business would be a duller place if rationality always won.

Given the degree of uncertainty, however, and the high costs of NPD, most managements still prefer a little rationality. They try to measure the risks and take a reasoned gamble on the ideas which promise best. If there are many potential new projects, some firms use a formal framework for screening. These may be quite complex: a summary of one used by a UK food firm is given below.

Screening criteria:

1 **The market:**
   - Potential size in launch year
   - Growth prospects next five years
   - Susceptibility to economic fluctuation

2 **The product:**
   - Consumer distinction
   - Consumer appeal

3 **Competition:**
   - Competitive advertisers
   - Own-label competition
   - Price flexibility

4 **The company:**
   - Product compatibility
   - Company strength
   - R&D
   - Production
   - Distribution
   - Sales force motivation

5 **Financial return:**
   - Estimated sales at m.s.p. in going year
   - Estimated gross profit margin
   - Marketing investment
   - Capital investment.

Each item is rated on a five-point scale, and each major heading is given a weighting; a total score can then be produced for each new product idea, and the various ideas compared.

Obviously this approach can be adapted to the individual company's circumstances. It is probably more suitable to firms with fairly stable markets and technology, and a large number of competing projects. Where either market or technical feasibility is highly uncertain, then the method risks giving a false sense of accuracy and validity to calculations.

In consumer markets, ideas can be subjected to concept testing, that is, exposing samples of target consumers to the concept and getting their reactions. The more fully the idea can be expressed (for example by producing mock-ups, a name and packaging), the more valid the test. Although no quantitative estimate of sales can be expected, a rough guide to acceptability can be obtained, and at least outright unattractive ideas can be identified.

In industrial markets, such techniques are less common, but on the other hand it is much more likely that the supplier and customer will work closely together over a long period on new product ideas.

Physical and communications development

Although these were listed as different stages, they are treated together here to underline the fact that they are in truth inseparable. As Stephen King has argued, we should be trying to develop a new brand not just a product. A successful new brand must be:

- salient to people's needs, wants and desires;
- a totality, a blend of physical product and communications (therefore you can't test the elements separately);
- a unique blend of appeals – to the senses, to reason and the emotions.

(King 1973)

Depending on the type of product and market, the physical and communications aspects will vary in importance; but even in highly technological products, the communications elements should not be forgotten or tacked on at the end.

It is perhaps a peculiarly British failing to think that aspects such as design are peripheral, additions to the 'real' product.

This leads directly to the central problem of how to ensure that the development process is as smooth as possible (the question of speed, though related, is returned to in a later section). The question of organization for NPD is strictly speaking outside the scope of this book, but it is too important to ignore. A great deal of evidence suggests that organization is the key to successful NPD, and that the key to organization is communication and co-ordination – in other words, teamwork. This sounds simple, but the fact is that many firms, especially very large ones, have separate departments which hardly communicate with each other, and expect the NPD process to go on in a linear fashion. The Ford Motor Company, for instance, had engineering and manufacturing departments which did not talk to each other face to face, and spent their time in mutual suspicion and recrimination (Pascale 1990).

The best teams, it appears, are small and contain members from the various functions. Some people recommend complete physical and organizational isolation of the team in a 'skunkworks' or cheap premises. Even IBM formed a completely separate unit (albeit a relatively big one) to work on the personal computer, away from the normal organizational pressures and constraints.

The leader of the team needs to be a 'product champion', with great skill and determination. He or she may be from any functional background, but must have a good grasp of both technical and marketing needs. A product champion needs to be able to carry the team through disappointment and over apparently insurmountable hurdles; and to persuade top management to continue supporting the project. Such people are rare, and when identified need to be encouraged. Failure must be acceptable, as not every NPD project can succeed.

It is the custom in some Japanese companies to have more than one team working on an NPD project (see the multiple approaches earlier in this chapter); the teams compete, and only as a clear winner begins to emerge does work stop on the unsuccessful candidates. Such an approach has to be bedded in a company culture which does not condemn people as failures if a project is cancelled, but judges them fairly on their efforts. Only such cultures can be truly supportive of innovation.

Market testing

The classical consumer marketing approach to NPD uses market research throughout the process. Concepts are tested with consumers; early versions of the product are tested on panels, perhaps in several variants; packaging may be tested separately, but anyway the product in its packaging is tested on consumers, probably against competition; the name and advertising approach are probably tested – in other words, every aspect of the new brand is tested with representative samples of consumers, and the whole marketing mix may be subjected to simulation (using some research measures and a computer model) or actual test marketing in a test area before the final launch. This care and willingness to spend large amounts of time and money reflect the risks involved, and the difficulty of getting it right.

At the opposite end of the spectrum are those firms (often, but not exclusively, Japanese) who argue that detailed market research is unnecessary; the only real test is the marketplace itself, so the only way to find out if a new product will sell is to put it on the market. This attitude is attractive to the action-oriented manager and company, and may work in some markets where development is rapid, there are many new products coming on stream, and it is extremely important to stay ahead of the competition. It assumes a vital link in the chain – a biddable and supportive distribution system. That condition exists for the present in Japan and a few other countries, but is emphatically absent in most western consumer markets. Manufacturers in many sectors in Europe and North America have a struggle to achieve adequate distribution for a small number of well-supported new brands, let alone a constant stream of new products, many of which will fail.

What then is the sensible approach? There may be occasions when secrecy and speed are crucial, and when management are confident of their product, when a launch can go ahead without any market testing. On the other hand, there are also many occasions when it would be foolhardy to put many millions of pounds behind a launch without at least some measurement of likely consumer reaction. How exactly that is carried out may vary, from informal tests with small groups through in-home blind (i.e. unidentified) testing, through major programmes such as that outlined earlier. The more original the product, the more important it is to gauge possible reactions, but the more difficult it is to measure them realistically. The guidelines, as with most market research, are to ask questions:

- What is the risk of failure?

- What might market research tell me, and how would it help?

- What would it cost, how long would it take, and how much do either of those matter?
- Would researching the brand allow competitors to catch up?
- Is research necessary to persuade someone – either management or distributors?
- If something does go wrong, will I know what, and what to do about it?

The last is one of the most persuasive of the questions, since it ought to be the ambition of firms to learn more about their markets and operations so that they make fewer mistakes in the future.

In many markets, of course, consumer methods of product testing are not appropriate. The approach, however, is; the same questions should be asked, though some of the answers may be different. As suggested earlier, in many industrial markets, the supplier and client may work together over a period on a new development. That in itself is a form of market testing, but it is still important to check in some way that what one particular client wants will also be attractive to other companies. Service markets also present particular problems for NPD, since it is often impossible to market test a new product without setting up at least a miniature version of the infrastructure. In other ways it is easier, particularly for those firms which control their own outlets, such as fast food businesses, or banks.

The old saying has it that fortune favours the brave, and that is certainly true in NPD. Personally, I should prefer to put money on those who are not only brave, but also sensible enough to have done some market testing too.

Final checks

Before a new product is actually launched, there should be a final, formal stage at which all the important issues are subject to a last check. It is probably helpful to have a checklist adapted to the company's particular situation, and to have a person assigned responsibility for each check. A general list, suitable for a consumer goods firm, would be:

- **Legal clearance**
  - trademark and copyright
  - name, pack design
  - content regulations
  - claims, advertising, promotion
- **Customer approval**
  - DPP, space management (see Chapter 14)
  - effect on category profit
  - terms
- **Production feasibility and costs**
  - pilot runs
  - costing checks
- **End-user check**
  - does it work, *in use*?

This last check is essential: the product must be put through all the stages of its journey from factory to consumer (at least in simulation) and must be actually used by representative consumers in a typical situation. There is no substitute for this; most people with experience in NPD can recount some horror story of unexpected things which went wrong only when the product had been released.

There should also be a complete financial analysis, as most of the figures which were largely assumptions earlier should have been firmed up. Typically, a firm will want to look at sales (net of cannibalization of existing brands), profit (again net of cannibalization), payback (years to recoup investment) and return on capital employed (ROCE). Some firms have targets and hurdle rates which a new product must meet.

These calculations should be subjected to sensitivity analysis. This means taking each major assumption which has gone into the calculation and testing the effect of changing it. What would be the effect on the outcome if the market growth rate turned out to be half that assumed, or double? The basic assumptions will be as to:

- market size
- growth rate
- selling price
- market share achieved
- investment
- fixed costs
- operating costs.

These can of course be elaborated and refined for each particular situation. Mathematical techniques can be used (such as Monte Carlo simulation), or simpler approaches such as taking optimistic, pessimistic and most likely estimates for each major assumption. The aim should be to get an idea of the spread of probabilities and thus the riskiness of the project. The exercise may also point up areas of particular sensitivity, on which more work can be done to reduce risk, or greater control exercised during and after launch. The motto should be: 'No surprises.' The use of spreadsheets makes such calculations easy, and simulation software that plugs directly into Microsoft Excel is available (for example, @Risk, from www.timberlake.co.uk/software/arisk/).

Launch

The main decision to be taken about the launch is whether to go all-out for the whole market, or to test the water in one area or segment first. A high level of confidence in success, and the nearness of competitors to a similar product launch, are likely to be factors pushing towards a full launch. Conversely, if there is some uncertainty about the product, or about aspects of the marketing programme, *and* there are few fears about a competitor launching a similar product in the short term, then a launch in only part of the market may make sense; the product or the marketing programme may then be adapted in the light of experience.

Although to a risk-averse company or manager the rolling launch may appear the most attractive option, the threat of competitive reaction is often a very real one; in many markets there is at least one competitor who is very good at being

a 'fast second', copying any innovation very quickly. A new brand launched successfully can become entrenched and difficult to dislodge – but the early period of life, as with most organisms, is the most vulnerable. Moreover, if the launch is successful, then profit opportunities are being lost for the period the product is not available to the whole market.

The effects of these probabilities and outcomes can be calculated using game theory or a decision tree. In a simple example, you could estimate the effect on the pay-off to you (profits), as follows:

	Competitor	
	follows	*does not follow*
Full launch	0	400
Rolling launch	100	200

You would then apply probabilities to the 'states of nature', i.e. whether or not the competitor follows. If you think the probabilities are 0.3 that the competitor will follow and 0.7 that they will not, the pay-offs are 280 (0×0.3 plus 400×0.7) for the full launch and 170 for the rolling launch (100×0.3 plus 200×0.7); the full launch is preferable. On the other hand, if the probabilities were 0.7 that the competitor would follow and 0.3 that they would not, the pay-offs would be 120 for a full launch and 130 for the rolling launch: the latter would be preferable. Techniques such as this will not make the decision, but they will help to clarify the choice. Again, software packages make the calculations easier. A comprehensive survey of decision analysis packages as at October 2000 is available at www.lionhrtpub.com/ORMS/surveys/das/das.html.

The other main point about the launch is that it should be thoroughly planned. We are accustomed to talking of successful operations as 'planned with military precision', and there are indeed lessons to be learned from military planning. Unfortunately, one of them is the expression SNAFU (situation normal: a foul-up – or words to that effect). Plans must be thorough and detailed, but they must also be flexible and allow for any contingency. The sensitivity analysis may have shown areas of the plan which are particularly responsive to unexpected occurrences, so contingency plans for those may be more thorough. It is impossible to plan for everything, but again 'No surprises' should be the aim. Some commentators believe that too much emphasis has been placed on strategic issues in recent years, and not enough on implementation (Bonoma 1985), and there certainly appear to be enough errors in implementation of NPD. Operational planning and implementation skills become paramount at this final launch stage.

Reducing time to market

Reducing product life cycles and increasing competition have been mentioned, and will be familiar to most managers. There is therefore great interest in ways of speeding up NPD, as well as other aspects of company operations. Many of the examples frequently quoted are Japanese, but not exclusively so:

- **Hitachi Dies**   Reduced time to produce die from six weeks to one day
- **US insurance company**   Reduced time to process claims from twenty days to five days
- **IBM printer**   Launched in half normal time
- **Quality Function Deployment** (see below)   Reduces NPD time by one third to a half
- **Toyota**   Produces new car model in three years, against Detroit's five years.

These and similar cases are examples of an approach known as 'fast cycle time' or 'time-based competition'. A full exploration is beyond the scope of this book, but an outline will be given here.

The main lesson seems to be that faster times to market are the result of a whole approach to business, not of one technique or a set of techniques which work like magic. There are characteristics of firms which can be identified and copied. They will probably:

- use Just-in-Time and Total Quality Control
- use computer models of their process
- have an excellent information system, widely accessible
- work to remove hurdles to faster progress
- study the causes of problems and seek to remove them.

All these, however, are only symptoms of an underlying attitude which can best be summed up as total commitment – to quality, cost and delivery; and to constant improvement. Everyone in every function, and at every level, works constantly to improve the way their operation contributes to quality, cost and delivery.

A vital facet of the way this must work in NPD has already been mentioned – teamwork and communication. It is essential that all functions work together, have access to all the same information, and communicate constantly. The techniques then become secondary, though they can be useful as a structure or a stimulant to thought. One particular technique which is relevant to NPD is Quality Function Deployment (QFD).

The crux of QFD is to relate consumer (or customer) attributes of the new product to engineering characteristics, so that marketing, engineering and manufacturing people engage in meaningful dialogue right from the beginning. QFD produces a diagram called a 'house of quality' (see Figure 10.2), which first translates a desired consumer attribute ('easy to open and close car door' in the example) into engineering attributes (energy to close door, check force needed on level ground, etc.), then attaches a relative importance to each, and the rates products and competitors' products on each attribute.

In the example quoted, it is possible to go on to produce quantified targets for improvement and associated costings. The main benefit of such techniques is in the thinking, discussion and collaboration between functions which it produces, and which are the real key to success.

The aim should be not just to get to market faster, but to get to market faster, and right first time.

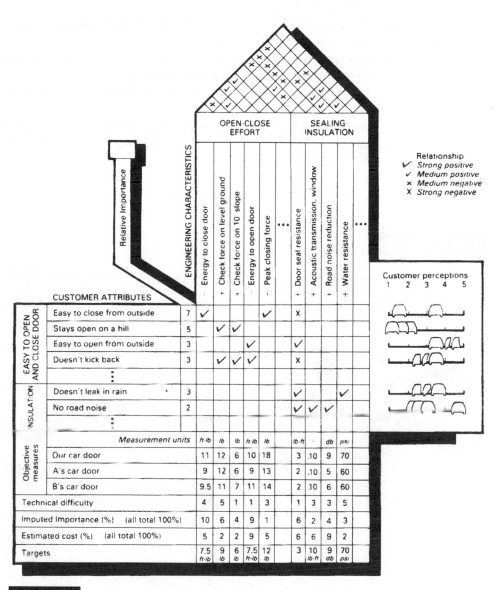

Figure 10.2 QFD: the house of quality

- There is a spectrum of new products, from totally new inventions to a product which exists elsewhere but is new to a particular company.
- New products are needed because old brands die, or because the firm wants more growth. The rate of failure of new products is very high, often because of internal organizational barriers to innovation.

- Specific reasons for failure are discussed, and the characteristics of successful companies described.

- Innovation is chaotic and untidy. Neat frameworks may help, but they are not complete solutions. Most have a series of stages: idea generation; screening; physical development; communications development; market testing; final checks; launch.

- The most important factors are probably setting the company's new product strategy correctly in the first place, and designing an organizational structure which will encourage teamwork.

- New approaches to management can radically reduce the time taken to develop and launch new products. Firms which do this successfully are described.

Further reading

Cooper, R. (1998) *Product Leadership: Creating and Launching Superior New Products*, New York: Perseus Books.

Cooper, R. and Kleinschmidt, E.J. (1990) *New Products: the Key Factors in Success*, Chicago: American Marketing Association.

Case study: Jennifer Rose 2

Apart from reviewing existing products, Jennifer Rose (see case described at the end of Chapter 9) has been told that the company is worried about its new product development record.

In personal computers, it does not see itself as a leader, but is happy to follow what other manufacturers introduce. It has, however, become increasingly slow at introducing its clones to market, and this is beginning to affect sales.

In audio systems, the company sees itself as a leader in at least some aspects of technology, but the culture of the R&D section is thought to be rather purist. Competitors are introducing new models faster, though the company's technologists insist that these products are of inferior quality.

The games market relies on innovation, and competitors from Asia are not only large but seem to be producing a stream of new products. The company still has its own niche, but is afraid that even this will be invaded soon.

Questions

1. What specific actions should Jennifer take in the next month?

2. What are the problems underlying the poor NPD record? What, if anything, can be done about them?

3. Evaluate the new product development process in your own organization. Examine one success and one failure, and draw conclusions from them.

Chapter 11 | Pricing

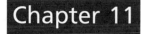

Impact of pricing decisions

In any market, price plays a central role in the exchange process. Even where the price is not fixed in monetary terms, a notional value is ascribed to the goods or services on offer. In some markets, prices are fixed, in others they are subject to haggling (or negotiation, as we may prefer to call it); in some markets, the price is stable over a reasonable period of time, in others it may fluctuate wildly within minutes or hours. In all cases, the price will have a major impact on at least one of the parties to the transaction.

If all business, reduced to its simplest, is about buying and selling, the price at which you buy and the price at which you can sell determine the profit or loss. Of course, there are many other factors, but price has a particularly direct impact on profits, as this example shows:

	Current position	Increase sales	Lower costs	Increase price
Sales revenue £mn	10.0	12.5	10.0	10.5
Direct costs	6.0	7.5	5.5	6.0
Fixed costs	3.5	4.0	3.5	3.5
Net profit	0.5	1.0	1.0	1.0

(Winkler 1983)

189

Each of the three options shows a doubling of profits:

1 Increasing sales volume by 25 per cent while holding fixed costs steady,
2 Holding sales steady while reducing direct costs by 12.5 per cent,
3 Increasing the average price by 5 per cent while holding volume and costs steady.

Increasing sales volume by 25 per cent is extremely difficult in most markets, and would involve at least some increase in fixed costs (sales force cost, for instance). Reducing costs is something which most companies strive for constantly, and this is right; but to achieve a significant reduction of 12.5 per cent, without any corresponding reduction in product quality and therefore a drop in sales, is asking a great deal. Increasing the average price achieved is not easy either, but it may be possible through varying the product mix and small, judicious rises on selected products; achieving a 5 per cent rise looks substantially easier than the other options, and the increase goes straight to the bottom line – profit.

To say that price is important, and that a business should try to set the price so as to increase profit, is to state the obvious. Economists have shown that profits can be optimized if the demand schedule and the cost equation for the product are known; the latter ought to be straightforward (though it is not always, as we shall see), but the former is a real problem. Your study of economics will have familiarized you with the arguments, which will be summarized here.

The demand schedule shows how demand for a product varies according to its price; usually demand increases as price decreases, and vice versa, although it is recognized that for some luxury products a higher price can produce higher demand. In practice it is extremely difficult to estimate a demand schedule with any degree of accuracy, given all the other influences on sales. If it can be done, then algebra will derive a profit function: this usually shows that profit has a parabolic relationship with price – profit goes up as price increases up to a certain point, then goes down again as demand falls away. The optimal price (giving the highest profit) can be plotted graphically, or found by using calculus. Another way of putting this is to say that the optimal price is found when the marginal cost (of making one more of the product) is equal to the marginal revenue (from selling one more).

Elasticity of demand

For marketing people, the most interesting part of all this is the demand schedule, and in particular the idea of the price elasticity of demand. This is defined as the percentage change in quantity demanded, divided by the percentage change in price; it is usually a minus figure, as demand is expected to fall with an increase in price. If the figure is minus one, then total revenue stays the same – for example, if quantity demanded falls 5 per cent when the price is put up by 5 per cent. (The percentage method is approximate, but will not lead anyone dramatically astray.)

If the price elasticity of demand is between minus one and zero, demand is said to be inelastic; total revenue will increase with an increase in price, and go down with a decrease. When demand is elastic, then a lower price will increase demand more than proportionately and total revenue will increase. In markets with inelastic demand, therefore, sellers will prefer to put prices up, while in those with elastic demand the temptation will be to reduce prices.

Of course, this grossly over-simplifies. In reality, there are differences between short-term and long-term price elasticities, and there are interactions between our price and other elements of the mix (quality, advertising, distribution), and between our price and those of competitors. Buyers may not switch from our brand because of a small price increase (and conversely may not switch to it because of a small decrease); in the longer term, however, if they are maintained, price differentials may lead to switching.

Given all the difficulties, then, can we apply any of the economic theory at all? In most market situations, it is very unlikely that we shall be able to optimize price mathematically; but we may be able to draw some conclusions about pricing strategy if we have at least some idea about the price elasticity of demand. Most managers have a view of their market, and a qualitative judgement about elasticity. This will be based on experience and observation, sometimes backed up by quantitative analysis (of past sales, or of sales in different geographical areas with different prices). In most cases, the drawback of these sources (apart from the level of uncertainty produced by all the interactions mentioned above) is that they cover only a very narrow range of price/demand situations and thus give little or no guidance in new market situations. However, they are better than nothing, and as with all marketing information, the collection of reliable data over a period of time must contribute to a greater understanding in the long run. Other methods of estimation are experimentation and surveys. A carefully designed experiment is an excellent way of testing price sensitivity, but is not available to everyone. A multiple retailer can do it easily, but in many markets it is not practical (for the effect of the Internet, see below). Surveys of buyer intentions may help, but are not always reliable. How marketing people may delve under the raw figures is examined in the next section.

Marketing View of the role of price

Marketing people must first of all also be business men and women: they must look at price in relation to costs and profits. This cost–volume–profit relationship is fundamental to an understanding of how the business works and how it makes (and loses) money; every marketing manager must be thoroughly familiar with it. Beyond that, there are specific contributions which marketing can make to pricing decisions; these fall into two groups – an external view of price, and price as an element of the marketing mix.

> **If the manufacturing and finance functions take an internal, cost-based view of pricing, it is essential that marketing reflects how price is perceived outside the firm, and particular by the three Cs – customers, consumers and competitors. Customers and consumers are looking for value for money, so marketing must work on how they perceive value, and how they perceive price; what we must offer is better perceived value for money than our competitors.**

This goes back to the earlier discussion of how the product fits into the customer's business or the consumer's life; what benefits is it actually delivering? From a marketing point of view, the price of a product is not just the figure on the invoice, but the total cost to the buyer of buying and using the product. This includes ordering and shipping costs, delivery and storage, and perhaps disposal as well as the prime usage.

When Ford in Europe were designing a new low-price car, they looked not just at the list price, but at depreciation, maintenance and insurance, to produce a total low-cost package for the buyer.

Sometimes, having identified these costs and benefits, it is marketing's job to educate buyers about them, as in Mercedes' campaign to show company buyers that their cars' high resale value makes them a sensible purchase when total cost is taken into account, rather than just initial price.

It follows that the other aspect of the marketing view sees price as just one of the elements of the overall marketing mix, and not separable from the others. Price then becomes an important function of, and tool for, positioning. Most markets have a very high-price, luxury segment, and a low-price, economy segment; many have a more complicated structure, but always with a range of prices.

Price may thus be a very important initial signal of what quality to expect, and it is essential that the price is consistent with the positioning. What marketing can help determine is the price–value expectations of the particular target segment; it can then help formulate and present the total product offering in a way which maximizes the perceived value against competition.

Some people, particularly in manufacturing, see marketing's role as one of always looking for the lowest price, or of 'designing down to a price'. The first should never be true, but the second is a valid approach; the difference is between what an engineer might regard as cheap and cheerful, and what a marketing person would see as fitness for purpose. The Japanese motorcycles which took over the world mass markets were very much designed down to a price: they delivered the benefits consumers actually wanted, at a price they could afford. They were also, of course, designed so that they could be manufactured in a way that would produce profits (at least in the long term).

It follows from this line of argument that pricing is a strategic decision: the level of price for a particular brand is part of its targeting at a specific segment, and it cannot be changed significantly without changing the whole strategy.

Pricing can of course also be used tactically; this aspect will be explored below in the section on competitive pricing.

In many markets, prices appear to be fairly heavily constrained by history and competition, and there is little freedom to alter them. In commodity markets, price is entirely a function of demand and supply; but even in heavily branded markets, a general level of price prevails, which it is difficult to break away from. As even small changes in price can have a dramatic effect on profit, however (as the worked example showed earlier), then much marketing activity is devoted to finding that small area and exploiting it. A higher price (and hopefully a higher profit margin) can be justified by perceived better value – by the sustainable competitive advantage, the unique selling proposition, the brand's point of difference.

These are matters of principle; in the next section we will go on to look at how prices are set in practice.

Approaches to pricing decisions

While the previous section stressed that the marketing view should always be directed outwards, and that pricing should be market-led, it is also true that the firm must cover its costs and make a profit to survive. Pricing decisions therefore cannot be made only on a marketing basis, but must take account of costs, profits and other company objectives. This section will look at methods of making pricing decisions.

Cost-plus

Since all costs have to be covered in the long run, it makes sense to look at costs in setting prices. It is not necessary that every product covers all its costs all the time, but it would be dangerous if too many were not contributing to profits for a sustained period (especially if no one knew that this was so). It is therefore common to use an approach which takes all the costs of making and selling the product, adds a profit margin, and uses the resulting figure as the price. This is most easily seen in retailing, where the retail price may be set by taking the manufacturer's or wholesaler's price and adding a standard mark-up. Manufacturers, however, also use the approach.

The cost-plus approach usually starts with standard costs of the product: an estimate of the total direct costs (labour, materials and components) divided by the assumed number of the product to be manufactured. This may be a straightforward calculation, but in a complex manufacturing situation it may become difficult, even impossible (for example, where there are thousands of different products and many common costs). In these cases, some assumptions have to be made and estimates used. This is acceptable, as long as everyone knows that they are being made, what they are, and what effect changes in the assumptions would have on the calculations.

It becomes even more difficult at the next stage, when indirect costs are added. This is an attempt to allocate direct fixed costs (investment in plant and machinery) and overheads (central salaries, office costs, etc.). Total costs are allocated to each product according to some measure such as relative volume, input costs, or labour costs. These allocations are invariably crude, and may be actually misleading. Research in recent years has shown, for example, that many firms use relative labour cost as the allocation method, but that it is an increasingly unreliable indicator of actual costs (Johnson and Kaplan 1987). Moreover, all allocations depend on an estimate of sales, which is bound to be inaccurate to at least some extent.

This leads to the logical problem of prices being fixed by costs, which are based on assumed sales, while actual sales are affected by the price set. Yet this method is more commonly used than any other. From a marketing viewpoint, it is acceptable that costs should be an input to the pricing decision, but not that they should be the sole determinant.

Marginal pricing and break-even analysis

An attempt to avoid the problem of allocating overheads is to look only at the marginal costs, that is the cost of making one incremental unit of the product. This approach is often advocated when all fixed costs have been allocated to normal production, and the opportunity arises to sell an extra batch – a one-off contract, or an unexpected export order, for example. A much keener (i.e. lower) price can be set if only marginal costs are taken into account.

The logic can also be applied more generally, to argue that what should be looked at is each product's *contribution* to overhead and profit. The contribution is defined as revenue minus variable costs (which can be regarded as marginal costs for all practical purposes). This avoids the overhead allocation problem, and also allows some prices to be set which are lower than might be called for by a full-cost approach.

Marketing managers are often tempted to use this approach, especially in product line pricing (see below), seeing it as more market-oriented: it is the market's perception of each product which should determine its price, not some arbitrary allocation of a particular firm's costs. This is true, and it is also a fact that there are situations when it makes sense for a firm to accept a contract which makes a contribution, but not an actual 'profit'. The dangers are apparent, however: too many pricing decisions taking account only of marginal costs may lead to a lowering of total company profit or, in the worst case, to revenue failing to cover all costs.

For marketing people, the trap to be avoided is that of setting a precedent with a major customer, so that a reasonable price giving a decent profit can never be achieved. Marginal pricing should be used in exceptional circumstances, rather than as a general rule.

The problem of overlooking profit can be avoided by break-even analysis. This takes the contribution per unit, and by dividing it into total fixed costs calculates how many units need to be made and sold to cover those fixed costs and start to make a profit. Break-even analysis is particularly useful in deciding on the price of a new brand. Different prices giving different contributions per unit can be used to give different break-even levels; these can be examined against market size and share estimates. Break-even analysis cannot give the right price, but it may show that at a given price, break-even would need a market share of 60 per cent; that sort of result should send everyone back to the drawing board.

Target pricing

This usually means pricing to achieve a target profit. Most firms have some idea of the profit they want to make on each product; it may be expressed as a percentage mark-up or margin, as an absolute amount, or as a return on investment.

Target	Example
■ Percentage mark-up	■ Variable costs plus 120 per cent
■ Percentage margin	■ 15 per cent of sales revenue
■ Absolute amount	■ Minimum of £3 million/yr.
■ Return on investment	■ 20 per cent ROCE (Return On Capital Employed)

How the target is expressed will depend on the type of business: percentage mark-up is often used in professional service firms, while return on investment is frequently found in manufacturing, for example. The targets may be combined, and an absolute amount is often set as a hurdle.

For marketing people, the question must always be, 'How will the market react to this proposed price?' The fact that a particular set of price and sales figures meets a target does not mean that those results can be achieved in the marketplace.

A market-oriented view of target pricing would be to ask: what benefits does this target segment want, and what price would represent value to them? We would then design the product or service to be sold at that target price (like the Japanese motor-cycle manufacturers).

Perceived value or product analysis pricing

This approach takes an explicitly market-oriented stance, by looking at the price from the customer's point of view, and trying to set a value *to the customer* of the various benefits offered. Product analysis suggests that the product should be analysed into its component parts, and each costed as if the customer were buying it separately. The sum of all these, perhaps with a small discount, becomes the price of the package on offer. The approach is particularly appropriate in contracting or tendering situations, and is the basis of package holiday pricing.

The more general perceived value approach can try to put a value on qualitative as well as quantitative differences, for instance on the reassurance of a well-known brand, as well as measurably higher quality.

From a marketing point of view, perceived value is the overriding consideration in any pricing decision. A great deal of effort should go into establishing exactly what value buyers place on the various benefits, and in presenting these (in all the marketing communications) to demonstrate that the price offers value for money.

Competitive pricing

For most firms, competition is likely to be an enormously important influence on pricing decisions. Only the truly unique product, well protected by patents, or a genuine monopoly, has real pricing freedom; even then there are probably regulators looking to curb 'excess' profits. It is worth repeating that it is marketing's job to create uniqueness and a local monopoly and thus to get away from a commodity situation, but the reality is that competitors can never be forgotten.

Exactly how much attention needs to be paid to competitors' prices in setting one's own depends partly on the market situation and partly on the firm's position and strategy. In some situations there will be long-term relationships in which supplier and buyer work closely together on the product or service; there may be a preferred supplier, or a small number of suppliers; switching costs may be high, so in this situation it is difficult for a new competitor to break in with a lower-price offer. In other situations price competition may be continuous and intense.

The other consideration is the positioning of the company. In most markets there is a price leader, recognized as such by most firms, whose general pricing levels are followed by everyone else. This may be the market leader by size, or the premium-price brand, or the low-priced mass market product. It is not always clear how and why a particular price leader emerges. The advantages of being in that position are that you can choose the timing of price changes to suit yourself, rather than having to follow others at what may be an inconvenient time.

The company probably also has an overall strategy which determines whether it is in the premium-price segment, the medium-price, or the economy bracket (it may of course have brands in more than one segment). This may mean that your price is always a given amount above (or below) a certain key competitor.

If there *is* a strong price leader in a market, then its behaviour can determine others' prices and hence profits. This can be helpful, in that the price leader can create a 'price umbrella' by setting a relatively high price; others can shelter under the umbrella and also make acceptable profits. The extent to which this can happen will depend on factors such as entry and mobility barriers, and the existence of substitutes (see Porter 1980).

Obviously this leads on to the idea of collusion between competitors: if all agree on a relatively high price level, all can pursue their own strategy and all can make profits, whereas if they all compete on price, all will suffer (the problem of a price war is returned to below in the section on strategy and tactics). Collusion is of course illegal, and if uncovered can lead to heavy fines by national or supranational bodies (the European Union has been active in this field). Nevertheless, there is a surprising convergence of price in many markets, so it appears that companies may decide separately that they will follow each other fairly closely. Once a general price level is set, it is difficult for an individual firm to break away from it without a very substantial price cut or a significant product improvement allowing a higher price. Many markets show orderly competition over long stretches of time, and it is a brave company (and one with deep pockets) which deliberately upsets price stability.

Other approaches

1   Geographical factors

In some markets, particularly industrial ones in which transport costs are significant, there is an issue of geographical pricing. The supplier must decide whether to let each buyer carry all transport costs, making the price higher for more distant customers; to average out transport costs, making prices relatively higher for closer customers and lower for more distant ones; to absorb transport costs and price accordingly; or to adopt some mixture of these. Charging the buyer all transport costs is known as FOB (Free On Board), while including all costs in the quoted price is known as CIF (Cost, Insurance, Freight); one or other may be established practice in a particular industry, as may others such as zone-based pricing or using a uniform delivered price. As with all such established practices, it is for the marketing people to look for opportunities for differentiation in providing a better service than the competitors.

2   Psychological pricing

This term refers to the effects (real or assumed) on buyers of particular prices. These are often referred to as 'shoulder prices' or 'price points', and commonly show up as prices just below a round figure – £19.95 instead of £20, for instance. People operating in particular market segments have firm beliefs about these price points, based on experience. As such pricing considerations may lead to charging a lower price than would otherwise be set, the effect should if possible be checked by controlled experiment. When the Euro is fully introduced, price points in all countries will change, and it will be interesting to see how firms and consumers react. Psychological factors also come into play with some cases of prestige pricing, where a very high price is set to suggest luxury, status or exclusivity. This happens not only in obvious categories such as perfume, but in other less obvious ones — even beer (Stella Artois is 'reassuringly expensive'). Such pricing must be part of a coherent and consistent mix and positioning (product quality, packaging, distribution, advertising and promotion). Unduly high prices may also be difficult to enforce in practice (see below).

3 Moral factors

Some people argue that pricing has a moral aspect (see Winkler 1983: 76) – that is, there is a notion of a fair or just price. This is most likely to arise in areas of state or local authority provision, such as housing or transport; but it can be raised in the field of, for example, medicine. There have been protests at the prices of new drugs which offer cures or alleviation for serious diseases. The extreme opposite view is that business has no moral duty at all; its only objective is to make the maximum return for shareholders. There is no single right answer to ethical dilemmas in this as in other cases, and each firm and each manager must take a considered view in the circumstances.

Channel and line pricing

So far, pricing has been considered as if a single product and a single set of buyers were concerned. In practice, the firm normally has to consider both intermediaries and end-users, and has to price a range of products. The two sets of decisions are often interlinked.

Channel pricing

In pricing for the channel or channels of distribution, the firm must balance the interests of the channel itself and those of the end-users or consumers against its own desire for profit. Distributors want products which their own customers want to buy, and a profit for themselves. Much of the struggle between supplier and distributor is about how the value-added available in the chain is to be split up, given what each party is providing.

This important topic is examined in more detail in Chapter 14; only the bones of the pricing issues are dealt with here.

There is normally an accepted level of margin between retail and wholesale/manufacturer price for a particular category of product. Typically these will be low for products with a high rate of sale (small, frequently purchased packaged goods, for example), and higher for slower-moving items such as consumer durables. They may range from 10 per cent to 30 per cent (and above in certain specialized categories). In any negotiation, the distributor is likely to regard the normal margin as the minimum; only an extremely strong brand which is guaranteed to walk off the shelves will be able to sustain a lower-than-usual margin. The margin may also be adjusted to reflect services the intermediary will perform, such as before- or after-sales service, staff training or promotion.

Discounts

Discounts are granted for a variety of reasons:

- volume
- timing (of purchase or payment)
- promotions
- carrying out agreed functions.

Volume discounts are the most common and basic; they reflect cost savings to the supplier (in ordering, invoicing and shipping costs, for example), but also act as an incentive to the distributor to sell more of the product rather than a competitor's. Volume discounts may become quite complex, with bonuses for achieving targets, and overriding discounts for annual sales levels.

Discounts for buying at a particular time are often aimed at evening out seasonal irregularities. Payment discounts are normal, and offer a small percentage off the invoice price for payment within a specified time. They need to be carefully calculated and controlled.

Promotional and other discounts (or allowances, as they are sometimes called) are straightforward on the surface, in that they offer a discount if the distributor carries out certain agreed functions: promotions, joint advertising campaigns, displays, price promotions and so on. As we shall see in Chapter 14, in practice they are a field of potential conflict as to whether the functions have in fact been carried out, or whether the money has just been pocketed by the distributor.

The reality is that all these discounts are part of the ongoing negotiation between the parties, each trying to improve its position. A key question for the manufacturer is whether or not to publish a price list and details of discounts available, or to leave everything to negotiation.

While some people argue for secrecy, there seems little doubt that an open price list has many advantages (not least in saving endless bargaining time), and should be adopted if the manufacturer is strong enough to sustain it.

Both general and detailed pricing to the channels should be regarded as part of the competitive strategy. Strong brands, as suggested, are needed by the retailers and wholesalers, and may carry a lower margin. Weaker brands, and new brands, may use promotional discounts to gain distribution or be given a temporary boost. Overall, the manufacturer should be trying to meet profit targets within the category.

It is here that the aspects of channel and product-line pricing overlap. The manufacturer may accept lower margins on some products within the line as long as other products make up for it, and this applies to channel pricing as well as more generally. Distributors may want a complete line of products, as that is what their customers will be looking for; correspondingly, some manufacturers will want distribution for their whole line, although some products within it may be less attractive to retailers than others. It is here that rigid attitudes to pricing (such as full-cost plus, for all products) are damaging. Flexibility is needed, and an overall view of the total profit to be achieved.

Line pricing

In pricing the product line, it is common that a range of versions is offered, from basic economy through various models with different features, to the luxury or top of the range model. This offers a choice of approaches to the supplier. The most common is that the profit margin is lowest on the stripped-down, basic version, and higher on those with more features; this approach can be seen in many car ranges. A pithy summing up of this policy is the previously quoted view that you should have 'one kind of product to advertise, one kind to sell, and one kind to make money on' (Ries and Trout 1986). The authors point out that,

> Conceptually, the burger chain advertises the burger, sells the french fries along with the burger, and makes money on the soft drinks.... If the kids drink enough of your 90-cent Cokes, you can almost afford to break even on everything else.

Pricing the range applies the previously-mentioned concepts of positioning within each segment, and psychological pricing. Often, there will be a model within each of a number of segments, each priced carefully at a price point. The strategy should be to have an entry in each segment which you wish to contest, positioned and priced so as to put your brands at maximum advantage against their competitors, while minimizing cannibalization between your brands.

The issue of control

A problem for any supplier selling through intermediaries is that the final price is set by the retailer, not by the manufacturer. Where a deliberately high pricing policy is adopted as a vital part of the brand's positioning, the manufacturer may be vulnerable if some retailers decide to discount prices. This has happened with high-priced perfumes – some low-price retailers have tried to sell exclusive couture-house perfumes at deeply discounted prices; the manufacturers have tried extremely hard to stop them, for example by refusing to supply them with the products. The retailers obtain supplies through the 'grey market' – from wholesalers who divert supplies from other destinations. The battle reached the law courts, with the retailers trying to force the manufacturers to supply direct. From the manufacturers' point of view, a carefully targeted marketing mix (including very high price and exclusive distribution outlets) is being ruined by the discounters' attack. Some consumers may be very happy in the short term, but the brands' cachet may be destroyed.

The same battle is played out on a lesser scale in other markets. The supermarkets have been active in trying to reduce prices, for example Tesco with Levi's jeans and Asda with over-the-counter (OTC) medicines. The position is confused in that special agreements in the EU allow car dealers and OTC medicine suppliers to control prices; manufacturers from outside the EU (e.g. Levi's) can also enforce their 'brand protection' pricing level, but manufacturers within the Common Market cannot. The manufacturer can only influence the retailers' pricing decision by the price at which they buy; they cannot control what actually happens on the shelves. This is yet another aspect of the need to manage the relationship, further discussed in Chapter 14.

Pricing strategies and tactics

Policy

The overall pricing policy of a company is a strategic decision – one that has long-term implications, should be made with great care, and cannot be changed easily. It is part of an overall positioning strategy.

Amstrad is a low-price supplier in each of the fields in which it operates – hi-fi, other consumer electronics, and personal computers – and could not suddenly change to the high-priced, premium end of the market. Similarly, a cheap Rolls-Royce is a nonsensical idea.

It is of course possible to change over time, and to enter new segments with a new pricing strategy; changing market conditions may also allow an alteration in previous policies.

Japanese car manufacturers were for many years known to offer well-equipped if dull cars in the mass market segments at a low price. Gradually, they have introduced more expensive models in some premium segments; and they have taken the opportunity provided by quota systems in some countries to sell more of the premium-priced models and fewer basic, cheaper ones. It is interesting to note, though, that both Toyota and Nissan, in introducing models in the expensive, executive bracket, have chosen completely new brands and names.

Pricing opportunities

If a firm's pricing policy is fixed, then, by its history and market situation, major alterations to strategy will be few. Opportunities will arise with the launch of new brands, and with price changes initiated either by the company or by competitors.

With a new brand, much will depend on the nature and in particular the distinctiveness of the brand. A new brand is traditionally said to offer a choice of 'skimming' or 'penetration' pricing. In fact, a brand which is similar to those already on the market (and many if not most new brand launches fall into that category) is restricted in its pricing to what the market dictates. It is really only a truly distinctive new brand which has the freedom to choose its price level.

Skimming

'Skimming' is short for skimming the cream from the market: setting a high initial price to maximize revenue while the brand has no or few competitors. Clearly this can be done only if the product offers genuine new benefits which are salient to buyers and for which they are prepared to pay. Often this means a new invention such as a drug, which can be patented. Other examples have been Polaroid cameras, electronic watches and calculators, and new artificial fibres. With industrial products, there must be some reference to existing materials or processes, and early buyers will be those companies which can make genuine savings or improvements using the new product. In consumer markets, there may be a segment of buyers who are prepared to pay high prices for novelty value or the prestige of being seen as an innovator; this happened with the first electronic watches, which did not tell the time any better than mechanical ones. Very high prices suggest high profits (assuming the costs of production have been worked out correctly); that will attract competitors, and it is a fine art to set price levels so as to earn good profits without attracting too much competition too early.

Penetration pricing

The alternative to skimming is to adopt a relatively low price which will develop the market quickly and give a dominating share to the innovator. If the market is expected to develop fast, and competition to enter quickly, then provided that the production costs support it, a penetration strategy makes sense; a dominating market share taken by the leader is extremely difficult to attack. An extreme version of penetration pricing is seen in some electronic components markets, and is sometimes referred to as 'riding the experience curve down'. Where manufacturing costs are expected to fall significantly through experience effects, the initial price is set below current production cost; the low price attracts high volumes, which drive down production costs rapidly, allowing lower prices, and so on. Needless to say, this is a high-risk strategy which needs courage as well as great skill in timing and implementation.

Price changes

The other area of opportunity in pricing is price changes, initiated either by the company itself or by competitors. At some periods, cost inflation has meant that most changes are rises, and that regular small price increases have become the norm. Recently, in the UK, some markets, such as food, have seen price deflation, which presents a mirror image. In competitive markets with little differentiation between brands, there is little opportunity to make any significant change from the level set by the main competition. Sometimes, however, a company can make a tactical decision to delay a price rise (in inflationary times, the equivalent of a price cut) and hope to pick up market share, or bring forward a rise and hope to make a little extra profit without losing sales. Good judgement of market conditions is needed.

> **The role of marketing is to be sure how price rises will be interpreted. If possible, price rises should be presented as reasonable and continuing to reflect good value.**

It is not always possible to introduce some added benefit at the same time as a price rise, though that is the best way of doing it, especially if the rise is higher than general inflation or than competitors'. A significant rise should be signalled in advance to customers so that they can prepare themselves and build the rise into their own pricing calculations.

Price cuts

Lowering prices occurs where input or production costs are falling. The timing of cuts may be dictated by competitors if you are not the price leader; where there is some freedom, careful timing can be used to gain share or extra profit as mentioned above. Price cutting is often used to attack the market leader, but it is a weapon which should be used with extreme care. The reactions of two sets of people must be gauged; competitors and customers/consumers. If a price cut is being used to gain share, it must be a significant one; if it is small, it is unlikely to make many buyers switch; if it is large enough to move the market, the main competitors will react. No one should want a price war, except the company which knows for certain that it will win by driving competitors out of business; this has happened in some markets such as airlines, but it is perhaps the most risky of all strategies. There is frequently a general weakness of prices in a particular market, caused by over-capacity, slack demand, or a combination of the two. This can degenerate into a full-scale price war if a major player decides that an advantage can be gained by slashing prices before anyone else. If stocks are high and increasing, this is a temptation, but the decision should not be taken lightly.

Again, the marketing task is to understand how the price cut will be interpreted and thus how buyers will react. If they perceive that prices will continue to fall, they will continue to hold off, as happened in the housing market in the UK in the early 1990s and the car market at the end of that decade. In other markets, they may interpret the cut as the sign that a new model is going to be introduced; some will wait for that. Sometimes a price cut will be seen as reflecting a lowering of quality. If none of these is true, buyers may move into the market, but only by bringing forward purchases. A company therefore needs to be clear about its objectives, and reasonably sure that a price cut will achieve them.

In reacting to price changes, every company should have a prepared policy and thus be ready to move quickly if necessary. A price leader will often have a policy which dictates that no one else should be allowed to take over that role; price changes will be reacted to strongly if they are seen as significant. Reaction need not always mean following the price change. A price cut by a competitor may be met by changing other elements of the mix – advertising more heavily, or making special offers (extra quantity packs, premium gifts, etc.). If a price cut is met, it may be met fiercely, with a swingeing cut at least in some areas; but such measures should always be short term, with a defined time limit.

Price followers have less freedom, although the same choices are in theory open to them. The important thing is not to be taken by surprise and have to work out a response from scratch. 'War-gaming' competitors' actions and reactions will pay off in response time.

Revenue management systems

A specific approach to managing prices is known as revenue management. Developed in the airline industry, it has spread into hotels, car hire, parcel delivery, car sales and online ticket sales. The airlines had a particular problem in that when an aircraft takes off, any unsold seat remains unsold for ever: the lost revenue can never be replaced. While a range of fares have always been on offer, it was difficult to make the best use of them when the number of flights a day was 10,000 or more: no human can cope with that degree of detail and complexity. The solution lay in mathematical modelling and computer analysis, which enabled fine calculations to work out the best price depending on the state of demand for a flight. When demand is high, the price remains high; the lower the demand, and the closer the flight time, the lower the price (bizjournals.com, 26 February 1999 edition, see also the site of software provider Talussolutions.com, now acquired by ManuGistics).

The fact that the same technique has been adopted by Ford to sell cars shows that it is applicable beyond perishable services. Ford has applied the approach to its product line pricing, with a significant positive impact on profitability (*Business Week*, 10 April 2000: 69).

The impact of the Internet on pricing

As we saw in Chapter 3, the general impact of widespread use of the Internet is expected to be a downward pressure on prices. This is due to greater transparency and ease of comparison, and the rise of auctions, reverse auctions, buying groups and exchanges. Bill Gates has referred to 'frictionless capitalism' suggesting that in the old economy, many firms made profits by exploiting the gap between suppliers' and buyers' knowledge of what was available at what price. In the new economy, this gap will disappear, and so will the easy profits, he argues.

Certainly, transparency will be greater. For example, it is common practice for direct marketers to vary the price offered to different classes of customers, so that new buyers are offered lower prices than those for loyal customers. When Amazon tried to experiment with this, the fact quickly became known, and the exposure forced them to withdraw.

On the other hand, it is not clear that the lowest price will always win most customers. As in the old economy, in some markets buyers will often prefer to pay a little more for good service, or reliability, or speed. Amazon does not offer the lowest prices for books, yet has easily the biggest share of the online market. Its Website is probably the easiest to use, and has many patented features such as One-Click Ordering. People trust its brand, and know from experience or word-of-mouth that its delivery will be fast and mainly accurate. They are prepared to pay more for the total package of benefits – just as they are in offline markets.

In both B2C and B2B markets, the evidence suggests that many buyers are using the Web to search for information – including price – then reverting to conventional methods to make the purchase. Car buyers in the USA increasingly use the Internet as part of the search process, but still want to go and look at cars, sit in them, and perhaps test them before actually buying. In B2B markets, the nature of relationships means that both buyer and seller want more than just an efficient transaction, so again the online procurement systems are only part of the total process.

What we still do not know is the extent to which the Internet economy will change buyers' attitudes and habits. It is possible that a greater proportion of customers will become price-conscious, because information is more widely available. They will know that, for suppliers, dealing online is very much cheaper than any other method (telephone, mail or bricks-and-mortar). They will expect to share some of those efficiency gains. But, as in banking, they may want to preserve the possibility of using multiple channels, and so may be willing to pay above the absolute cheapest price, which an Internet-only banker can offer.

What this suggests is that, although patterns are still emerging, and we do not know what the final state will be, the Internet will not completely destroy the role of price within the marketing mix. It will exert downward pressure on prices, and some marketers will have to find ways of resisting that (as the luxury perfume manufacturers are doing by using the law in Europe to prevent cheap online selling of their brands), but that is no different from the situation with discounters in traditional marketplaces (indeed, the perfume makers have had exactly the same battle with bricks-and-mortar retailers such as Superdrug).

More generally, there is a danger that selling over the Internet will lead prices down to uneconomic levels. There is a parallel with the deregulated airlines in the USA. After deregulation in 1978, the 1980s saw a rash of new airlines offering ever cheaper prices. For a time, this seemed an unmitigated benefit to customers, but problems soon began to appear. The spectacular bankruptcy of one of the most prominent low-price operators, People Express, crystallized the danger, and many other cut-price airlines followed. As we saw earlier, those that remained, and the mainstream operators, developed sophisticated computer models to ensure that they balanced selling as much capacity as possible with covering their costs and maximizing revenue where they could (for example, amongst price-insensitive segments such as business customers). The same danger – of relying on discounting – applies to Internet pricing, and it seems likely that similar solutions will need to be adopted.

Key learning points

- **Pricing is central to business, and crucially affects profitability.**
- **The marketing view of price is that it should be seen from the viewpoint of customers, consumers and competitors. Customers and consumers are looking for value for money, so marketing must work on how they perceive value and how they perceive our price; what we must offer is value which is perceived as better than our competitors'.**
- **Price must also be seen as part of the marketing mix; it is an important signal to the market of what quality to expect, and it must be consistent with the brand's positioning.**
- **Approaches to setting a price are: cost plus; marginal pricing (and break-even analysis); target pricing; perceived value or product analysis pricing; competitive pricing; others (geographical, psychological). The advantages and disadvantages of each are described.**
- **In pricing the product line, it is possible to set different levels of profit for different models within the line; often the basic model has the lowest margin, and the top of the line the greatest.**
- **The Internet will make pricing information more widely available, and may produce downward pressure on prices, but buyers will not always choose the cheapest product.**

Further reading

Diamantopoulos, A. and Matthews, B. (1995) *Making Pricing Decisions: A Study of Managerial Practice*, London: Chapman and Hall.
Winkler, J. (1983) *Pricing for Results*, London: Heinemann.

Case study: MML

Midlands Materials Ltd (MML) is a medium-sized manufacturer of chemicals sold to other manufacturers for incorporation in their products. They currently have about 35 per cent of the market in their region, as far as they can tell. Bill Rogers, the marketing manager, is trying to work out the price to charge for next year. The price had been increased substantially this year as margins had been under pressure for some time; the board was demanding better profits. The MML price is now some 15 per cent above its competitors'.

The levels of MML prices and sales for the last few years have been:

	Price per lb	Sales '000 lb
This year	1.20	4.6
Last year	1.00	5.4
Two years ago	1.00	4.6
Three years ago	1.00	3.4

Bill thinks the total market has been increasing: his best estimate is that it has gone up by a third in three years. He feels that the market as a whole is slightly price sensitive, and that MML's share is too; he estimates that MML's share has dropped from about half the market to its present level.

Questions

1 What price should Bill recommend, (a) if competitors raise their prices to MML's level, and (b) if they remain below?

2 What information would help Bill to make his pricing decisions in future, if it were available?

3 How are pricing decisions made in your organization, and by whom? Could the process be improved by any of the approaches outlined in this chapter?

Chapter 12 | Marketing communications

The communications mix

Advertising is, after the product itself, easily the most visible part of marketing. We are all bombarded by advertising for much of our waking lives: on television and radio, in newspapers and magazines, on hoardings, through direct mail, and so on. We are all consumers of advertising, sometimes more willingly than others; we all have views on advertising, and can talk about favourite (and most annoying) advertisements. All this may blind us to what advertising is actually all about, and what its role is.

Two things must always be borne in mind: advertising is just one part of the total communication sent out by companies; and it is only part of the overall marketing mix.

As we talk of the marketing mix – the combination of different elements we use to achieve our objectives – so we think of the communications mix, which combines all those methods of communication that an organization uses to reach its various audiences.

We saw in Chapter 4 that there are many aspects of the environment, the industry and markets, customers and consumers, of concern to a company. Each organization therefore has many target audiences, and many ways of reaching them. The audiences may be summed up as:

- Shareholders, investors, bankers, the City
- Customers, distributors, agents

- Consumers
- Suppliers
- Government agencies
- Competitors
- Opinion leaders
- Employees, current and potential.

For any firm, there are probably other audiences, too – a wide range of different people. In this book, we are concerned only with those who are directly related to marketing, and so will ignore topics such as investor relations and communicating with employees, important as these communications are.

To reach our target audiences, we have available a large number of communication methods. Just as we summarize the marketing mix as the Four Ps, each of which can be further broken down, so we can summarize the communications mix as:

- Advertising
- Internet
- Promotion
- Personal selling
- Public relations
- Other publicity.

Each of these will be dealt with separately, mainly in this chapter, but with a separate chapter devoted to the important topic of personal selling. The 'other publicity' heading covers a very wide range of activities, since companies have been extremely creative in finding ways of communicating their messages; everything from matchboxes to deck-chairs, racing cars to tennis players, hot air balloons to the air itself, has been used. Not all the possible media can be listed here, and certainly not discussed; each should be treated the same way, and subjected to the same tests of efficiency and effectiveness: what are they trying to achieve, how well do they do it, how do they relate to the rest of the mix?

The problem with asking such questions is that communication shares many of the measurement problems of all marketing variables, but with the additional one that we understand very little of how communication actually works. One psychologist, having studied the subject exhaustively, said that his only conclusion was amazement that, given all the difficulties, any communication took place at all! There is a considerable body of literature, and of course a huge reservoir of experience, but there is still much that is uncertain. All of us have personal experiences demonstrating some of the pitfalls; imagine the total number of messages sent out by a firm in the course of a year, and the potential for distortion and error. We receive information about a firm not only from the formal messages it sends out in the form of advertising, sales brochures and so on, but also from experience of its products, word of mouth, stories in the press, the state of its lorries, perhaps even the road manners of its drivers or the politeness of its switchboard operators. The information we take out may not be what is intended; for example, the information we get from an advertisement may be affected by the clothes the actors are wearing, the furnishings of the room portrayed, our personal memories aroused by the music, all interacting with a whole range of other personal experiences, attitudes and beliefs. Total control is impossible; but it therefore becomes even more important to control what is controllable.

Each company must analyse its target audiences, and decide what messages it wishes to send to each; it can then choose the best combination of media to achieve its aims efficiently. The nature of the mix chosen will clearly vary greatly, depending on the nature of the firm and its markets. Companies selling to consumer mass markets may use large amounts of advertising, and relatively little personal selling; those in technical industrial markets, on the contrary, may spend a lot on the sales force and exhibitions, but almost nothing on advertising (these are relativities – personal selling and advertising may each play a vital role, even though it is relatively small). The questions, to repeat, are the same: who is the target audience, what is the message we want to communicate to them, what is the most effective and most efficient way of doing it?

What do we know about how advertising works?

Most people have an implicit view of how advertising works, probably something to do with information and persuasion. Those in the field have elaborated models, such as the famous USP (the Unique Selling Proposition), or DAGMAR (Defining Advertising Goals for Measuring Advertising Results). A common model – implicit or explicit – is the hierarchy of mental states: this assumes that consumers pass through a succession of mental states, from ignorance about a brand, through awareness, interest, belief, conviction and purchase. An early formulation was AIDA: Attention, Interest, Desire, Action. The DAGMAR approach also assumes some such hierarchy, as the goals defined are normally the intervening communication goals such as awareness, or recall of advertising. The problem is that there is very little or no evidence to support these models.

The most comprehensive attempt to summarize what we actually do know about advertising's workings was made by Vakratsas and Ambler (1999). They reviewed more than 250 articles and books, and reached some important conclusions. First, they produced a taxonomy of the models they found. They divided them up into:

Model	Sequence of effects
Market response	No intermediate effects
Cognitive information	'Think'
Pure affect	'Feel'
Persuasive hierarchy	'Think' – 'Feel' – 'Do'
Low involvement hierarchy	'Think' – 'Do' – 'Feel'
Integrative	Hierarchy not fixed
Hierarchy-free	No particular hierarchy

From the results reported for these models, they drew twenty-five conclusions, too detailed to reproduce here, and suggested five generalizations.

1 *Experience, affect and cognition are the three key intermediate advertising effects, and the omission of any one can lead to the overestimation of the effect of the others*. The

experience of actually using a brand is an important, often the most important, influence on brand choice. Feeling (affect) plays a part in decision-making, as well as thinking (cognition). Any model that leaves out one of these will produce misleading results, usually by exaggerating the importance of one or more of the remaining variables.

2 *Short-term advertising elasticities are small and decrease during the product life cycle.* Most of the studies reviewed focused on fast-moving consumer goods (where most advertising money is spent), so this conclusion *may* apply only to them. There is also an influential countervailing view that short-term effects can be measured, and may be significant (Jones 1995).

3 *In mature, frequently purchased packaged goods markets, returns to advertising diminish fast. A small frequency, therefore (one to three reminders per purchase cycle), is sufficient for advertising an established brand.* This is a useful finding for planning campaigns, though we must recognize that much of the repetition that we see reflects the attempt to increase the reach of a campaign (increasing the percentage of the target population who are exposed to an advertisement).

4 *The concept of a space of intermediate effects is supported, but a hierarchy (sequence) is not.* Cognition (thinking) is more important for high-involvement goods, affect (feeling) for low-involvement goods, and experience for mature, familiar products. Therefore, it is sensible to think of a three-dimensional space, with all three represented and different products positioned in different parts of the space. A linear sequence, with one effect (say, positive attitude) following from a previous one (say, belief) and leading to purchase, is not supported.

5 *Cognitive bias interferes with affect measurement.* This is a serious methodological problem that affects all attitude research. Asking about a feeling causes the respondent to think about it, and that disrupts the attitude. We should bear this in mind in planning and interpreting any attempts to measure affective responses.

Taken together, these findings should influence all those working in and with advertising. The hierarchy of effects model, in particular, has been very widely used, either implicitly or explicitly, but this research shows that it is not valid. This is especially important when we try to measure the effects of advertising, which we discuss below.

Roles and tasks of advertising

The main task of advertising is to increase profits, but that does not help much in understanding it or making decisions about it. It must, however, be in our minds, as unless advertising is helping to create short- or long-term profits, it is wasted.

The next step is to say that advertising creates sales.

Having said that, a glance through a range of advertising in different media will quickly show that a huge variety of things are going on. We must therefore look at advertising in its context; it cannot be divorced from the setting of its originating organization, market situation and marketing mix. A particular campaign may be trying to:

- introduce a new brand
- inform about a product modification

- remind users of benefits
- get users to use more
- get non-users to try the brand
- suggest new uses
- inform about a special offer
- increase the perceived importance of certain attributes of the brand
- stress advantages against competitors
- present technical information
- stress general company attributes (size, reputation, reliability, etc.)
- and so on, *ad infinitum*.

It will be clear to perceptive readers that such a list is conceptually confused. We should analyse the role of advertising at more than one level:

- What are the marketing objectives?
- What is advertising's contribution (as compared with that of the product, pricing, promotion and distribution)?
- How exactly will advertising perform this task?
- What are the specific communication objectives of the advertising?

Thus we might have a situation in which the marketing objective for a brand is to increase market share by three percentage points by retaining existing buyers, getting them to use more, and attracting non-buyers to try the brand. The role of advertising is to remind existing buyers of the benefits of the brand and reassure them about its quality, to suggest new uses; and to inform both existing and potential new buyers of new pack sizes and special offers as they occur. The advertising campaign will continue its previous theme of quality, value-for-money, and suitability for all the family, using the same family which has been established in previous years as warm, humorous and 'just like us'. Specific communication objectives would be set for each message for each target group (recall of brand name amongst housewives aged 25–34, for example).

Such an approach, which is common, has the virtue of being logical, and ensures that the advertising is seen to play its role within the total mix. It does, however, beg a number of questions. The discussion of consumer behaviour and buying patterns in Chapter 4 and above showed how difficult it is to understand exactly how advertising works:

- Objectives for advertising have to be set in communications terms (to be meaningful to the people who have to produce the advertisements),
- What we are looking for is changes in behaviour (buying more, buying the brand at all),
- What is mainly missing is the link between the two. It must be stressed again that we simply do not know what the connection is between attitudes and behaviour; yet much advertising is trying to form attitudes.

This may of course be over-complicating matters. Most brands are bought for fairly simple reasons, and the main determinant of their success is how good they are at delivering the main salient benefits. Advertising then becomes important only in reminding people. This squares with the view that advertising's role can be summed up as ATR – Awareness, Trial, Repeat buying (Ehrenberg 1988). As Ehrenberg and his colleagues have shown, most buyers in most markets buy a repertoire of brands; they do not buy one all the time, then suddenly switch to another. Most people are familiar with the brands on the market, but they need reminding, and of course new consumers need to be informed. This approach is consistent with ideas such as cognitive dissonance, since much advertising is aimed at existing buyers to reassure them that they have made the right decision; and it is consistent with the fact that many markets in which advertising expenditures are heavy are ones characterized by low involvement – the product does not play a hugely important role in the consumer's life, and the choice between very similar brands is also unimportant. In such situations, advertising may be contributing to consumers' perception of the brand's personality, and preference for the personality may be the basis of brand choice.

In another situation, advertising may contain dense technical information, and may be physically filed away for reference at a later date; or it may introduce a company and its products so that when a sales person calls, he or she is not totally anonymous; or it may be asking for a specific response, such as the return of a coupon. What is important is that the company should be absolutely clear about what the advertising is trying to do in the particular situation.

Deciding on the budget

There are four main decision areas involved in using advertising:

1 The size of the budget
2 The media to be used
3 The content of the message
4 The creative treatment.

All interact with each other, and could be seen as part of a circle which can be broken into at any point. For example, the company might decide that to do justice to its new product, its benefits must be demonstrated using sound and movement; that indicates television, and that in turn implies a certain minimum size of budget. Alternatively, you might start with the message to be communicated; if it is fairly complicated, that may determine that it must be in the form of a press advertisement, and so on. We are starting the discussion here with the decision on budget, but it must be remembered that the other decisions are related, and the process may be iterative: a subsequent decision on media and treatment may lead us back to reconsider the size of the budget.

The main methods companies use to set their advertising budgets are:

■ Percentage of sales
■ What we can afford
■ Competitive parity
■ Objective and task
■ Mathematical models.

Percentage of sales

The most common method is still the percentage of sales – either last year's, or forecast future sales. This method is simple and straightforward, but suffers from a similar logical difficulty to cost-based pricing, discussed in the previous chapter. It is assumed that advertising influences sales, but in this method sales are predetermined and influence advertising. Despite this problem, the method is used by many companies, particularly where the budget is small relative to sales.

What we can afford

Spending what we can afford is also an approach which is used when advertising is seen to be relatively unimportant. After the sales forecast has been produced and all other costs deducted, an amount for advertising is set aside. A little thought, however, will suggest that in such circumstances, the advertising is likely to be traditional and to have little impact – similar advertisements to last year's (and the year before), in the same publications, 'Because that's what we always do'. Such campaigns may of course still fulfil a useful function in reminding buyers of the company's continuing existence.

Competitive parity

Competitive parity is more likely to be used in markets in which advertising is heavier, and it is felt important not to be left behind. This happens in many consumer goods markets, and frequently the advertising budget for a brand is related to its market share. In stationary markets, with fairly small and slow changes in market growth and shares, this approach has a certain logic to it. Normally, it is felt that the brand leader needs to spend proportionately less as a share of total advertising to maintain its market share, while conversely a brand trying to improve its market share will have to spend proportionately more.

Objective and task

The objective and task method tries to assign money to the tasks specified for the advertising. This is a logical approach, with the major proviso discussed earlier, that it is frequently impossible to specify the link between communications objectives and behavioural results. Thus setting as an objective: 'Increase in recall of advertising message by target audience from 30 per cent to 40 per cent' is fine; but it does not translate directly into a marketing objective of increasing brand share from 14 per cent to 16 per cent, for example.

It should be said that there are commercially available models which claim to make such links: they will claim to be able to translate advertising expenditure through awareness and recall figures to trial and repeat purchase and thence to market share and sales. Like most such services, they seem to work sometimes, but not always; they are worth investigating for a company which has large advertising budgets but not the resources or time to develop its own models.

Mathematical models

It is this last approach which offers the best chance of producing better decisions on advertising budgets. Previous discussions have underlined how difficult it is to measure the response curve of sales to marketing instruments such as price or advertising. What can be done over time is to experiment with different levels of advertising in a controlled way, and to build results into a mathematical model of your market. It goes without saying that this approach demands substantial resources, expertise and patience. Major marketing companies have been doing it for many years; unfortunately for students of marketing, they do not publish the results, so we simply do not know how successful they have been. Some results are now available from controlled experiments in the USA; these are summarized in Vakratsas and Ambler (1999).

The overall approach to budget setting is intimately tied up with the way advertising's effectiveness is measured. This is discussed later in this chapter.

Message and treatment

Deciding on what advertising should say and how it should be expressed are areas on which large amounts of time can be spent, but on which little guidance is available from theory and evidence.

The overall advertising strategy should flow from an analysis of the brand's situation and the company's marketing strategy. This definition of what should be communicated to whom is so important that some people have argued that it should be done by only the most senior managers, because only they have a sufficiently deep understanding of all the factors.

They also have a reservoir of knowledge and experience of their customers and consumers, of what works and what does not work in their market; this knowledge may or may not be backed up by data on buyer behaviour and the effectiveness of different advertising appeals. The strategy should be based on an empathy with the buyers and users, a sensitivity to their needs, and an understanding of what they expect from the company and the brand. It should be an important part of the brand's differentiation from its competitors.

Many approaches to message selection set out a framework, such as rational, sensual, emotional ('What do we want them to believe about the brand? What appeals to the different senses does it make? What do we want them to feel about it?'). Such frameworks are helpful, as long as the statements that emerge connect with the marketing situation and the behaviour and motivation of buyers.

Detailed translation of the overall advertising strategy into specific messages and advertisements is the creative part of the process, carried out by specialists in the company's advertising department or agency (see the section below on using an agency); but it is always the responsibility of the company's senior managers to approve whatever is produced. The advertisement has two main jobs to do: to attract the attention of the target audience, and to communicate the desired message. Attracting and keeping attention is not easy, given the tremendous clutter in many media and our short attention span. We can probably all think of advertisements which succeed brilliantly in gaining our attention, and even keeping it, but which on consideration have failed to deliver a relevant message. On the other hand, advertising which does not stand out and therefore does not get beyond the attention threshold cannot communicate anything.

To produce high quality advertising thus demands high levels of creativity and skill. The manager judging it may use some criteria, such as:

- Does it meet the brief?
- Is it consistent with the company and brand image?
- Does it communicate the main message clearly?
- Does it address the target audience's concerns (not ours)?
- Does it talk the language and use the tone of voice appropriate to a dialogue between us and the target audience?
- Will it stand out?
- Will it work?

It will be appreciated that many of these judgements are difficult to make (and the last almost impossible), but nevertheless a judgement must be made. Some companies use fairly tight guidelines (every advertisement must have a unique selling proposition, a reason why, and a closing pack shot, for example); others are much more flexible. Only experience and patient collection of data will help with these difficult but important decisions.

A personal view, which cannot be substantiated, is that probably the creative element in advertising follows a normal distribution. Most advertising campaigns are around the average, the creative aspects having a relatively small impact on sales. At each end of the distribution are a few very good or very bad campaigns, which have a real and dramatic impact. Famously good campaigns include the Avis campaign 'We're number 2 – we try harder' in the USA and the Tango orange drink campaign in the UK. About the only famously bad campaign generally acknowledged was that for Strand cigarettes in the UK (the commercials were well-made, very distinctive and memorable; but the slogan, 'You're never alone with a Strand' rebounded, in that the target audience of young men were unwilling to associate themselves with loneliness; the brand failed). Readers will have their own experiences.

Media selection

The main advertising media are television, the press (newspapers and magazines), radio, cinema and posters, although as mentioned earlier there are very many others which are used from time to time, and recent years have seen a proliferation of new media, including the Internet and now interactive digital TV. Which media are chosen will depend on the other decisions, though it sometimes happens that the media decision is made first ('We must be on television because all our competitors are'). Clearly, the main criteria for selection are the extent to which a medium reaches the target audience, and its efficiency. We return to the problem of integrating the different media below.

For many industrial markets, specialist journals are the ideal and probably only practicable means of reaching tightly defined targets. It is important that all the different buying influences are identified and targeted: for instance, you may want to reach the engineering director through a professional engineering journal, the finance director through *The Accountant*, and the managing director through *Management Today*.

Similar considerations apply in some consumer markets, with specialist magazines reaching defined groups. A glance along the shelves of a newsagent will show a huge variety of publications dedicated to enthusiasts for gardening, cooking, photography, fishing, personal computers, hi-fi and so on, often with subdivisions within each. Selection should be made on the basis of readership data, if available, and cost.

Other small target audiences are local ones, which can be reached by local radio or newspapers. Radio was rather slow to develop in the UK, but is now well established; it is much more widespread in some other countries. The nature of the audience will depend on the targeting of the station's programming; many UK stations provide mainly pop music, and the audiences are young people. Local newspapers are likely to reach a broader audience, and are used particularly by advertisers such as retailers.

In many of the cases discussed so far, the advertiser has little choice, often because the budget is limited. A larger budget and/or a broader definition of target audience opens up other media, and other considerations.

Efficiency

Efficiency is measured simply (in theory) by cost per thousand target audience: what is the cost of reaching 1000 of my target audience once in this medium? Obviously, data need to be available for such calculations to be made. Most major media publish very detailed audience data, concentrating mainly on demographic data and possibly purchasing in some markets. It therefore helps if target audiences are defined in these terms, even though that may imply some translation from your marketing definitions ('traditional housewives who believe cleanliness is of over-riding importance').

Effectiveness

Effectiveness brings in more qualitative influences, in particular the nature of the message and treatment. Some types of message and treatment choose their own medium; a detailed explanation of a complex investment plan must go into the press, probably a serious newspaper or magazine. This example brings out the two aspects of the effectiveness decision: intrinsic qualities of the medium, and the effect of context. The intrinsic qualities of the press mean that detailed arguments can be presented in semi-permanent form, and readers can return to an advertisement to study it. That applies to any form of press; however, some people believe that some subjects gain or lose by the context of the actual press vehicle chosen; in the example, the arguments about an investment plan would gain seriousness and weight by being in the context of a 'quality' newspaper rather than a tabloid (regardless of the target audience considerations).

Similar influences may help determine broad media choice, though in the case of television, the decision is likely to be affected by competitive considerations, the effect on retailers, and the sheer impact which only television can have in a mass market campaign.

The other main aspect of media scheduling is timing. In some markets there are seasonal patterns which effectively determine the timing of advertising, which is scheduled to coincide with (or just precede) main buying periods. Experience suggests that trying to advertise counter-seasonally is expensive and unlikely to be successful, but every market is different and yours may be the exception to the rule. It is worth thinking through buyers' purchasing and use processes to see what can really be changed.

With or without seasonality, advertisers have a choice of advertising steadily throughout buying periods, or in bursts of concentrated activity (known as 'drip' or 'burst' strategies). The advantage of bursts is that while advertising is going on, you can appear to dominate, relatively at least; this may be a way of making a limited budget go further. There is little evidence for any general rule saying that one or the other is right; as always, the parameters of the particular situation must be examined.

Measuring advertising effects

It follows from the arguments adopted earlier that the way advertising effects are measured depends on what you think the advertising is doing. All the decisions discussed – budget, content and treatment, and media selection – have a potential impact on sales and profits. It is in your interest, therefore, to measure the effects of your decisions so that you can improve the quality of future decision-making. It may not be worth measuring everything, as the cost of doing so may outweigh the benefit; but the impact of major decisions should be quantified if possible.

Some things are much easier to measure than others: the size and composition of the audience for a particular media vehicle is fairly easy to measure, while the profit impact of spending three million pounds rather than two and a half million is not. It was suggested earlier that managers have underlying, implicit models of how they think advertising works; which model they use ought to determine the methods selected to measure its effects. The subject is complex and controversial, with many claims made for particular methods, and a great deal of secrecy. The summary which follows is therefore a personal one, with which many in the industry would disagree.

- What communication is taking place using a specific advertisement can be checked qualitatively through small group discussions; major distortions and misunderstandings can be picked up and corrected. How much people like a particular advertisement or approach can be checked, but no quantitative conclusions can be drawn.

- There are methods which claim to quantify the effects of an advertisement before it is launched, but these claims are of doubtful validity.

- After a campaign appears, many communications objectives can be measured – for example, recall of brand name and of advertising, recall of specific claims, belief of claims, rating of the brand on a list of attributes, feelings about the brand and the advertising. This sort of measurement is very common, and large spenders frequently use a selection of them regularly to track what is happening. They claim to derive benefits from this process, but there is no theoretical basis and little actual evidence to link such measures with sales and profits.

- The measures chosen reflect the manager's underlying model of how advertising works; often this is not realized, and the model is not made explicit. In those circumstances, decisions made on the basis of the measures are not rational.

- The effect of major advertising decisions can be quantified by careful controlled experimentation in different geographical areas. This applies to questions of budget, drip or burst pattern, media choice (sometimes), and actual advertisements. Such experimentation is difficult (sometimes impossible) and expensive, and should be seen as a long-term investment; many successful companies do it.

- New technology using cable television and smart cards allows simulated markets to be set up in a city; experiments can be run and detailed effects tracked. Such wired cities exist in the USA and are appearing in Europe. They offer great possibilities, though they will always suffer the drawbacks of being possibly unrepresentative.

To sum up, there are situations in which the effect of advertising can be measured. For example, when press advertising is used to stimulate coupon response, the cost per reply (and further calculations, such as cost per conversion or sale) can be measured exactly.

However, in most cases it is extremely difficult to say precisely what a specific advertising campaign is contributing to sales and profits. When advertising forms a large part of total spending, it is worth devoting time and effort to the measurement of its effects; but it should be recognized that the undertaking will be long and complicated.

Using an advertising agency

Where advertising forms only a small part of a company's budget, it may be produced in-house by an advertising department and placed directly in the relevant media. Most advertising, however, is produced and placed by a specialist advertising agency.

Because of the way they developed historically, advertising agencies in Britain were for many years paid not directly by the client, but by taking a commission from the media owners with whom the advertising was placed; the commission was normally 15 per cent for major media and 10 per cent for others. Recently this system has begun to break down, for two main reasons: the bargaining power of large clients, and the rise of separate media buying houses. Large clients, spending many millions of pounds, are now sophisticated buyers of services; many negotiate fees for work carried out by their agencies, rather than allowing them a consistent percentage of billing. The appearance and success of independent media-buying firms, which act rather like wholesalers but buying advertising time and space in bulk from owners and then re-selling it to clients, has further weakened the logic of the old commission system. The current situation is therefore a mixture; where a client is happy to let the agency carry out all the functions of creation, media planning and buying (together perhaps with the supply of other marketing services such as promotions and market research), the commission system may be retained as it is simple and effective. A large client may buy specific services from several different providers, including an advertising agency, an independent media buyer, and a promotions agency, each for a negotiated fee. A few accounts now operate on a payment-by-results basis.

Some radical commentators claim that the traditional advertising agency's day is over, and that the future belongs to wholly new methods of marketing (see Chapter 1). There is little sign that this is yet happening, though it is true that some of the work previously done by advertising agencies is now carried out by others, such as marketing agencies or specialist groups of talented individuals.

Although an agency may have a variety of titles and ways of organizing itself, it normally has four main functions:

- account direction
- creative

- production
- media planning and buying.

Many also have a function called account planning, which brings together market research and marketing analysis as support and guide to advertising development.

- The account director and his or her team are responsible for client contact and for co-ordinating the efforts of the other functions so as to meet the client's objectives.
- Creative teams, as the name suggests, think up the actual advertising campaigns for client approval; the team usually contains a words person (the copywriter) and a pictures person (the visualizer), although in practice the roles may not be sharply demarcated.
- The production department is responsible for ensuring that finished advertisements are produced on time and to the required standard, often by outside specialist contractors, and delivered to the media owners for printing/transmission.
- Media planners analyse data and plan the best schedule to meet campaign objectives within the budget, while buyers separately concentrate on getting the best deal on price and placing within the media vehicle.

The client's role, as with the buying and management of any service, is to choose the most appropriate agency in the first place, and to ensure that they are properly briefed. It must remain the client's function to define the overall advertising strategy, based on the marketing strategy for the brand. The brief should contain clear marketing objectives and a statement of what the advertising is expected to achieve within the overall plan. As the previous discussion will have made clear, there are differing views as to how advertising works, and the client's particular beliefs will inform the way in which the brief is formulated. For example, some briefs will contain a statement of the brand's unique selling proposition and reason why: the agency's job then is to translate these into memorable advertising. Other briefs will contain a description of the brand's positioning and some communications objectives, such as percentage increase in brand awareness, proportion of target audience recalling the advertising's main message, and so on.

The relationship between client and agency, like any supplier–customer relationship, works best when founded on trust and co-operation over a long period. A good client makes all relevant information available, even the most confidential and commercially sensitive; the agency is clearly briefed, and decisions on advertising are made quickly and unambiguously – but the agency is left to make its specialist contribution without undue interference in detail. For its part the agency produces good quality work on time and to the brief, and performs its other functions such as media buying efficiently and competitively. The difficulty of judging quality in advertising has been mentioned, and is at the centre of client–agency difficulties. The personalities involved are vitally important, but change frequently in both marketing departments and agencies, at junior levels anyway. It then becomes even more important for senior managers to take responsibility for what may be major strategic decisions.

Other forms of promotion – what they can and cannot do

The ingenuity of people trying to sell goods and services is endless, and so therefore are the methods of promotion which are thought up. Problems of definition are rife, but are really not important. For our purposes, sales promotion will be defined as all means of promotion not specifically classified as advertising or personal selling. The main components are:

- public relations
- publicity
- sponsorship
- packaging
- displays of product
- point-of-purchase promotion
- demonstrations
- free samples
- premium offers, such as extra product, gifts, etc.
- competitions
- exhibitions and trade fairs
- other material (films, brochures, leaflets).

Public relations

As already mentioned, public relations has a wider application than marketing, and is concerned with making sure that all the company's target audiences receive the desired messages. In marketing terms it is often thought of as a support medium, although there are cases when it becomes central; for example, a margarine brand which cannot claim directly in its advertising that it helps lessen the danger of heart disease may use PR to place general messages to that effect through editorial mentions.

Publicity

Publicity is used to keep the company's name before the public, and to reach specific audiences through, for example, press receptions. Sponsorship, which might be included under this general heading, is also used to generate media coverage. Sponsorship has grown enormously in recent years, often as the only way an advertiser can obtain television coverage – either because direct advertising of the product in question is not allowed on television (e.g. cigarettes), or because the advertiser's budget is too small for a complete campaign (e.g. all the smaller sponsors whose names appear on racing drivers' overalls). Apart from reminding potential buyers of the company's existence, sponsorship may transmit messages about the company or the product – associating it with Formula 1's image of speed, masculinity and power, for instance. If the target audiences of the brand

and of the sponsored activity are similar, and if the messages are congruent with those of the overall marketing strategy, then sponsorship may be an effective and efficient tool. Looking at many sponsorship activities, one is tempted to conclude that the chairman's hobby has been important in determining the choice of sponsorship – opera against horse racing, for example. Of course, sponsorship frequently gives opportunities for corporate entertaining, so it may also contribute to another part of the total marketing campaign, helping to build personal relationships with individuals who would otherwise be difficult to reach with conventional advertising or promotion.

Packaging

This may be thought of as part of the product, or as a means of promotion. In some markets, such as cosmetics, it is central to the brand's positioning and appeal; in others, it is merely a way of protecting the product during transport. Any packaging must be functional, in that it must protect; it should also be designed to make it easy for both intermediaries and final users to handle, and it should if possible fit the brand's positioning, even if it is almost entirely functional. Brands which are displayed on retailers' shelves need their packaging to be not only functional, but:

- consistent with the overall brand message
- readable
- recognizable
- different from competition
- if possible, offering some distinct benefit.

The last is difficult; it is only occasionally that a brand such as Toilet Duck has packaging which is in itself a competitive difference.

The example leads us back to the basic marketing principle, that we must always think of the product-in-use: can the packaging help the consumer to do the job better, more easily, more enjoyably?

These days, other considerations such as biodegradability and reducing environmental damage generally also play their part. In some countries, such as Germany, there have been serious moves to eliminate or reduce packaging, and this seems likely to spread.

Most of the other categories listed – displays, competitions, offers – are normally thought of as sales promotion. They may be targeted at consumers or at the trade. They can add interest and excitement, or they may have a very specific marketing objective – to induce non-triers to try the brand, or to encourage repurchase and loyalty, for example. All the evidence suggests that promotions are almost entirely short-term in their effects. They may (indeed should) have an immediate effect on sales, but that effect will not last long. In the worst case, a promotion will merely induce people who were going to buy anyway to buy more now; but they will buy correspondingly less in the next purchase period. In the best result, some of the new buyers attracted by the promotion will remain as purchasers subsequently; although sales may fall back after the promotion, they will not fall all the way back to their previous level, and some permanent gain in market share will have been achieved.

It is therefore vital that the objectives of a particular promotion are carefully thought through. It must be consistent with the overall strategy, and must fit in with advertising and sales plans; it should enhance the brand, not cheapen it. Too much promotion may indeed weaken a brand, if it leads consumers to think – even if only subconsciously – that the central brand proposition must be weak if constant promotion is needed to persuade people to buy.

Direct marketing

Direct marketing has grown out of the traditional techniques of direct mail and mail order. There is no single definition of what is and is not direct marketing. Some of its components and alternative names will give an indication of its scope and content:

- **Direct mail** The use of letters and promotional material sent by mail to named individuals,
- **Mail order** A distribution system in which buyers contact sellers by mail (or, nowadays, telephone or fax) and receive direct delivery of goods ordered,
- **Direct response marketing** Any approach which asks the target audience to take action (return a coupon, make a telephone call, etc.),
- **Telemarketing** The use of the telephone to contact prospects,
- **Database marketing** The use of a database (normally on a computer) to store customer records and target direct contacts,
- **E-commerce** Using the Internet to sell goods and services.

Two of these terms sum up the essence, and the reason for the dramatic growth in recent years of the techniques:

direct and **database.**

Direct marketing cuts out intermediaries and establishes direct contact between supplier and customer; the use of computerized storage and analysis permits more efficient and effective promotional effort.

The example in Figure 12.1 shows what can easily be done with this method. It was received in October 1992 as part of the regular mailing I receive from the supplier from whom I buy office materials. Printed on the front cover of the fifty-six page catalogue (and with a reminder on the back cover) is an individualized offer. It shows that I bought bubble jet cartridges on 24 July 1992, and offers me the chance to buy more at a special price – lower than the one inside the catalogue – and gives an individual 'private sale' number. The fact that we all know that this is produced by a computer does not lessen its appeal: they know I buy bubble jet cartridges, and they are offering an incentive to buy again *now* at an advantageous price. (On another occasion I also received a letter from the managing director when I had bought nothing for six months, asking if something was wrong with their service.)

Figure 12.1 Example of database marketing: Viking

This demonstrates how the database can record customer details on purchases and use them to stimulate reordering, as well as to keep track of potentially lost business (it is always much more expensive to gain new customers than to retain existing ones). Anyone who has ever bought something from a leading exponent of consumer direct mail, such as Readers' Digest, will be familiar with these features.

It has been suggested that a fully fledged database marketing system should have the following features:

1 Each actual or potential customer is identified as a record on the marketing database. Markets and market segments are not identified primarily through aggregate data, which cannot be broken down into individual customers, but as agglomerations of individual customers.

2 Each customer record contains not only identification and access information (e.g. name, address, telephone number), but also a range of marketing information. This includes information about customer needs and characteristics (demographic and psychographic information about consumers, industry type and decision-making unit information for industrial customers). Such information is used to identify likely purchasers of particular products and how they should be approached. Each customer record also contains information about campaign communications (whether the customer has been exposed to particular marketing communications campaigns), about customers' past responses...and about past transactions....

3 The information is available to the company during the process of each communication with the customer.

4 The data base is used to record responses of customers to company initiatives.

5 The information is also available to marketing policy makers. . .to decide. . .which target markets or segments are appropriate for each product or service and what marketing mix. . .is appropriate for each target market.

6 In large corporations, selling many products to each customer, the data base is used to ensure that the approach to the customer is co-ordinated.

7 The data base eventually replaces market research. Marketing campaigns are devised such that the response of customers. . .provides information which the company is looking for.

8 [As well as developing a large customer data base and ways of accessing it to handle transactions]. . .marketing management automation is also developed. This is needed to handle the vast volume of information generated by data base marketing. It makes higher quality information on marketing performance available to senior management, allowing them to allocate marketing resources more effectively.

(Shaw and Stone 1988)

Shaw and Stone admit that few companies have yet reached this final stage, but many are using the approach outlined in the first six paragraphs. Obviously, the advent of cheap computer power and sophisticated software has made this feasible.

Although firm figures are not available, it is clear that direct marketing is growing very fast; expenditure on direct mail alone has been estimated to be increasing at some 30 per cent per year in the UK, much faster than promotional spending in other media. Direct marketing can and does use other contact methods, particularly the telephone, another rapidly growing medium (see below). The range of companies using the approach has also grown. As the examples quoted suggest, direct mail has been used for years in business-to-business marketing, and by a few practitioners in selling to consumers. In recent years financial services have become major users, and industries from retailing to capital goods manufacturers have adopted the approach. Even some branded goods manufacturers have begun to experiment with direct marketing in the field of toiletries, which has been almost exclusively the province of heavy television campaigns in the past.

It is worth saying a little more on telephone marketing, since it is playing a major role in some fields, and taking over at least some of the tasks of personal selling, dealt with in the next chapter. The telephone is now used for a wide variety of marketing jobs; it can:

■ research, evaluate and test new markets

■ identify prospects and their potential value

■ generate leads and make appointments for sales people

■ sell products and services

■ service existing customers

■ launch new products and services

■ handle responses generated by advertising

■ process orders and enquiries

- handle complaints
- build, maintain and exploit marketing databases
- invite people to events
- update mailing lists
- communicate important company/product/service information
- raise awareness or funds.

(Stevens 1991)

As several of those headings suggest, the telephone can often be used most effectively in combination with other elements, particularly sales people. A combination of telephone for routine contact, and soliciting and taking reorders, with sales people in the field for other tasks which are best performed by personal contact, is rapidly becoming the norm in areas which previously used large field sales forces. The relative costs are such that it probably costs over £50,000 in total to keep a sales person in the field, and a personal call might therefore cost around £50; a telephone sales call might cost roughly £10.

The advantages and disadvantages of the telephone have been summed up as:

Advantages	Disadvantages
Targeted	■ More expensive than some other techniques
Personal	■ Comparatively low volume
Interactive	■ Intangible
Immediate	■ Sometimes intrusive
High quality	■ Easily misused
Flexible	
Measurable and accountable	
Testable	
Intrusive	
Cost-effective	

(Stevens 1991)

Cost is of course relative: telephoning is cheap compared with a personal visit, as we have seen, but it may be expensive compared with direct mail or a mass advertising campaign. Obviously, the specific situation needs to be analysed in each case to see whether using the telephone would be appropriate, effective and efficient.

Direct marketing must be seen as one of the major growth areas in the coming years. Its advantages are selectivity, the ability to target selected groups with specifically chosen products and marketing mixes, and the facility to monitor existing customers – generally to use accumulated knowledge of individuals' behaviour to better meet their needs with products and services.

At present, the approach needs a response from customers to start the database, but with the coming of smart cards it may be that purchasing in shops will automatically trigger a record in a supplier's computer. Future vistas include complete home shopping via electronic networks, with marketing offers targeted to your screen and purchases made through a keypad. This may sound like either heaven or hell, according to taste.

Integrated marketing communications

Although it has been stated before, it is worth hammering home the point that all advertising and promotion should be coherent.

Everything should be driving in the same direction, giving a coherent overall message, reinforcing and not working against the other parts of the marketing mix and the total strategy.

As different parts of the mix may be designed at different times, often by different people in different agencies, it is easy to lose sight of this – but somewhere there must be a controlling mind which judges everything against the brand's positioning and the company strategy. The task has become more complex – but, therefore, even more vital – with the proliferation of new media, and the growth of direct marketing and e-commerce.

Consistency over time has also been stressed, and is worth underlining. All the great brands show great consistency over time, and this is reinforced by consistent advertising and promotion.

Neither of these exhortations should exclude creativity, and both coherence and consistency may sometimes be interpreted broadly. Two of the great consumer promotions were the Esso tiger tail and the Persil rail tickets. Neither look at first sight to fit the above requirements very closely. It could be argued, however, that both do in fact show coherence. The Esso tiger was part of an overall strategy designed to differentiate the brand from other (identical) petrols; it implied power, and the promotion added fun and liveliness. The Persil promotion offered real value, and perhaps by offering opportunities to visit distant relatives enhanced the family context which is central to Persil's long-term positioning.

Perhaps we should say that, along with coherence and consistency, we should look for creativity which never goes against brand values, and if possible enhances them.

Key learning points

- **Any organization has many target audiences, and many ways of reaching them.**
- **Marketing has several methods, together known as the communications mix. The main methods are: advertising, promotion, personal selling, public relations, other publicity.**

- Advertising can have a range of roles and tasks. Although its aim is to increase sales and profits, these effects are very difficult to measure.
- The main decisions to be made about advertising are the size of the budget, the media to be used, the content of the message, and the treatment. They interact with each other.
- There is a huge variety of forms of promotion and publicity. All should have clear objectives, and should be consistent with the overall marketing strategy and the positioning of the brand.
- Direct marketing using computer databases is growing rapidly, and has many advantages.

Further reading

Cox, K. and Enis, B. (1973) *Experimentation for Marketing Decisions*, Aylesbury: Intertext.
McCorkell, G. (1998) *Direct and Database Marketing*, London: Kogan Page.

Case study: Alcohols Unlimited

Alcohols Unlimited is an importer and wholesaler of wines and spirits. James Rudd, the marketing executive, has noticed the swift rise of imported beers and novelty drinks sold on a fashion basis to young people; these have captured a small but significant volume share of the market, and sell at very high prices.

James thinks that there is an opportunity for AU, and has found a continental supplier of a new alcoholic drink with fruit and herbs, of a quality he thinks is at least adequate ('They can't really tell one from another when the drink is cold and they are in the mood', he feels). He has named the drink 'Luna', and has had an attractive label designed for the distinctive bottle.

He is now wondering how to promote 'Luna'.

Questions

1 What target audience should James select? Be as specific as possible in terms of age, sex, social class, location and life style.
2 How might AU reach this audience, using only a small budget (less than a quarter of a million pounds)?
3 Design an advertising slogan and a sales promotion for 'Luna' which will differentiate it from competitors.
4 How does your organization communicate with its audiences? Evaluate the various elements of the communications mix.

Chapter 13 | Personal selling

Although the word 'selling' has unfortunate connotations for some people (perhaps particularly in Britain), it is in fact basic to most activities; we are all selling something some of the time. In the business context, very many people may be involved in some way, however slight, in influencing whether or not a particular sale is made. Telephonists answering the phone, secretaries taking (or forgetting) messages, accountants dealing with queries, delivery people handling goods, factory workers talking on buses – all may contribute to the total communication which their firms' customers receive.

In this chapter, we are concerned with those whose job is specifically to do with selling, but we should not forget that they must always be seen in the context of the firm as a whole.

The exact role and importance of personal selling for a particular firm varies enormously. An old but still useful classification suggested that the role of a sales person might be any of the following:

- delivery (milk)
- inside order-taking (some retail sales people)
- outside order-taking (some manufacturers or wholesalers)
- customer liaison but not order-taking (pharmaceutical companies calling on doctors)
- technical consultancy (many engineering companies)
- creative sale of tangible products (cars, double glazing)

- creative sale of intangibles (insurance, professional services).

The list is in ascending order of the creative contribution of the sales person to the sale. Many sales people cover more than one of the roles, of course, or different roles at different times.

In general, where spending on advertising is low, the sales force is likely to be very important; indeed, it could be said that for most companies outside the field of branded consumer goods, the sales force is the most important part of the communications mix. Even for consumer goods manufacturers, the sales force, though much smaller now than previously (see next section), is still vital in achieving sales objectives.

Whatever its precise role, the sales force has a number of tasks to carry out. It has to:

- communicate (information about products, prices etc.)
- sell (persuade customers to buy, or to buy more, or to take specific products or ranges)
- service (deal with queries, help with problems, ensure deliveries)
- maintain and develop the relationship (through crises and successes)
- feed back information (on customers and competitors)
- find new customers and opportunities.

Apart from all this, sales people are the main contact between the company and its customers; they are its representatives in the fullest sense, and the way they behave (and the ways in which they are selected and trained), will have an enormous impact on how the company and its products are perceived.

The changing role of the sales force in consumer markets

Not many years ago, the typical sales force in a consumer goods company probably numbered several hundred sales people – up to a thousand in some cases. The reason was that they called on – and sold to – virtually every retailer stocking their products. There are still a few such organizations, in markets such as snack foods in which van sales people call on a huge variety of outlets – pubs, clubs, canteens, kiosks and so on, as well as many smaller retailers. All the others, however, have changed beyond recognition.

The cause of this – the rise of retailer multiples with enormous buying power – is examined in more depth in the next chapter. Here, we will just note that many fast-moving consumer goods manufacturers today have very small sales forces. National account managers deal with the major multiples' head office buying teams, and the job is much more to do with negotiating and managing the relationship than with selling techniques in the old-fashioned sense. The multiples have learned that, on the whole, it is more efficient for them to take all major buying decisions centrally, leaving little discretion to the individual store manager. In these circumstances, it becomes less and less productive for sales people to call on stores; indeed, some retailers severely discourage manufacturers' representatives from entering stores on business.

There are, of course, still some areas of retailing in which substantial proportions of the total market are accounted for by independent shops, and therefore where sales people still have a role. The Co-operative movement is still important in many markets, and is (perhaps to its detriment) still organized in regional societies; they and their stores can profitably be called on by the sales force. Wholesalers and symbol groups (such as Spar or Mace, in which independent shops trade under a group symbol and identity) may also repay visits.

In most cases, the role of the sales force of a consumer goods manufacturer is now much more like that found in industrial markets: a small number of high-quality people are targeted on a small number of customers who account for a very large proportion of the total business.

Telephone selling may be used for routine contact and order solicitation if ordering is left to store managers. As for contact with the shops themselves, a team of merchandisers (less qualified, less well-trained and lower-paid than fully fledged sales people, often part-time and therefore cheaper all round) may be employed to check stocks and displays. The very large sales force, with its attendant organizational structure of area and regional sales managers, has more or less disappeared for ever.

Decisions on size, allocation and organization

Size

The decision on the size of a sales force (and indeed its allocation) is similar to all decisions about marketing budgets: you should invest the economically optimum amount. This may be simpler in the case of the sales force, in that one can start with some accessible numbers: how many customers need to be called on? Assuming that experience will tell you how often each firm needs to be called on, and how many calls a sales person can make in a day, simple arithmetic will lead to a sales force size.

Some refinement can be added by separating existing customers from potential new business; how much of the total effort is spent on each will reflect the firm's current position and strategy for the future. Obviously, an aggressive growth strategy will demand greater efforts in prospecting for new business.

This sort of approach was probably used to arrive at the current size of the sales force, and provided that it is reviewed to ensure that it remains up to date with changes in the structure of the customer industries, it may lead to an acceptable solution. In times when there is extreme pressure on profit margins, however, every part of a company's operations will be subjected to intense scrutiny, and probing questions will be asked of the sales force; keeping a sales person on the road is expensive. The basic questions are:

■ Are we calling on the right companies?

■ Are we calling on the right people in those companies?

■ How will changes in the market and in the industry affect our selection of target customers?

■ What would happen if we changed the frequency of calling?

- What exactly is achieved by the sales call?
- What parts of the total set of tasks carried out by the sales people could be carried out differently?
- Would it be as effective, and more efficient, to use telephone selling or direct marketing?

Normally, a sales force will not have the personnel to call as often as they would like on all the firms they would like to visit; the total resource is rationed out according to the importance of current business. Asking the sort of questions listed above could release some of that total resource to be reallocated more efficiently.

For example, the frequency of calling on selected customers is often set by custom and practice; this is true for both existing and new business. Careful experimentation might show that some customers do not need to be called on as often as is the case at present; equally, it might be found that increasing the frequency of calling improves the probability of gaining new business from a particular set of customers.

The important thing is to question existing practice, and to try to measure the effects of change; the results could lead to an increase in the size of the sales force, as well as to reallocation or reduction.

Of course, all this must be set within the overall marketing context. Product, pricing, advertising and distribution decisions all impact on what the sales force is trying to achieve and how it carries out its tasks.

Allocation

Allocation of sales force effort to different segments follows the same logic. The question is, 'What would happen if we allocated more, or less, effort to each segment?' One manufacturer found itself with some spare sales force capacity when a major customer decided to move to central warehousing, cutting out the need for sales people to call on individual stores. The sales people were redeployed to the Co-operative societies, previously a neglected area, and sales volume there increased significantly (Randall 1994). Again, accepted practice should be challenged, and experiments carried out with different ways of doing things.

The other factor to watch is new and developing distribution channels. There is often a dilemma between concentrating effort on the current providers of sales and profit, and devoting time and support to new channels which are currently small but which may grow to be important later. Such channels may be expensive to service now, but early support to members may pay dividends in the long run. Continuously seeking efficiencies in all aspects of sales operations is the only way to free up resources for such development work.

Organization

The sales force may be structured by territory, by product, by market or customer, or by some combination of these.

Territorial structure

A territorial organization is very common, and is simple to understand; the country is divided up between sales people, and each has responsibility for everything in the allocated territory. Actually defining the territories is not quite so simple, as sales people not unnaturally want to see equality in both workload and sales potential. Customers and prospects are not always spread evenly across the map, and obviously travelling distances and times vary considerably between different parts of the country. Computer programs are available which can apply mathematical models to this problem, but experience and commonsense are also valuable inputs.

Market structure

Where a company has a wide range of products, and particularly where they are technical or specialized in nature, a territorial division may not be adequate: an individual simply cannot cope with the spread of specialized knowledge required. In these circumstances the total product range may be divided up, and a sales person or even separate sales force is allocated to each division. Against the gains from this arrangement must be set the disadvantage that several sales people from one manufacturer may call on the same customer, adding to costs and possibly causing confusion in customers' minds.

One way of overcoming this problem is to divide the sales force up by market or customer. Thus a manufacturer selling to several different industries would split the sales force along industry group lines; any one sales person would call only on companies of a similar type, and thus would be able to build up knowledge of the customer industry and the applications of the manufacturer's product range. In extreme cases, where there are a few very large customers, one or more sales people may be devoted to a single firm.

NAM structure

As has been mentioned above, this has happened in consumer goods, but it is also developing elsewhere. It is sometimes referred to as a National Account Manager system, as one national account manager is responsible for co-ordinating all the company's contacts with the customer; there may be other sales people calling on subsidiary parts of the customer, or there may not, but it is the NAM's job to manage the relationship with the customer and negotiate the major terms of the contract.

In large, complex suppliers, the sales force structure may be organized according to more than one of the arrangements outlined – for example, product type within territory. The more complex the structure, the greater the need for co-ordination (and, for large and important customers, for a NAM).

Telephone selling

Telephone selling has already been described in the previous chapter, in the context of direct marketing. It straddles both fields, in the sense that it can be seen as a whole new strategy (it has its own name, 'telemarketing'), or as just another way of carrying out the personal selling function.

Certainly, cost pressures have meant that in many companies telephone sales people have replaced parts of the field sales force. This has happened in companies as diverse as oil suppliers and food manufacturers. Where much of the 'sales' function is in fact routine collection of orders on a regular basis (say weekly or monthly), then that can be carried out by telephone quite adequately and at lower cost. The huge growth in the use of telephone call centres, both for sales calls and for customer service, has produced a whole new industry. Some field sales people may be retained to continue customer relationship building, and to introduce new products, sell in major promotions, and generally carry out any tasks which cannot be done by telephone.

The Internet and e-CRM

The Internet has taken over some of the direct contact for many firms, and may be allied with a Web based CRM (customer relationship management) system, referred to as e-CRM. The need to maintain and develop the personal relationship means that humans should still be involved.

Sales force management

In many ways, the job of managing a sales force is exactly the same as that of managing any other function. The major difference is that the sales people are mainly working on their own out in the field rather than in the next office. Many sales representatives are doing a difficult job in trying circumstances; they must be accustomed to rebuffs and failure, and they need a special set of characteristics. Motivating and controlling them may therefore be a complex task.

One leading text on sales management lists no less than thirty facets of the sales manager's job:

1 Interviewing, selecting and recruiting sales [people]
2 Sales training and development
3 Remuneration of sales [people]
4 Sales [people's] expenses
5 Control of sales [people]
6 Training staff in telephone selling
7 Sales forecasting
8 Budgetary control
9 Profit improvement in selling
10 Marketing policy and profits
11 Sales manuals
12 Successful sales bulletins
13 Sales competitions

14 Sales conferences and meetings

15 Exhibition selling

16 Merchandising

17 Market research

18 Direct mailing

19 Public relations

20 Speaking in public

21 Letter writing

22 The use of consultancy organizations

23 The computer as a marketing tool

24 Human relations for management

25 Audio-visual training

26 Dealing with complaints

27 Diplomacy

28 Personal presentations

29 Product launches

30 Quotations

(Strafford and Grant 1987)

Which of these fall into the job description of any single sales manager will of course vary according to the size and type of firm. Some of the tasks seem to stray into the marketing area, but in many firms, particularly smaller and medium-sized ones, the sales manager is probably the marketing manager too. Sales automation software has helped to make many of the routine tasks simpler or more efficient (see, for example, www.epicor.co.uk/products).

Some of the areas of responsibility are certainly common to any manager; planning, organizing, motivating, communicating, controlling, and so on – all these are basic to all management jobs, and are covered in detail in other courses and books. Here we will comment briefly on some of the areas specific to sales management.

Recruitment and training

Given that sales people are seen to require special characteristics, recruitment and training loom larger in sales management than in some other functions. The nature of the sales function covers a wide range of situations, and it is impossible to specify what makes a good sales person. Every sales manager will have his or her own recipe. Sales people need product knowledge and selling skills; the balance between the two will vary with the nature of the firm and its products and markets. Most sales people believe that it is better to take someone with the right general characteristics (personality, motivation, character) and to train them in both selling and product knowledge, rather than relying on years of experience of the particular products. Given the choice, they would take someone with proven selling skills and give them the product knowledge, rather than the other way round.

Our experience tells us that most industrial companies would benefit considerably by recruiting money-motivated, successful, well-trained salesmen with insurance or photocopying experience.

(Strafford and Grant 1987)

Training will concentrate on the two areas – product knowledge and selling skills – but these days the changing role of the sales force discussed earlier will mean that negotiation skills may be as important as old 'hard-sell' techniques. Where national account managers or other senior sales staff are carrying a substantial responsibility for the relationship with a major customer, they may need further upgrading of management knowledge and skills (for example in finance and accounting, marketing and business strategy, or planning techniques).

Target-setting

The setting of objectives (targets or budgets), and the control of operations through the year, are likely to feature more strongly in sales than elsewhere. As is discussed later (in Chapter 18), the setting of targets is a sensitive matter in sales and marketing. Although it is easy to try to set a low target, so that later performance looks good, experience suggests that sales people are much more likely to set very ambitious goals for themselves. A balance must be struck between what will stretch people and what is achievable. As the sales people's remuneration is often linked to the achievement of targets, and their motivation is closely linked to both, target-setting is crucial. Sales managers must try to ensure that they have a significant influence on sales targets, rather than having them sent down from above. When that happens, and the targets are seen to be impossible (and this does occur, even in well-known and apparently well-run companies), the effect is very demotivating.

Remuneration

The question of remuneration is also different in sales from elsewhere. Sales people may be paid a straight salary, a commission, a bonus, or some combination of the three. A straight salary is paid when the sales function is solely representative, when the sale process is long and complex, and when a particular sale cannot be attributed to an individual sales person; a fully salaried sales force represents a high fixed cost compared with some other arrangements. Where sales may result from the efforts of a team, then a bonus may be paid to all the team members when certain targets are reached (a bonus is usually a fixed amount, and a commission a percentage of sales). Commission is usually regarded as a major motivator; it may vary from a low to a high percentage, account for more or less of the total remuneration package. The greater the effect the individual's efforts may have on the probability of a sale, the larger the commission element may be. On the other hand, the larger the commission element, the more the sales person will concentrate solely on getting sales, rather than other tasks such as service or relationship building. The package adopted must therefore be tailored to the nature of the sales force's overall function. Commission-only sales forces do exist, and represent the lowest fixed cost possible; the commission rate, on the other hand, needs to be reasonably high so as to allow sales people to earn a living, and this will be reflected in variable cost. Commission-only sales forces frequently have a very high staff turnover, as many people cannot cope with the nature of the job; the approach is therefore applicable only in situations where either little specialist knowledge is needed, or brief training can bring entrants up to speed quickly.

Motivation

As mentioned earlier, motivation may be a particular problem for a sales manager, since the staff are mainly travelling and selling; some sales people work almost entirely from home, communicating with head office by post and telephone, or by computer. Though money is a motivator, and the remuneration scheme very important, sales people also need other forms of support. The job itself should be interesting, giving the individual responsibility wherever possible. Achievement should be recognized in ways other than just money; although some of the more extrovert manifestations of American sales culture seem alien to the UK, they represent a real attempt to give recognition where it is due. Published league tables, Sales Person of the Month, prizes, pins and badges, all may be appropriate in the right culture. If they are thought inappropriate, the sales manager must find other ways of communicating individually to staff.

Key learning points

- Personal selling is very important in many companies, especially when little is spent on advertising.
- The role and size of the sales force in consumer goods manufacturers have changed dramatically. Sales forces are now much smaller, and concentrate on high-level negotiations, and managing the relationship with major retailers.
- All sales forces have a number of tasks: to communicate (information etc.); to sell; to service (deal with queries etc.); to maintain and develop the relationship; to feed back information; to find new customers and opportunities.
- The main decisions to be made about the sales force concern its size, allocation and organization.
- Sales force management has many features common to any management position, but also has some unique characteristics.

Further reading

Donaldson, B. (1998) *Sales Management: Theory and Practice*, 2nd edition, Basingstoke: Macmillan.
Stevens, M. (1991) *Handbook of Telemarketing: Strategies for Implementation and Management*, London: Kogan Page.

Case study: Broxton's

Dick Stephens is wondering what to do first. He has recently been promoted to general sales manager of the frozen foods manufacturer, Broxtons. The product range includes vegetables, fish, prepared meats and ready meals. They are sold direct to retailers, and through wholesalers and cash-and-carry outlets. They also sell to institutional buyers, which is where Dick has been working for the last few years. The company makes mainly branded products, but also makes some own-label brands for retailers.

Broxtons' sales force numbers 200 full-time sales people and a varying number of merchandisers. The average age of the full-time representatives is almost fifty, and they have received little formal training. Some redundancies were declared last year, including the previous general sales manager, and morale is low. Total sales have been falling as retailers' brands have taken an increasing share of the market.

Dick's brief is to recover sales volume and to make cost savings of 20 per cent within two years.

Questions

1 Recommend what actions Dick should take in the first three months, and over the next year.

2 Is the brief reasonable? What factors would help to make it achievable, and to hinder it?

3 Could the sales effort of your own organization be made more efficient? More effective?

| Distribution

Channel types and functions

Every manufacturer needs to distribute its products to customers and/or consumers. Some do this directly: an industrial manufacturer with a small number of customers, or a supplier of components to a larger manufacturer, a very few manufacturers of consumer goods (such as Avon, which sells and distributes cosmetics directly to buyers in their homes); Dell has had enormous success in selling computers direct to both businesses and consumers. The great majority of firms, however, use intermediaries. There may be one or more levels between manufacturer and customer or consumer:

- **One level** Manufacturer-retailer-consumer, or manufacturer-distributor-industrial buyer
- **Two levels** Manufacturer-wholesaler-retailer-consumer, or manufacturer-agent-distributor-buyer
- **Three levels** Manufacturer-wholesaler-jobber-retailer-consumer.

Functions of intermediaries

The economic reason for the existence of intermediaries is that it is more efficient. If every manufacturer in a market were distributing separately to every buyer, the numbers of channels of communication would be enormous; the interposition of a distributor cuts down those numbers drastically.

There are many different functions performed by channel members:

- **Physical distribution**   The transport and storage of goods.
- **Matching**   Making available the assortment of goods and services desired by the channel member's customers.
- **Time and place**   Making those available at the time and in the place desired by customers and consumers.
- **Finance**   Financing all the above.
- **Transferring title**   Ensuring that legal ownership passes to the final buyer.
- **Risk-taking**   Bearing part of the risk inherent in business.
- **Research and prospecting**   Finding out what potential buyers want.
- **Promotion and selling**   Persuading potential buyers to buy.
- **Service**   Pre- and after-sales service.
- **Support services**   Insurance, documentation, management.

In any given industry, these functions may be carried out by manufacturers themselves, by various types of intermediary, and by external agencies (for example the financing, insurance and some aspects of promotion will be done by firms outside the industry). Within each industry there is likely to be an established pattern of distribution, with recognized channel members carrying out the functions traditionally allotted to them; but these patterns may vary from industry to industry.

Channel structures

Structures also change over time. For instance, there has been a growth in what are called 'vertical marketing systems', in which there is a greater degree of control between the different levels of the system than in a conventional system in which all members are independent businesses making their own decisions. A vertical marketing system may reflect vertical integration by a manufacturer (such as brewers in Britain owning the pub outlets). Another form is the contractual system in which there are legal ties between channel members, such as wholesaler–retailer voluntary (symbol) chains. Finally there are franchise systems, which cover, for instance, Coca-Cola's franchised bottlers, motor manufacturers' franchised dealers, and a wide variety of businesses from fast-food outlets through hotels to car hire and print shops. (For a fuller discussion, see Kotler 2000.)

Generally, it is best to assume that each channel member is an independent business trying to survive and make a profit, with its own objectives and strategy. Using Porter's notion of a value chain (Porter 1985), it is helpful to think of the whole chain from raw materials through components and finished products to distributors and final consumers as one value chain system. Many of the issues revolve round how the total value created by the system is divided between the members. Every member is trying to optimize the way they perform the activities within their part of the chain, and sell on at a price which optimizes their margin. Competitive forces and the structure of the industry will help determine how successful each is.

However fragmented or integrated the system is, the positive way forward for any member is to look on it as a symbiotic system in which all members live together. An approach in which the suppliers and distributors are seen as partners or allies, rather than enemies, must be fruitful.

Channel strategy: selection and management

There are two problems in talking of channel strategy. One is that, as mentioned above, there is almost certainly an existing structure in the industry, and an established way in which the company distributes its products. The second is that distribution is probably dealt with by several different people in the firm – production, physical distribution, marketing, sales, and finance will all have some contact with distributors, and may make decisions without consulting colleagues.

Selection of strategy

As to the first problem, there is a case for reviewing an established strategy. General Motors set up an entirely new chain of distributors for its new Saturn models, quite separate from the existing one; in the UK, Daewoo set up its own chain of outlets. There are also opportunities when expanding into new territories or new markets to look afresh at channel choice.

- The first criterion for choosing a distributor is that it should provide access to your target customers/consumers. Referring back to the overall marketing strategy, are you aiming for a mass market, or for defined segments? What are the characteristics of your target buyers, compared with the profile of the distributor?

  —A mass market strategy (for snack products, disposable pens, cigarettes, etc.) demands distribution in every possible outlet.

  —A premium brand aimed at the top end of the market (expensive perfumes, premium cognacs) should be available only in stores which contribute to the exclusive image and which are patronized by the wealthy potential buyers (though see the discussion in Chapter 11 on control).

  —In between, there is a range of more or less selective channel strategies, depending on the product and its positioning.

- A second consideration is the level of service needed to support the product. In both consumer and industrial markets, products which demand a high level of service will be stocked only by those distributors who can provide it to the manufacturer's (and customer's) satisfaction.

- Third, the financial criterion: how profitable to you would each distributor be? There may be a trade-off between volume and margin, but in principle each distributor should offer an acceptable profit overall.

If there is a choice between apparently similar channel members (for example agents or wholesalers), then apart from access to target customers, the criteria must be the same as would apply in choosing any business partner: size, financial soundness, reputation, management competence, services offered.

Of particular interest, given that any distributor will be selling your competitors' product as well as your own, is commitment: how much effort will they put behind your products? This will partly refer back to how good your products are, their pricing and what advertising support you are giving them, and partly to the terms negotiated with the distributor.

It is probably better in the long run to rely on high-quality products and a supportive relationship, than on offering a better margin than competitors: every lowering of manufacturers' selling price comes straight off your bottom line, for every product sold.

Channel management

Managing channel members, as previous discussion will have suggested, is a matter of managing the relationship so that both partners see that they are gaining from it. It is clearly helpful to define precisely what is expected of each partner, and to set objectives for the distributor and for yourself. This is the area often referred to as 'customer service'; unfortunately, the term is used differently by different companies, sometimes narrowly to refer to measurable actions performed by the manufacturer in providing supply of the product, at other times to refer to the whole relationship or to trade marketing (see section below on coping with retailer power).

Components of customer service

One author, using the narrower definition, suggests the following components of customer service for a manufacturer dealing with retailers:

- Frequency of delivery
- Time from order to delivery
- Reliability of delivery
- Emergency deliveries when required
- Stock availability and continuity of supply
- Orders filled completely
- Advice on non-availability
- Convenience of placing order
- Acknowledgment of order
- Accuracy of invoices
- Quality of sales representation
- Regular calls by sales representatives
- Manufacturer monitoring of retail stock levels
- Credit terms offered
- Customer query handling
- Quality of outer packaging
- Well-stacked pallets

- Easy-to-read use-by dates on outers
- Quality of inner package for in-store handling and display
- Consults on new product/package development
- Reviews product range regularly
- Co-ordination between production, distribution and marketing.

(McDonald 1999)

This list, it should be noted, refers only to what the supplier will do for the retailer, and reflects the balance of power discussed in the next section. It is a useful start, but there should equally be a list of what the retailer will do for the supplier. This would in some ways be a mirror image of the supplier's service, but would concern itself much more with the stocking, handling and display of products. Making clear requests, consulting on any changes required, and not making unreasonable demands, would all be welcome to suppliers, though it is not certain that retailers would be willing to promise them. Distributors in other industries are much more likely to see that they have duties to suppliers as well as to customers.

If one defines customer service from the point of view of the distributor's customers (who may be other firms, or consumers), then it becomes easier to see what a supplier might ask. Consumers want availability of brands, a choice of brands and varieties, quality and freshness (or up-to-dateness), value for money in pricing, convenience, and service (advice, finance, delivery, after-sales back-up, or whatever is appropriate). In some fields, they may want a pleasant shopping experience; in others, some may want the lowest prices possible, for which they will trade off other elements such as range of choice or ambience. In any field it seems reasonable to demand agreed levels of stocking and availability; where appropriate, as in many industrial markets, it would be possible to agree service levels. In any market, the amount and nature of promotional support to be given by each partner should be agreed.

Once objectives are agreed, their achievement should be monitored. Those objectives which can be measured should be: items such as timing and reliability of deliveries, percentage of orders correctly filled, level of stock-outs, average facings and display given, can all be measured and compared on a regular basis with targets. These and other, more qualitative elements, can be reviewed annually.

To return to an earlier point, the manufacturer may be locked into an existing distribution system, or may have a free choice of channels. Either way, channel choice is a strategic decision: it involves a long-term commitment which cannot be changed quickly. Once the decision is made (or the current situation accepted if there is no alternative), it is up to the manufacturer to make the best of the relationship through careful management. It need not be a zero sum game, with gains for one party being reflected inevitably in losses for the other. With luck and good management, it can become a win-win situation.

The importance of distribution suggests (again to reiterate an earlier point) that companies should take it more seriously as a management task, and should integrate the various elements currently dealt with separately; only then can a strategic view be taken and effective action planned and carried out.

Coping with retailer power: strategic implications for manufacturers

The retailing revolution

Although retailing, like all human institutions, is always changing, the 1980s and 1990s seemed to experience a particularly rapid development; many talked of a 'retailing revolution'. The most noticeable aspects of this change were the growth of very large outlets in several fields (supermarkets and superstores, DIY, electrical, furniture etc.); targeted 'life style' chains (e.g. Next); the decline of traditional department stores and the rise of galleria concepts; the spread of out-of-town shopping centres or malls in towns and cities; the appearance of new convenience stores, for example on petrol stations; extended opening hours, including Sunday trading; and a general increase in the excitement levels and profiles of retailers. There were also technological developments, discussed below, which will have a profound impact.

Much of the excitement and growth reflected a general rise in economic activity and prosperity: people had more money and were willing to spend it. This changed dramatically in the early 1990s, as most industrialized economies slowed or declined. Some of the most prominent retailers of the 1980s came to grief, and few made anything like the profits they once did. The later 1990s saw recovery for many, but at the turn of the century some established names, such as Marks & Spencer, were in deep trouble, while newcomers such as Matalan sprang to prominence. From a manufacturer's point of view, however, this is not the major change, or the main issue.

For marketing people, the major change is the swing in the balance of power between manufacturers and retailers. This has been caused by the rise of multiples which have gained increasing market share at the expense of independent retailers. Taking the UK, the top four supermarket multiples (Tesco, Sainsbury's, Asda and Safeway) have over half the packaged grocery market between them; their share is still increasing. The picture is similar in other European countries. In other sectors, the share of multiples varies from a fifth to over four-fifths. Very large retailers such as Boots or WHSmith have huge shares of some product fields. These shares give the retailers enormous buying power.

Allied to this growth has been an increase in the sophistication of management. Whereas some years ago the calibre of managers in retailing was not as high as in the large manufacturers, this has changed; buying and marketing groups in retailers are well qualified, well trained and highly motivated; operations management is extremely good, producing high service levels at low costs. Retailers have unparalleled access to detailed data from their scanning systems and loyalty cards.

Part of this process has been the centralization of buying decisions. Sophisticated buying groups, with huge volume to give them power and good back-up to help with analysis, can make better deals than individual store managers. While not all multiples practise central buying, and others give at least some discretion to local managers, the trend is very much to central decision-making.

The manufacturer–retailer relationship

All this has completely changed the relationship between manufacturers and retailers. Some years ago, the major consumer goods manufacturers looked on retailers as merely the distribution channel. Manufacturers owned the brands, knew all about consumers, created new products, spent large sums on advertising to pull brands through the distribution chain. They decided what promotions to run when, and told the retailers what they had to do.

Now the situation is almost reversed. A large multiple will account for a much bigger proportion of any supplier's total sales than the other way round ('I account for 15 per cent of your business, you account for 5 per cent of mine: let's talk terms'). The retailers have complete control over their space, for which there is severe competition; they sell it dearly. The margins demanded by retailers have increased, either overtly or in the form of volume discounts, promotional allowances, overriders, or a variety of other terms which all involve the manufacturer giving more money. Some retailers claim that they should be controlling the marketing, since they know the consumers better, and are more efficient at putting brands on the shelves than manufacturers.

All this has been a culture shock for some managers in manufacturing firms, and they have been slow to adapt. The old ways of doing business are no longer adequate; new strategies and forms of organization are needed.

Basically this means applying marketing principles to customers as well as to consumers. This author has suggested a checklist of steps that manufacturers should take in adapting to the new situation. Apart from understanding consumers, the forces driving the market, and competitors, you must:

- **Understand your customers** Who they are, what their strategies are, where your brands fit within those strategies, what their problems and opportunities are and how you can help them.

- **Build an information system** This will include information on customers and competitors. Because of the demands of the new customer relationships, it will also include internal cost data from manufacturing and distribution, perhaps in new forms; it should include customer profitability data.

- **Analyse your brand portfolio** Be realistic about the future of each of your brands, given the data on consumers, customers and competitors you have gathered. Which will definitely survive as major brands, which will need a lot of remedial help, which are in danger? Check that you will generate the cash necessary to support the brands in the way that will be needed.

- **Develop a brand strategy** Decide on the actions needed over the next few years to achieve your objectives; decide on whether or not to make retailers' brands.

- **Develop a customer strategy** Take a stance on whether you will be a strong independent, a partner, or a responsive supplier. Target the major customer groups and accounts, deciding on a strategy for each.

- **Fix clear objectives for brands and customers** Decide what is needed to achieve your objectives, set budgets and allocate responsibility for decisions on spending. Make people accountable.

- **Think customers** Make sure that customer thinking penetrates deeply into the company, into all the departments whose activities do affect the relationship even if they are not yet aware of it.

- **Rethink your organizational structure** Make sure that your structure helps you to deliver the information and actions needed to implement your strategies. List the tasks that relate to customers and allocate them to those best able to carry them out (not necessarily those whose job it has traditionally been).

- **Build business teams** Make sure that everyone who contributes to the total delivery of a brand to customers and consumers is involved. Make sure that information flows within the team, so that action can be co-ordinated.

- **Implement a training programme** Ensure that NAMs and others dealing with customers are fully trained in Direct Product Profitability and space management systems (see below), and in negotiation skills. Use training to implant customer thinking and build teams.

- **Review recruitment and selection policies** Decide what sort of people are going to be needed, not just today but in the future in your new organization. Plan to have them available and prepared.

(Randall 1994: 171)

The point is that manufacturers must see retailers as partners, and be proactive in looking for ways of working with them, however strange this may seem.

Of course, there will never be a full and true partnership, since the two parties are competing for a share of the value added available. Further, some retailers are competing directly with manufacturers through their own-label brands. In such circumstances, there will necessarily be the need to maintain arm's-length dealing, at least in some areas. Greater co-operation in general can only be good for both. (ECR, or Efficient Consumer Response, is an attempt to get all the parties in the grocery industry to work together; it has had some success in both North America and Europe.)

Two things may be said in conclusion:

1 Manufacturers who succeed in serving their customers better than competitors will gain a competitive advantage.

2 Those who ignore the new demands of customers will suffer.

Impact of new technology on retailing

All the examples in this section are taken from Randall (1994) Chapter 5, to which readers are referred for a fuller discussion. While references here are mainly to retailers, many of the principles apply equally to wholesalers and other distributors.

Information technology has had just as much impact in retailing as elsewhere in business; some of it is visible, but much that is extremely important is hidden. Since development is so rapid, some of the applications described here will have been overtaken by events within a year or so. Quite how some developments will work out is not yet clear;

but the main lines are well established. The major application areas will be described briefly.

EPOS and scanning

Most people are familiar with electronic point of sale (EPOS), particularly when allied to scanning. Scanning equipment uses a window, wand or gun to capture electronically the data recorded on each item by bar codes. The bar codes are a common system agreed by the Article Numbering Association, and now appear on outers and inner packs used by wholesalers and cash-and-carry outlets. Although scanning is not a necessary part of EPOS, it obviously speeds up transactions. With EPOS, the till becomes in effect a computer terminal, and every transaction is recorded in a back-office computer. This local computer can be downloaded daily to a central headquarters as well as being used for local applications. EPOS systems are now installed in a very wide variety of retail and wholesale outlets.

It can readily be seen that EPOS systems produce enormous amounts of data, and potentially very valuable information. They can be linked to stock control in real time, and in more advanced applications fed directly into reordering programmes. They provide detailed feedback on sales of every item, allowing extremely detailed and precise measurement of sales patterns and the effects of price changes, promotions and indeed any experimental variable.

This information is very useful to the retailers, and of great interest to manufacturers too. It is another sign of the swing in the balance of power that retailers now have much more information (of one sort, anyway) than manufacturers. Some retailers sell their data, and the ideal position would be for a central market research firm to set up a syndicated system for each major market. There are some moves in that direction, but it seems likely that there will always be some retailers who refuse to co-operate, thus limiting the usefulness of the aggregated data.

EPOS systems do have some drawbacks, in that they may cause extra work in bringing in any changes, such as promotions; this may make retailers even more reluctant to accept what their suppliers want them to do, or may make them charge even more for the service. On the other hand, some forms of promotion, such as 'four for the price of three' or BOGOFs (buy one, get one free) are much easier, as they can be programmed into the system; the till will count the items, no matter the order in which they appear.

EDI and other acronyms

Electronic Data Interchange (EDI) allows a retailer and manufacturer to link their computers directly, allowing rapid communication and, it is hoped, fewer errors. Many firms now use EDI for orders, and some are using it for invoicing and queries. Eventually payment will be made this way too. There are cost savings potentially available to both partners, and possibly some savings in stock levels. It is, moreover, an excellent example of partnership between manufacturers and retailers; some who have experienced it have found that it generated greater co-operation throughout the trade marketing area.

Clearly a problem in any system is getting computer systems to talk to each other. The Article Numbering Association has led the way in introducing TRADA-COMS, a procedure for structuring data and messages so that they can be exchanged between any system. A further development is TRADANET, which is an electronic mailbox that allows members to deliver and collect messages between them and their trading partners in complete security.

There are still many problems to be worked out, but the direction is clear. It is very much in the interest of manufacturers to be aware of developments so that they can prepare their own systems, and ensure that they are not unwittingly causing problems to their customers.

The Internet and extranets

EDI is quite expensive, and using an extranet is simpler and more flexible. This will probably take over entirely from EDI in due course.

Direct product profitability (DPP)

DPP is really management accounting applied to products moving through the distribution system. Traditionally, both manufacturers and retailers have concentrated on the gross margin (the difference between retail selling price and manufacturer's selling price). DPP looks at all the costs involved in moving the product through transport, warehousing, handling and storage in the shop. The differing nature of products (size, shape, density), the width and depth of the range (number of sizes, flavours, etc.), the selling characteristics (high or low turnover) will all affect DPP in addition to the margin and volume. Products with identical gross margin may turn out to have different DPP. A standard model produced by the Institute of Grocery Distribution is widely used in the UK.

Many manufacturers now use DPP calculations routinely to check whether there are any negatives for the retailers in changes they may be considering. They will tell their customers if there is a good story ('This packaging change enhances your DPP by so many per cent'); sometimes, they will make changes specifically for DPP reasons, for example by redesigning an inefficient package – but they must be careful not to damage the brand's appeal to consumers.

So far, DPP seems not to be used in negotiations, as retail buyers' performance is still measured on gross margin, but this may change. As with EDI and extranets, DPP may be an area in which the partners can work together to their mutual benefit.

Space management systems

The availability of good data and cheap computing power has led to space management models, which try to help retailers make the complex decisions about precisely what products to stock, where, and in what quantities. Essentially, the model takes a category (often one fixture or bay of shelving) and examines the effect on overall sales and profit of different ways of filling the shelves. Inputs are stock level required, policy decisions (e.g. no pack weighing more than 5 kg above shoulder height), the effect of different shelf position on sales (using judgement or scanning data), and product and margin data. The model ranks brands according to the criterion selected (sales, gross profit, or some more complex profit return figure); when space is limited (which it always is), the lowest-ranked brands drop off the bottom of the list when capacity is reached.

Space management systems can evaluate particular layouts or search for an optimum. The output is in the form of planograms (a drawing of the proposed shelf layout) and tables of detailed statistics. Current developments will allow such single-store category applications to be aggregated to look at all the stores in a multiple.

The models are obviously of use to retailers. Manufacturers also use them to check the effect of proposed pack changes or the introduction of new varieties and new brands. Clearly, when space is at a premium, and manufacturers are fighting for what they see as adequate display of their brands, it is vitally important for them to see things from the retailers' point of view. The output of space management systems will therefore continue to be used, hopefully in a positive way by both partners; at worst, manufacturers must be prepared with defensive arguments.

The future

At present, all the systems described are separate. One future development must be towards greater integration. One package which claims to integrate accounting and merchandise control offers:

- links to EPOS and scanning
- inventory and sales performance by category
- price ticket generation
- price change control
- open-to-buy forecasting and planning
- store transfers
- back-door control
- invoicing and cash control
- salesperson performance control.

Other developments include greater automation within shops, and teleshopping, mentioned in a previous chapter. The introduction of smart cards may allow the development of direct marketing by retailers, as they will be able to build up a database of individuals' purchasing from their EPOS system and link it to addresses. Already some controlled experiments in the USA allow the effects of marketing mix elements to be measured in a test town using this methodology.

The message for all those marketing to and through retailers is that they must be aware of developments, perhaps even slightly ahead of their customers in understanding the implications of these messages, and ready to use them in serving their customers better while meeting their own objectives.

The impact of the Internet on distribution

As we have seen, the Internet offers great opportunities for channel partners to communicate with each other. In theory, it will enormously improve the chances of optimizing the flow of information and goods through the entire chain. A consumer order or purchase could, in this ideal world, be transmitted instantaneously up the chain, to the intermediaries, their suppliers, and those who supply them (with components and raw materials, for example). Stock levels would fall throughout the system and efficiency would rise, giving better customer service, and more profit to be shared by the partners. The theory has yet to be fully realized in practice, and there are many problems in implementation, but there is no doubt that this is the area in which the Internet will produce huge and lasting change. All participants in the chain should be aware of this, and working to achieve the potential rewards.

There is, however, another effect. Because the Internet offers another, and very direct, channel to customers, many firms are tempted to use it. Like any direct channel, it offers the chance to cut out the intermediary's margin and keep it for yourself. This, of course, raises the old problem of channel conflict: your existing channel partners will not be pleased at losing this business, and may react by refusing to handle your products. When Compaq tried to emulate Dell in selling direct, they antagonized their existing dealers, as had tour operators in the 'old' economy in trying to bypass travel agents.

The answer is to work towards a solution that embraces the technology and its benefits, but shares them with all the partners. Some high-tech firms are doing this already. National Semiconductor offers all participants a very rich e-commerce site, with detailed technical information available to end-users. Online purchasing is available, but only of excess stock. Distributors initially experienced 'an explosion of emotion' when this was announced, but were mollified when they understood more fully. Moreover, they now realize that they receive very high-quality leads from the company (National Semiconductor passes 3,000 leads a day to its distributors; Andersen 2000). This 'Collaborative e-Commerce' is a promising way forward. The Internet enables the creation of very rich information and communication communities, in which all partners can share. End-users can gain both information and more choice and flexibility. Distributors can enhance their relationships with both suppliers and customers.

Key learning points

- **All manufacturers need to distribute their products, and most use intermediaries.**
- **The number of tasks to be carried out by the channels of distribution is large, and in different industries these may be split in various ways between different channel members.**
- **Each channel member should be understood as an individual business with its own objectives and strategy, but working in a symbiotic system in which members depend on each other.**
- **The relationship between supplier and distributor should be managed so that both gain from it.**
- **The growth of retailer multiples with huge buying power has major strategic implications for manufacturers.**
- **Manufacturers need to understand their retailer customers, analyse their own brand portfolio, develop a strategy towards their customers, and change their organization structure and methods of operation.**
- **The Internet will play an increasingly important role in supply chain management.**

Further reading

Berman, B. (1996) *Marketing Channels*, New York: Wiley.
Randall, G. (1994) *Trade Marketing Strategies*, Oxford: Heinemann.

Case study: Alcohols Unlimited 2

Alcohols Unlimited, described in the case study at the end of Chapter 12, distributes its products through:

■ multiple wine merchants (such as Bottoms Up);
■ specialist wine merchants;
■ specialist wholesalers;
■ grocery wholesalers and cash-and-carry outlets;
■ supermarket multiples.

James Rudd has asked his assistant, Gill Griffin, to work out how to distribute 'Luna', the new drink. Gill is not sure how many of the existing outlets are suitable, or which ones will accept the product. She knows that the prices demanded by the supermarket multiples are always very keen; but while better margins may be obtainable in multiple wine merchants, some of them are controlled by major brewers, and may resist AU's product. She has decided to visit a sample of the different outlets to see what sort of ambience they provide, what sort of customers they attract, and what competitive products are stocked.

Questions

1 Evaluate the various channel options open to AU, and recommend a policy.
2 Follow Gill's example, and visit a sample of outlets. What are your conclusions? Do they affect your recommendation in question 1?

Marketing of services

Difference between services and products

Services now account for the majority of the economic activities of most industrialized countries. The marketing literature, however, concentrated for many years almost entirely on physical products. Obviously this is because that is where marketing as a separate function developed earliest, and where it has been most intensively applied, particularly in the field of fast-moving consumer goods. As both academics and practitioners have turned their attention to the increasingly important services markets, the question has been debated, 'How different actually are services?'

When we examine them, we can see that there is not such a clear-cut line between services and products as might be thought. As we have seen, many products in fact include large elements of service in their delivery. Looked at from the buyer's point of view, services may form a vital part of the total bundle of benefits which is sought, particularly in industrial markets.

Equally, many services include a large contribution from hardware: hotels, airlines, fast food outlets are all classed as services, but the physical elements in the offering are a very large part of what customers buy. What is different is that as buyers we do not receive ownership of the physical elements of a service, but merely rent them for a period. Otherwise, it seems that there is a spectrum of product–service offerings, in which the physical element plays a decreasing role from one end to the other.

That is one of the ways in which services can be classified. Classification is a helpful approach, since the range of services is so wide that generalizations about them may become vague. Many classification schemes have been put forward. One of the more useful is based on the following questions:

1 What is the nature of the service act?

2 What type of relationship does the service organization have with its customers?

3 How much room is there for customization and judgement on the part of the service provider?

4 What is the nature of demand and supply for the service?

5 How is the service delivered?

(Lovelock 1983)

For each of these questions, Lovelock sets up a matrix to classify services, and draws insights for marketing. An example is shown in Figure 15.1.

If customers have to be personally present for the delivery of the service, location and convenience become important, and the physical surroundings play a large part. If the transaction is at arm's length, the 'factory' is never seen by the customer, and only its efficiency in delivering output is important. This and all the classification schemes help to focus managers' minds on the nature of the process; they may help to pinpoint areas of dissatisfaction and guide the search for improvements.

	Who or what is the direct recipient of the service?	
	People	*Things*
What is the nature of the service act? *Tangible Actions*	Services directed at people's bodies: • health care • passenger transportation • beauty salons • exercise clinics • restaurants • haircutting	Services directed at goods and other physical possessions: • freight transportation • industrial equipment repair and maintenance • janitorial services • laundry and dry cleaning • landscaping/lawn care • veterinary care
Intangible Actions	Services directed at people's minds: • education • broadcasting • information services • theatres • museums	Services directed at intangible assets: • banking • legal services • accounting • securities • insurance

Figure 15.1 Understanding the nature of the service act
Reprinted with permission from the *Journal of Marketing*, published by the American Marketing Association, C.H. Lovelock, 1983, vol. 47, Summer, pp. 9-20.

Characteristics of services

There is general agreement in the literature that the main characteristics of services are:

- Intangibility
- Inseparability
- Variability
- Perishability.

Intangibility

As we have seen, intangibility is relevant only to the pure service element; the hotel bed and the hamburger are very tangible. The problem of intangibility is that it is difficult to communicate and display exactly what the product is.

Inseparability

This refers to the fact that production and consumption of the service are inextricably intertwined. The implications of this are that the consumer is involved in production. Further, in many cases other consumers are also involved at the same time, as in most retailing situations. This may be a positive aspect of the benefits delivered (in a theatre or club), or it may be a potential negative aspect (waiting in queues at the post office). Whether the buyer is physically present or not, the product comes into existence only when it is bought; it cannot be mass produced in advance (although the physical components may be, to some extent).

Variability

Variability (often called heterogeneity in textbooks) is a result of the fact that services are usually delivered by human beings, whose performance is necessarily variable; quality control is extremely difficult.

Perishability

This means that the service cannot be stockpiled. If a seat is unfilled when the plane leaves or the play starts, it cannot be kept and sold the next day or next week; that revenue is lost for ever. In some cases, such as insurance or banking, it could be argued that potential stocks remain, in the sense that the service is there to be sold every day as long as underwriting or loan capacity exists. Retailers can keep stocks of products for the duration of their shelf-life – a day for fresh produce, several months for clothes, longer still for furniture. Most services, however, are clearly time-dependent in a way that physical products are not.

Implications for marketing

Intangibility and variability

A central problem in marketing services is the intangibility and variability of the product. Although it is not always easy to measure exactly what people want from a physical product, and what benefits they gain from it, at least the physical product itself can be seen, felt, used. We know that quality control in the factory can ensure that within very narrow limits the product will always be the same, and that a bar of soap bought in one shop will be the same as one bought in another shop at a different time in a completely different part of the country. That is not true for what has been called 'the service experience', however, since every experience is different.

One answer to that is to try to industrialize the service, as recommended early on by Levitt (1972). There are some very successful examples of this approach, notably the McDonald's hamburger chain. All hardware and materials can be standardized, as can the processes of production. Policies and rules can be set down for every action taken by the personnel in delivering the service, and performance measures can be used to control quality.

Where service operations can be standardized, this approach can lead to great efficiencies as well as to control over variability.

Many service organizations will react against the concept, sometimes seeing it as the negation of the very idea of service. The opposite extreme is customization – producing a different service for every customer. Some professional firms such as lawyers would claim to offer this, but even they have some aspects of service which can be standardized, as the entry of new competitors into the conveyancing market has shown.

Many if not most service providers could probably industrialize at least part of their operations, to the benefit of both themselves and their customers. This raises the question which will always be central to the delivery of services: how do you standardize what staff do, while leaving them pride and responsibility in the job?

The whole direction of most organizational development today is towards giving individuals greater responsibility and control over their job – empowering them, to use the jargon. There will be a fine balance, particularly when the drive of operations is towards greater efficiency while the marketing department may be trying to achieve greater customer satisfaction (i.e. responsiveness). One answer is to try to ensure standardization and quality control of the basic elements of the service, while allowing individual freedom to go beyond what is expected, to try to 'delight' the customer (the latest idea being that it is not enough in this highly competitive world to satisfy customers, we must delight them). Some advertising for international hotel chains which uses examples of how staff went beyond the call of duty to help a client show this approach.

This leads on to two other connected issues: how to communicate the benefits of your service brand, and the expectations gap.

Communicating the brand benefits

Earlier chapters showed how difficult, but how necessary, it is to differentiate your brand from competitors' brands; with an intangible service, it is even more difficult. The idea that you should stress what is tangible leads to the sort of airline advertising which focuses on pretty stewardesses: perhaps unfortunate if the literal meaning of tangible is taken at face value, and anyway the subject of severe criticism from many quarters.

As with any brand, the main effort must be in the search for a real point of difference which will motivate buyers, which you can deliver (see below), and which is difficult for your competitors to copy. Almost everything in a service offering can be copied, as an idea cannot be patented; the very rapid spread of 'air miles' as a promotion to build loyalty is a good example. A pre-emptive claim, established in the minds of the target market, may work for some time at least, even if competitors can also deliver that benefit.

Some evidence suggests that personal experience and word-of-mouth are even more influential in services than in physical product purchasing. This would lead to attempts to stimulate word-of-mouth ('Tell your friends!'), and to the use in advertising of real or simulated recommendation.

If the service experience is central, this leads back again to the people who deliver it. The messages we receive as customers from an organization embrace all the communications: not just advertising, but the information contained in staff appearance and behaviour, and in the hardware – the premises, the decor, the cleanliness, the logo, the packaging, and so on.

That in turn leads on to the expectations gap.

The expectations gap

It is dangerous with any product to arouse expectations which experience of the product fails to fulfil. Given the variability in service quality, that danger is all the greater.

One model suggests that there are five expectations gaps:

Consumer expectation

Gap 1

Management perception of consumer expectation

Gap 2

Translation of perceptions into service quality specifications

Gap 3

Service delivery

Gap 4

External communications to consumers

Gap 5

Expected service

(Parasuraman *et al.* 1985)

It is clear that on the old 'Chinese whispers' principle, the potential for a wide gap to have opened up by the end of the line is very great. The more the people designing marketing campaigns and advertising are divorced from the actual delivery of the service, the greater the danger; this issue is returned to in the next section below.

A good example of the danger was a campaign launched some years ago by the British clearing banks. Having learned from research that most people were scared of their bank manager, they tried to overcome this by running a television campaign showing, in a humorous and friendly way ('The bank manager in your cupboard') how approachable these managers really were. Unfortunately, when customers went to see their bank manager, they found exactly the same person who had been there all along: perfectly polite, no doubt, but not able to deliver the service customers had been led to expect.

All communications must, therefore, be consistent with reality. They may certainly use emotional imagery as well as rational product differences, as long as the experience of the service matches the promise. The more tangible or measurable the promise can be made, the better.

Other elements of the marketing mix

Pricing

Pricing is generally thought to be problematic for services, given the difficulty consumers have in evaluating them. Many service providers seem to use a cost-plus approach; this at least ensures that all costs are covered. Parity with competitors, or positioning in relation to them, is another obvious way, and again seems to be widespread. Where the services are very similar to those of competitors, then some parity must be expected. The difficulty comes when there are differences between the product offerings. Consumers may not be able to articulate their judgement of the relative value of different services and service levels; sometimes only experimenting will give an answer, and that can be dangerous if too high a price is chosen. This is an area in which considerable further research is needed.

Distribution

Distribution may or may not be an issue. Where there are outlets, they are clearly important. They should be efficient, but they must also be consistent with the overall product and its desired image. It will be interesting to see, for example, if the new-style banks with open, modern layouts and decor affect consumers' perceptions of the service offered. Given the cost of retail outlets and staff, it is worth examining the extent to which some or all of the services could be delivered another way – by post, telephone or computer, for example. The First Direct banking service launched by Midland has no branches at all; all transactions are carried out over the telephone. This was the first sign of a clearing bank actually putting the marketing concept into practice (see below), by targeting a particular segment with a specific set of benefits. Whether this method of distribution is consistent with what consumers expect of a bank remains to be seen. The telephone and Internet banks that have sprung up have not always been as popular as their promoters hoped: many customers seem to like having a choice of channels – Internet, telephone *and* physical branch.

Positioning

Finally, the concept of positioning: there seems no reason why services cannot be positioned within a market just like physical products. Some hotel chains certainly have clear positioning, and even clear product portfolios: Novotel and Ibis, for example, are clearly positioned hotel brands. In these cases, where there appear to be real market segments which can be targeted with significantly different offerings, normal marketing techniques can be applied. It is more difficult when there is little differentiation between competitors – but that is equally true of product marketing.

Generally speaking, then, we can conclude that there are some crucial differences between the marketing of products and of services, but that the same basic principles apply. Providers must still strive to understand their customers and consumers, and to develop and deliver what they want better than competitors can. The elements of the mix are used in much the same way, and they must still be consistent, coherent, and targeted at the chosen segment.

Organizational issues

One organizational issue has already been touched on: the tension between efficiency and control on the one hand, and empowerment on the other. In some service companies, it is possible to imagine the whole staff as forming the marketing department: they each contribute, in some way, to the delivery of the service. It is for this reason that firms which want to improve their product often see training as part of the answer. British Airways' wholehearted commitment to service was demonstrated by putting every member of staff through a customer care programme. The results were perceptible by customers, and were reflected in winning ratings in customer surveys; this in turn helped to stimulate word-of-mouth, and contributed to the change in image which has helped BA to improve its financial performance significantly (unfortunately, BA later ruined this through heavy-handed management that led to damaging industrial disputes). It is important to realize, however, that training some staff is only part of the answer: the commitment must run right through the organization, from top to bottom.

British clearing banks were mentioned earlier. It is the author's personal view, as an outside observer and as a consumer of their services, that they still have not really taken on board the marketing concept. They have moved from the product-oriented stance they have had for most of their history towards a selling orientation; they have learned that they have a captive audience to whom to sell lots of other financial services, and they bombard us with glossy leaflets. They also spend money on television advertising campaigns, and they are spending more on revamping their premises to look more like estate agents. But has their basic attitude to delivering quality services to their customers really changed? There seems little evidence. They have had to respond to new competitors by offering interest on current accounts, they are finally using new technology to make some of our tasks as consumers easier, and in general their service has improved. Cost-cutting measures, however, often endanger the progress achieved (e.g. by closing branches).

This seems to be symptomatic of a general problem in service companies, that the marketing department is peripheral: it is in charge of producing the glossy communications, but not of deciding what the product portfolio should be.

In some ways it appears that the more successful a service company is, the more powerful its operations department becomes; marketing is then in danger of being merely the icing on the cake, and will lose any argument against operations or finance.

The situation is not dissimilar to that found in many industrial companies, and indeed to that prevalent in fast-moving consumer goods firms thirty years ago. However, it may be just a matter of time before services providers learn that marketing really does apply to them. Those who are first to embrace the concept fully, to implant it deep in their culture, will gain a competitive advantage.

The other organizational issue is that of coping with growth. Small firms, led by founders who keep a close eye on delivery and standards, grow. The larger they grow, the more the problem of quality control and standardization grows. The problems outlined earlier of control versus creativity looms larger. One answer, and one which seems to find an echo in other fields such as new product development, is to organize in small teams and push responsibility as far down the line as possible. What patently does not work is a huge bureaucracy of management and inspection. Another parallel which suggests itself is that of Japanese approaches to quality control: in Japan, there are no large teams of inspectors examining the final product and sending faulty ones back for expensive rectification; instead, each team of workers is responsible for the quality which leaves its work-station.

For large organizations, the trick must be to find the balance between a minimum of rules (to produce a service which is recognizably our brand) while leaving room for individuals to motivate themselves in the pursuit of quality.

Key learning points

- Services now account for the majority of economic activities in most industrialized countries. The line between manufactured products and services is not clear cut. Services cover a wide range, but can be classified in various ways.
- Services are characterized by intangibility, inseparability, heterogeneity (or variability) and perishability. Each has implications for marketing.
- The way each of the elements of the marketing mix may be applied to services is discussed.
- There is often a tension between efficiency and control on the one hand, and empowerment of staff on the other.
- Superficial adoption of a 'customer care' approach will not work if commitment to customer service does not run deeply throughout the organization.
- There is a danger of creating an expectations gap between what marketing communications promise and what the service actually delivers.

Further reading

Hoffman, K.D. and Bateson, J.E.G. (1997) *Essentials of Services Marketing*, Fort Worth: Dryden.
Zeithaml, V.A. and Bitner, M.J. (2000) *Services Marketing: integrating customer focus across the firm*, 2nd edition, New York: McGraw-Hill.

Case study

Questions

1 Choose a clearing bank or building society (preferably one you use yourself). Analyse its service offering: what services does it offer, to whom? How are they marketed?

2 From your own experience, and from interviews with other customers, try to evaluate the quality of the services.

3 Make recommendations as to how the bank could improve the marketing of its services, based on this chapter and on your investigations. See if the local branch manager would discuss your findings.

Chapter 16 | Business-to-business marketing

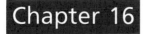
Business-to-business, or industrial marketing is concerned with selling to other organizations, rather than to consumers. Its application is wider than just business, covering marketing to institutions (hospitals, schools, etc.) and governments as well.

The range of products involved is also wide, embracing the extractive industries, raw materials of all sorts, heavy machinery and equipment, lighter equipment and tools, consumable supplies and services.

There are some overlaps with consumer markets, both in actual products (organizations and households both buy cars and toilet rolls), and in the type of product (copying paper and other supplies are similar to frequently-bought, low involvement consumer products).

Traditionally, however, and especially from the industrial side of the fence, business-to-business marketing has been seen to be different. Many of those differences have been alluded to throughout this book; here we will pull together those scattered references and discuss what essentially separates the two.

One leading author states that there are four major differentiating factors:

1 **Functional interdependence** There is a greater need for communication and co-operation between functions, and marketing depends more heavily on other departments for its success.

2 **Product complexity**   Industrial products are more complicated than their consumer equivalents, and this complexity extends to other elements of the relationship between manufacturer and buyer.

3 **Buyer–seller interdependence**   The two are more closely engaged in a relationship which extends beyond the transaction itself.

4 **Complexity of the buying process.**

(Webster 1991)

To these could be added a number of other characteristics:

■ Purchases are usually less frequent

■ The average price paid per transaction is likely to be much higher

■ An industrial product may be much more crucial to the buyer's business, which may depend on it for successful performance

■ Reciprocity of buying is often a feature of the buyer–seller relationship

■ Sellers may service a wide range of very different markets, each with different needs and buying processes

■ These different markets may react differently to the elements of the marketing mix

■ Manufacturers may need to understand not just their immediate market, but several levels, perhaps as far as end-users.

Thus we can say that, although the general principles of marketing will always apply, the detailed applications in industrial markets may differ from those familiar in consumer markets. The rest of this chapter will look at some of those differences.

The buying process

The section in Chapter 5 on organizational buying behaviour summarized the general level of knowledge. Here we will look more closely at the buying process. From the previous discussion, it is worth repeating two salient points:

1 The complexity of the process in industrial situations is reflected in the fact that there are normally several people in the buying company who influence the outcome – these members of the Decision Making Unit (DMU) must be identified.

2 The industrial buying process is not strictly rational, since human beings are always involved, but it is more explicitly rational than many consumer decision-making processes.

This explicitness is seen in the procedures adopted for anything more complicated than a straight rebuy, and perhaps even then when the rebuy concerns the supply of a major component or important material.

Explicit procedures, often in the form of detailed checklists, are used to evaluate suppliers on a range of characteristics; sometimes a field visit to the supplier is made, and the vetting can resemble a detailed audit of the whole business.

Buyers are interested in quality and price, of course, but they are also interested in reliability of supply, delivery, and service.

Buying companies also use rigorous value analysis of every element of their production process, and this will include scrutiny of the value provided by each supplier. This may lead to make-or-buy decisions on various elements, when the criteria will again include not only quality and price, but availability, flexibility, and security of supply.

The more analytical approach is also demonstrated in the adoption of computer-based models for Materials Requirements Planning (MRP and its derivatives), which produce detailed schedules of exactly what is required for any production run. To some extent, this has been superseded by other approaches to manufacturing, and in particular by Just-in-Time and total quality. As mentioned in Chapter 5, many large manufacturers have fundamentally reappraised their relationships with suppliers; they are seeing them much more as partners, or even as members of a strategic alliance working towards common goals. JIT and total quality cannot really be adopted in a vacuum: suppliers are necessarily deeply involved. This leads away from an adversarial, arm's-length relationship to one of much closer and deeper co-operation.

That is the leading edge, of course, and many manufacturers are no doubt still acting in the old ways. There will always be some conflict, since the parties are engaged in the same struggle, as described in Chapter 14, to get a greater share of the total value added. It is noteworthy that at the same time as Ford is supposedly trying to build close partnerships, General Motors has unilaterally made demands on all its suppliers for significant cuts in prices.

Segmentation

Segmentation in industrial markets has parallels to that in the consumer field. The equivalent of consumer demographics is segmentation by industry type, size, and location. Buying habits are paralleled by product applications, and these two sets of criteria are what most firms seem to use for segmenting markets.

Although suggestions for more complex or micro-segmentation have been made, there are virtually no actual applications reported. Probably the task is quite complicated enough without adding still more difficulties.

A more down-to-earth recent approach has been developed by McKinsey, the management consultants. They have produced a 'Strategy Game Board' using the questions 'Where to compete?' and 'How to compete?' The choices for the first question are 'Head on' or 'Niche', and for the second 'Same game' or 'New game'. The resulting strategies are:

	Same game	*New game*
Niche	Re-segment the market to create a niche	Create and preserve a unique advantage
Head-on	Do more of the same, better	Exploit unique advantage industry-wide

McKinsey found five types of strategic market segments:

- end-use
- product
- geographic
- common buying factor
- customer size.

These do not, on the face of it, take us much further forward. Other findings are more interesting:

> Their experience led them to conclude that industrial marketing companies in general have difficulty developing and implementing niche marketing strategies for several reasons. There is a reluctance to concentrate effort on a few market segments because of the fear of losing sales volume, and a tendency to focus on sales volume rather than profitability... McKinsey experts saw a tendency to place too much emphasis on segmentation *per se* rather than on the development of strategies for competing successfully in those segments. There was also an observed lack of understanding of how to resegment markets, leading to either too few segments and therefore inadequate opportunities to achieve real competitive advantage, or too many segments and therefore confusion and misdirection.

(Webster 1991)

The marketing mix

Product

There is no fundamental difference in the way the product should be seen in industrial marketing. It is likely to be more complex, and technical issues are likely to be higher on the agenda.

The problem is likely to be that too much attention is paid to technical issues and not enough to customer needs.

This is mainly due to the fact that market thinking has been adopted more slowly by industrial companies than by fast-moving consumer goods manufacturers. The marketing function is often seen as peripheral – there to sell the product once the engineers have developed and produced it (cf. services).

It was, however, from an industrial company that one of the best definitions of marketing thinking has come – the previously quoted saying of the chairman of Carborundum – 'Our customers don't want grinding wheels, they want metal removed.'

This epitomizes the marketing approach to product development and delivery; it starts from the customer and asks what problem they want solved, only then moving on to how we can help them do it. It leads to a reappraisal of our product range, and also underlines the importance of the service element in

industrial marketing. Our product should be a package of products and services which help our customers run their business better.

If our customers are themselves adopting JIT and total quality, we shall anyway be deeply involved with them. This pattern of collaboration already exists in successful companies.

Communications: advertising and personal selling

It was suggested earlier, in the chapter on personal selling, that the sales force is likely to be much the most important element of the communications mix for industrial companies. Sales people are at the boundary between the closely-working partners, and although that suggests a much wider set of contacts between firms, the sales person must always be the co-ordinator and channel (just as the NAM operates between consumer goods companies and retailers).

Sales people may be few in number, or many (as in office products, for example); they are probably technically qualified, though they should also be trained in selling. Their role may involve negotiating and bargaining (and they should be trained in those, too). Above all, they are managing the relationship over a long period, and that should be their main focus.

Advertising is likely to be of relatively little importance, though it can have a vital back-up role. There is a well-known advertisement for McGraw Hill business publications which shows a buyer greeting a sales representative with the words:

I don't know who you are.
I don't know your company.
I don't know your company's product.
I don't know what your company stands for.
I don't know your company's customers.
I don't know your company's record.
I don't know your company's reputation.
Now – what was it you wanted to sell me?

(Quoted in Kotler, and Webster, among others)

Particularly in new markets, or ones where your company is not well-known, advertising is an essential part of the total communication. There is evidence that adequate advertising support can increase the effectiveness and reduce the cost of the personal selling effort.

Advertising can also be used to reach those members of the DMU whom the sales person does not, and can target a different and relevant message to each. For example, different messages could be sent via advertising to the finance director and the chairman, while the sales effort concentrates on the technical people and the purchasing department.

Exhibitions and trade fairs are other important tools for industrial marketers. These, all being elements of the communications mix, need to have their objectives set and the results measured. Given the nature of the DMU and the complexity of the buying process, the targeting of the total communications mix must also be fairly complex – but perhaps even more important.

Distribution

Distribution is more often carried directly in industrial than consumer marketing. There are also channels which carry out similar functions to those described in Chapter 14, although they are slightly more complicated. The main types of intermediary are:

- **Manufacturer's representatives or agents** Do not take title to the goods, work on commission, normally have an exclusive geographical territory, with a long-term contract. These are the main alternative to a sales force, particularly in markets too distant or too small to justify full-time employees. The danger for the representative is that if they are too successful, the manufacturer will take over direct sales and distribution, so there is a fine balance in motivating them. Agents may be the same, or may work on shorter-term contracts with less commitment.

- **Brokers** Do not take title, work on commission. These are usually firms which make markets and set prices (cf. stockbrokers), usually in a commodity market.

- **Industrial distributors** Take title and work on margin. Similar to wholesalers; builders' merchants would be a familiar example. They may be general, carrying a wide range of products, or specialist.

- **Value Added Resellers (VARs)** These have appeared so far mainly in the computer industry, though they do exist in other areas; as the name suggests, they add value to the products they distribute, by combining hardware and (in the computer case) software. They frequently specialize in an industry, developing packages tailored to the needs of organizations in that field.

The issue of motivation and control of distributors is exactly the same as in consumer markets, except that there is not so much concentration and thus buying power in industrial distribution, and on the other hand manufacturers do not always have strong brands which the distributors need to carry. The same argument for strong branding applies, and the ideal position for any manufacturer is to have the products which are the best in their field, are recognized as such by buyers, and are therefore demanded by name. This leads back to the role of advertising, which can clearly help in gaining distribution and motivating dealers.

There is also an issue of competition between the manufacturer and the distributor, when the manufacturer sometimes deals directly with a customer as well as through the distributor. This may happen when a particular customer is very large, or has special needs. There are no magic answers to such problems. Distributors need to be convinced that the manufacturer supports their business if they are to continue putting effort behind his or her products; but customers are also sometimes very demanding. Each case has to be decided on its merits, with a strategic review every so often. The danger is that without an objective review, a previously agreed strategy can be whittled away bit by bit, leaving the manufacturer with the worst of both worlds.

The Internet, online exchanges and B2B

The Internet has had more impact on B2B than B2C markets (see Chapter 3); the great majority of online buying is B2B, and this seems likely to remain true. One of the major new phenomena of the turn of this new century has been the explosion of online exchanges, which aim to allow many sellers and buyers to congregate in cyberspace to conduct business. The exchanges offer a variety of ways of transacting: auctions, reverse auctions, aggregate auctions (like consumer buying groups), catalogues, RFQs (Request for Quote) or RFPs (Request for Proposal), matching buyers and sellers (as in a stock market), and value-added services, such as portals or software. There are currently two main types of exchange:

■ *Horizontal exchanges*, such as Commerce One's Marketsite or the Ariba Network, aim to reduce the participants' costs of procurement of what are known as MRO (maintenance, repair and operating) supplies; they are mainly for large companies.

■ *Vertical exchanges* also try to reduce the cost of purchasing, but for companies within an industry, such as Metalsite for the metal industry or ChemDex for chemicals. The major manufacturers own some well-known examples, as with Covisint, set up by the major car makers.

Exchanges offer clear advantages, particularly transparency and access to new buyers and sellers. On the other hand, they may lead to price wars. For both sides, they may detract from the relationship, or at best offer a way of gathering information before continuing to work with a long-term partner.

As with so much of the Internet, the early years have seen a proliferation of sites, many of which are bound to consolidate or fail. In any one industry, it seems probable that only one main site can survive, and the coming years will see a shakeout. Firms must work out for themselves what are the true costs and benefits of joining an exchange before committing themselves to it.

More generally, firms in B2B markets can gain through better linkages, especially through the supply chain. All parties can gain rapid access to up-to-date and accurate information – on product availability, or stocks, for example – and pass it on. Orders can pass seamlessly through several stages in the chain without intervention or delay, reducing costs and improving performance. Some commentators see the emergence of 'virtual organisations', linked electronically but with few of the boundaries between firms that we see now.

It is important that marketers remain in touch with these developments, and make sure that essential elements, especially the precious relationships, are not damaged.

Convergence of industrial and consumer marketing

It has for some years been the author's opinion that industrial and consumer marketing are converging.

Industrial marketers are increasingly adopting consumer techniques of market research and branding, while consumer manufacturers are having to adopt the relationship management approach of industry to deal with retailers. The functional interdependence quoted as typical of industrial marketing is also becoming increasingly vital for consumer firms, both in dealing with retailer power and in new product development.

There will always be differences in emphasis, of course, but the principles will be the same and the practice will look much more alike.

Key learning points

- **Industrial or business-to-business marketing covers a wide range of industries and markets. It overlaps with some consumer markets, but is usually thought to be different.**

- **The main factors differentiating industrial marketing from consumer are: functional interdependence; product complexity; buyer–seller interdependence; and the complexity of the buying process.**

- **Other differences are: purchases are less frequent; the average price per transaction is higher; an industrial product may be more crucial to the buyer; reciprocity of buying is often a feature; sellers may service a wide range of different markets and these may react differently to the elements of the marketing mix; manufacturers need to understand not only their immediate customer, but several levels beyond that.**

- **Differences between consumer and industrial marketing in the use of each element of the marketing mix are discussed.**

Further reading

Ford, D. (1997) *Understanding Business Markets*, 2nd edition, London: The Dryden Press.
Hutt, M.D. and Speh, T.W. (1997) *Business Marketing Management*, 6th edition, Fort Worth: The Dryden Press.

Case study: Finefilter Ltd

Finefilter Ltd is a company with a turnover of just over £10 million, 70 per cent of it in the UK. It specializes in filtration systems for a particular application in one area of the chemical industry. Recently it has begun to realize that its knowledge and skills could be more widely exploited, especially in reducing pollution. Both national, European and American rules on the levels of pollution allowed to escape into the environment have become stricter, and this trend looks likely to continue.

The R&D section of Finefilter has been working on adapting its expertise to new application areas; it is confident that it could develop systems which would at least meet probable future legislative requirements in treating both liquid and gaseous emissions from factories. Detailed costings have not yet been carried out, but the manufacturing people feel that Finefilter's unique technology will enable them to produce systems which offer better performance than existing products, at a price only slightly higher.

A venture capital company has expressed an interest in providing the substantial increase in capital which the expansion into new markets will require. The sales manager, David Barnett, is considering how to go about developing a strategy. He currently has four specialist sales people; there are no marketing staff. He has tentatively identified the fields of effluent treatment in chemical plants, filtration of water and other liquids used in manufacturing processes, and a variety of applications in water and sewage treatment in water companies (those supplying domestic and industrial water and treating the waste).

Questions

1 Outline the information David should collect to help him in his decisions.

2 What marketing issues will he have to confront in developing the new markets? How should he proceed?

3 What relationships does your employer have with other organizations (businesses or not-for-profit organizations)? Analyse one of these relationships, using concepts from the chapter. Do any practical suggestions emerge?

Chapter 17 | International marketing

Why go international?

We are all familiar with the fact that our world has become much more international, and that business is particularly open to international influences. It is worth pausing to ask why a business should go international, since its objectives and motivation will affect how it goes about it, and how it judges success and failure.

The obvious reason to start doing business outside the home country is to make more profit: international markets are seen as an opportunity. Sometimes the trigger is a feeling that the home market is saturated; or that there is excess capacity which could be used elsewhere – production capacity, or financial, or even human.

As international markets have developed, two new and interrelated pressures have appeared: from manufacturing, and from competitors. The argument is that as competitors develop international manufacturing strategies, they have access to increasing economies of scale; in order to compete, even in our home market, we need to have the same economies of scale, and to achieve those we need to be in international markets too. This argument may be defensive or offensive – we need to develop international markets in order to maintain our competitive lead.

For many service firms, it is the move of their clients into international and global markets that has led their own expansion – banks, for example, or accountants or advertising agencies. Another motivation is the desire to balance risk: when one country is in recession or its market in decline, others will be growing. Finally, the technological revolution in communications, especially the Internet, offers new opportunities to internationalize.

Excess capacity and an opportunity or threat are not enough for successful internationalization on their own: the firm needs a competitive advantage in its new overseas markets just as much as at home.

Although there are complex theories of international trade and comparative advantage, these do not need to play a major part in the firm's decision-making process. The firm will ask, is it worth doing business in that country? Can *we* do business there? How do we do business there? We are concerned with fundamental marketing principles applied to many countries instead of one.

What is international marketing?

The question then arises, is international marketing any different from domestic marketing? Surely we just apply the same analytical frameworks and use the same marketing techniques in new countries as in new markets? At one level, the answer to the latter question must be 'Yes': the principles and techniques are the same. There is a case to be made that countries are just markets, or even just segments of markets, and they should be treated as such. A company used to targeting different segments with different marketing mixes will have no problems with new countries.

This approach may be regarded as either superficial or profound; superficial, because 'It just doesn't work that way, countries are all different'; profound, because 'If you look deep enough, the principles are the same, it's just the applications that vary'. The problem with the 'no difference' view is that it presupposes an ideal marketing person in the home country who is capable of understanding markets, customers and consumers in a foreign country as well as those at home. It turns out that this is extremely difficult; the more distant a country, either physically or psychologically, the more difficult it is to understand that country in the depth required by successful marketing.

Clearly there are technical issues to be dealt with, such as tariffs and taxes; more importantly, there are cultural and social issues, of which language may be taken as an exemplar for the moment. If these are solved, then it may be that an international company is practising multi-domestic marketing, that is, a marketing strategy and set of marketing mixes designed separately for each country without reference to each other; in that case, there is little need to discuss the topic of international marketing as such.

Beyond that stage, however, there is the key issue of the extent to which the marketing effort can be standardized, and while it could be argued that this applies to segments within a country, the international dimension does appear to add a new level of complexity.

In this chapter, as with services and industrial marketing in previous chapters, we will look at those areas in which there are real differences between domestic and international marketing.

The international marketing environment

All the factors in the environment need to be scanned, but obviously on a broader scale. As the level of analysis overlaps to a considerable extent with overall business strategy, comments here will be brief.

Political factors

Political risk may be an important factor, since host governments may take decisions which nullify a company's strategic intent. It is clear that some countries are much less stable than others, and they represent a real risk. Even in stable countries, attitudes of government towards inward investment and foreign goods vary tremendously. Assessments of political risk can be bought from specialist agencies. The overall trend is towards greater openness, as countries realize the benefits that this can bring, and many old ideological barriers have crumbled. Each country under consideration, or in which a business is already established, nevertheless needs careful scrutiny and review to check that profits can be repatriated, and that no undue checks will be placed on development.

Within the marketing field, it is important to be aware of existing and possible future legislation. Regulations affecting particular products (such as pharmaceuticals and food) vary from country to country, and may change at any time. Frequently there are special requirements for packaging and labelling; restrictions on advertising vary; and in some countries there are detailed controls on promotions that are allowed. Tariffs and taxes will have an impact on pricing.

There are of course also supranational bodies, especially the European Union, which regulate the conduct of business.

Economic factors

Economies clearly vary in their stage of development, and in their rate of growth, rate of inflation and so on. Stage of development may be a first stage of screening (see below) for some products which need an advanced, wealthy economy to provide a market. For long-term decisions, future development is the key, and is obviously closely tied in to the political situation and the aims of the current and likely future governments. Again, forecasts can be bought from specialist agencies, and the publications of bodies such as the OECD (Organization for Economic Co-operation and Development) can be studied. Economic forecasts are notoriously unreliable in detail, but there is often broad agreement about overall trends.

Social and cultural factors

Culture is one of the areas of the environment which plays a much more important role in international marketing analysis than in domestic marketing analysis. By culture we mean all those habits, attitudes and beliefs which we learn as we grow up in a particular society. Culture has a powerful influence on our thinking and behaviour, and is the more important in this context because we are mostly unconscious of its working. Cultures differ significantly, and if we want to understand customers and consumers in a foreign country, we need to understand their culture. A pessimistic view is that no foreigner can ever fully understand another culture; marketing people need to penetrate far enough not to make foolish mistakes – and perhaps they need to use local managers who do understand.

Language is the most noticeable difference between countries. Most research on the topic suggests strongly that some grasp of the language of a country is absolutely essential as a gateway to its culture (Randall 1992). No single manager can be fluent in more than a few languages, but the implication is that for every country there must be someone who understands the language well and who has inputs to any decisions made.

Apart from language, the important elements of culture are:

- religion, which deals with intimate convictions
- varying attitudes towards time, wealth acquisition and risk-taking
- organization of relationships in the form of social and cultural stratification, family units
- level of education
- technology and material culture development in general
- aesthetic values.

(adapted from Bradley 1999)

Most people are now probably aware of the existence of cultural difference; most managers know that doing business in the Middle East, the Far East or South America is significantly different from normal western European practice. This awareness is the first stage, and is helpful as long as it is more than superficial. Texts on international marketing, and informal conversation with practitioners, will throw up plenty of horror stories of how western business people have offended their hosts and lost contracts through their ignorance of cultural norms. Even within western Europe, however, there are cultural differences (for an entertaining and instructive exposition in management terms, see Mole (1990) *Mind Your Manners*, tellingly subtitled 'Managing Culture Clash in the Single European Market').

The problem with culture is that it runs so deep that we are not even aware that we are filtering our perceptions through a barrier of our own. We start out with stereotypes of other nations (part of our national culture), and we have to work hard to see evidence objectively. We are frequently unaware that behaviour which we would regard as absolutely normal if we thought about it at all is, to a foreigner, odd or offensive. For example, interpersonal distance (the physical gap between us and the people we are talking to, at which we feel comfortable) is fairly standard between European countries and North America, but other cultures (Middle East, South America) have a much shorter distance. It is said that a culturally mixed gathering viewed from above looks as if a complex dance were taking place, as the westerners continually retreat to a distance at which they feel comfortable, continually pursued by those from other cultures trying to get closer. Probably no one is aware of what is going on.

Even in looking at apparently unambiguous things such as consumer durables, we must be aware of potential cultural differences. A bicycle is an item of leisure equipment in the USA, a basic method of transport in the Netherlands or China, and a status symbol in some African societies.

Marketing people need to understand and cope with cultural differences at two levels: the interaction between them and the foreign managers and government officials they will necessarily have to deal with; and the customers and consumers they will need to analyse in order to develop their marketing plans.

They also need to know that culture changes, often slowly but sometimes very quickly and discontinuously (as in eastern Europe during the last few years); it needs to be monitored.

The other major issue for marketing is the question of whether cultures are becoming more alike: are we moving towards a culturally homogeneous world? There are many ways in which all human societies are similar; there have been attempts to identify 'cultural universals' (see Keegan 1999: 61) which cover a wide range of human behaviour. Patently, there are still significant differences, but the world has been made a smaller place by modern communications. This issue is returned to below, in the discussion of globalization.

Technological factors

Technology is prima facie international; it is tempting to think that the markets for industrial and technological products do not suffer from the cultural differences outlined above. Clearly, there are differences in levels of technological development; what is appropriate technology in Japan may not be so in Africa. However, there are still the issues of dealing with managers: their culture is different, and their ways of doing business are different. Moreover, the way technology is actually used does in fact vary from country to country. It is essential to understand how the technology fits into the customer's world, how it will be used, what sort of people will be using it; it is too easy to assume that attitudes and behaviour will be the same as in the home country.

Globalization and harmonization

If all countries were completely different – their government systems, their economies, their cultures, their markets – then they would all have to be treated differently; international marketing would be multi-domestic marketing. If, on the other hand, most countries were really rather similar, and in particular their markets were similar, then markets could be looked at globally.

Theodore Levitt, in a famous article (Levitt 1983) argued just that: that many markets are already alike, and that others are growing more similar as economies converge and international communications reach more and more people. In this 'global village', brands must become global; those that do will gain such a competitive advantage that rivals will never be able to compete. Not surprisingly, many disagreed, and the debate continues today.

The truth probably lies somewhere in between the two positions: there are a few world brands, and many regional brands, and there are many markets which are quite local in character and have no international brands.

Cars, computers and electronics are examples of markets that not only allow globalization (because usage is fairly standardized), but probably *demand* it (it is becoming increasingly difficult to compete without global scale).

US consumer brands, such as Coca-Cola, Disney or McDonald's, tend to support Levitt's argument, because they are in markets which are relatively culture-bound. The normal view is that the more culture-bound a market, the less amenable it is to standardized marketing: food, for example, is thought to be culture-bound to a much greater extent than the market for VCRs. Coca-Cola and McDonald's vary very slightly across the world, but are essentially the same brand, marketed in the same way everywhere. It is also true to say that the positioning of these brands varies: a McDonald's meal is humdrum in many western markets, but a treat or status symbol in developing ones. Those loath to accept the globalization thesis argue that both are examples of American culture (even of cultural imperialism) dominating local cultures: they are bought not because they are suited to local tastes, but because they represent America: buying these brands, and others such as Levi Strauss jeans, means identifying with American culture and all that it represents.

If that is true, then the success of a few American brands world-wide does not mean that other, non-American brands can also succeed. Japanese and German products succeed because they are well-designed, well-engineered quality products which meet people's needs and give value for money; they happen to be in markets which are fairly standard; companies in more culture-bound markets do not succeed to the same extent (Japanese companies have not yet cracked the global cosmetics market, for example).

There is clearly a trend in many markets towards greater harmonization; in Europe this can be seen in many laundry, household, toiletries and confectionery markets. This must reflect convergence on the part of the consumers in those markets, but is driven by competitive pressures as much as anything.

This leads to the question as to why companies should be looking for harmonization. The ultimate aim must be greater profit and one of the drivers is certainly costs.

If economies of scale are available, then harmonization is attractive as long as it does not weaken the brand.

A minor example of potential gains is that one company found that it had sixteen different containers across Europe for the same household cleaner brand; standardizing the cap alone saved several hundred thousand pounds a year.

The proviso in the highlighted sentence above contained the crux of the argument: will harmonization harm the brand? Countries *are* different, and local management will always have adapted brands to their local conditions (at least partly to demonstrate their value as marketing managers). Harmonization is bound to mean changes, which may mean that the brand becomes less acceptable in some countries. A new brand avoids this problem, but if it is designed for international markets, it may represent the lowest common denominator.

No general answer is available for this dilemma. Supporters of harmonization point out that the possible effect is always checked in each country; if the results would be disastrous, that country is left alone; the benefits of harmonization are such that some risks are worth taking.

The other pressure for standardization is that of control. Where local management has total control over product policy, then profit opportunities may be missed. Procter and

Gamble lost profit opportunities for over ten years in some countries because local management delayed launching a brand which had been successful elsewhere.

Finally, there is a view that apart from economies of scale in manufacturing (which is a major driver of standardization), there are economies of scale in marketing ideas. Getting the brand right, with the positioning and marketing mix properly targeted and well executed, is a difficult and challenging task; not every brand group in every country is capable of it. Proponents of this view like to see the right branding developed in one country, and then rolled out unchanged as far as possible to every country.

The argument will continue. The trend towards greater control will undoubtedly continue, and the trend towards harmonization will certainly carry on in some markets. What is appropriate for any particular market must be determined with care, in relation to cost and market factors, and in the knowledge of what competitors are and will be doing.

The degree of globalization or harmonization is fundamental to so many marketing decisions that it has been discussed at this point. We will now return to the other decisions which a company has to make when entering or operating in international markets.

International market intelligence

Gathering information on many markets is necessarily more complex than for one – but it is even more important to gather information on foreign markets, since these markets will by definition be less known to us, so we will need information more. Secondary data are available from many sources. Economic data can be found through the United Nations, World Bank, OECD and other supra-national organizations. Governments, particularly in the industrialized nations, supply large amounts of data at both country and industry level; many have a separate department devoted to exporting and foreign trade (see, for example, www.tradepartners.gov.uk, www.dti.gov.uk, fco.gov.uk). Commercial sources, such as Business International and Euromonitor may be useful. For industry data, it is worth trying companies such as the EIU (Economist Intelligence Unit) (www.eiu.com, and www.ebusinessforum.com/index for e-commerce). *The Economist* and *Financial Times* (www.ft.com), Government departments and embassies publish or can find a great deal of information, as may Chambers of Commerce, trade associations and specialist databases. An Internet search is likely to throw up more potential sources than you can deal with, but practice will develop your skills. As always with secondary data, you have to evaluate what you find for validity, timeliness and accuracy; with international data, you have additional problems of comparability. The reliability of many countries' data is suspect, and caution is the order of the day. Still, it is preferable to have some data than none.

In collecting primary data, the difficulties of normal survey research in one, advanced country are compounded when trying to replicate the research across many countries. The problems of culture and language are major barriers. In addition, there are problems of construct equivalence, measure equivalence and sampling equivalence (see Craig and Douglas 2000).

Market selection

Whether a company is looking to enter international markets for the first time, or is an experienced one, deciding on market extension for its products, the choice of which markets to enter is crucial. There are three ways of approaching the decision:

- opportunistic
- traditional
- systematic.

Opportunistic

Many companies have entered markets haphazardly, for example because a distributor from that country has approached them, or a potential customer has contacted them spontaneously.

Traditional

The traditional approach has been typical of many British firms in the past: they sold in nations of the British Commonwealth, because of traditional loyalties, cultural links (key decision-makers having been educated in Britain, for example), and because language difficulties were few.

Both haphazard and traditional methods may lead to success, but they are obviously risky, in that the markets chosen may not be the most suitable or most profitable.

Systematic

A systematic approach then seems desirable. Since not every country in the world has equal potential, and most companies could not cope with launching simultaneously in a large number of countries, an initial screening is the first stage. The exact criteria used for this screening will clearly vary according to the nature of the company's product range:

- Geographic distance may be relevant to most firms, though its relative importance will vary.
- Psychological distance – the gap between the two cultures – may be a deciding factor.
- Economic status will also be widely applicable, though the exact way of measuring it will need to be adapted to different companies; consumer goods firms will be more interested in disposable income per capita, and machine tools manufacturers in levels of industrial investment.
- Demographics and their industrial equivalent will then be brought in.

The initial screening should reduce the number of countries to a manageable level. The market or markets relevant to the company can then be measured. Since this is a strategic decision, a reasonably long-term view must be taken, and the potential over several years be estimated. This is not always easy, particularly where demand is currently low. The old story of the two salesmen sums it up: one comes back and says, 'No one wears shoes, there's no market'; the other says, 'No one wears shoes, there's a huge market'. The factors driving the market must be identified, and forecasts of those factors evaluated. Experience from other countries may be used, though the underlying causes of market development should also be examined; superficial analogies may be dangerous.

Assessment of market share

Once the potential market in each country is established (this may eliminate further candidates), the potential market share attainable by the company must be assessed. This means applying basic marketing analysis: industry structure, market shares, strengths and weaknesses of competitors, distribution systems, consumer behaviour or organizational buying processes. Above all, it is a question of trying to assess how your particular product range will fit into this market. Are there similar products already, competitors with similar strategies to your own? How will existing competitors react? In cultural and marketing terms, is the country ready for your product? If the product is relatively unfamiliar, what adjustments will buyers have to make in order to incorporate your brand into their business or life? Will the nationality of your country be a help or a hindrance? Most of this analysis should be straightforward, with the proviso that the cultural barriers mentioned above will be in operation; it is essential that distorted perceptions should not affect a clear judgement. Local inputs will be of great value.

Depending on the country, the information available may be of variable quality. In most industrialized countries, both government data and commercial market research will be freely available (and government statistics in some countries are rather superior to those in the UK). In other cases, statistics will be rarer, and perhaps not so reliable; market research may be more difficult, for geographical or cultural reasons.

At this stage, a dual segmentation may take place – of countries, and of markets within selected countries. Some segmentation or prioritization of countries will probably be necessary, unless the company is large enough to enter all at once. Segmentation should be on the basis of fit between the company and the market potentials established. For some products, it may make sense to start with those markets which are geographically closest; in other cases, the nearest markets may offer very little immediate potential. It is likely that countries will fall into some 'natural' segmentation which is common to many products: stable government, wealthy economy and open markets characterize the industrialized countries, and they will form a priority segment for many companies; they are also likely to be the most crowded and competitive markets.

Which countries, or groups of countries, are chosen will depend to some extent on the company's objectives in wanting to go international in the first place. A firm wanting to dispose of excess production of a declining product will choose differently from one seeking to exploit a real technological advance.

Market entry strategies

A fundamental decision, before the choice of entry strategy to each country, is whether to go for a broad or a deep approach, i.e. to market in a broad selection of countries with relatively few resources committed to each, or to choose a few countries and market there in depth. These options have been referred to earlier as 'skimming' and 'penetration' strategies (Ayal and Zif 1979). Since these terms are so well established in the field of pricing, they are not used here. At this stage, there is simply not enough knowledge to state confidently that a broad or a deep strategy is preferable.

The choice depends on a number of factors, including the size and resources of the firm, the nature of its overall strategy, the nature of the markets under consideration and the strategies of competitors. The decision process will be iterative, as in all planning processes, as there is interaction between the elements of the decision. For a fuller discussion, readers are referred to Bradley (1999: Chapter 11).

As a generalization, we may say that the principles of product and market development apply, and that familiar products in familiar markets are least risky: the more unfamiliar the markets, the greater the risk (and probably the more resources will be required). The marketing entry strategy must be tailored to the firm's existing strengths and weaknesses, as well as to its aspirations.

The main methods of entering foreign markets are:

- exporting
- licensing
- joint ventures and other alliances
- foreign direct investment.

Exporting

Exporting is often the first method adopted by a company new to international markets, as it is relatively simple and carries low risks. Its success must depend on the firm's ability to deliver some competitive advantage in the export market, even after the extra costs of transport and possibly tariffs. That this is possible is shown by the great success achieved by many exporters of many nations. When Perrier can profitably export bottled water to the USA, it may be seen that the competitive advantage may be one conferred by marketing as well as by technology or low cost.

The advantage of exporting is that any economies of scale obtainable, whether from manufacturing or from elsewhere in the value chain, are maintained by keeping production in one country. Problems of management control and quality are also minimized.

Exporting may be indirect or direct. With indirect exporting, the exporter is essentially passive, selling to a broker or agent in his own country; the agent takes care of everything overseas. With direct exporting, the market selection process outlined above should have been applied, and a careful market study made of the countries selected. The marketing strategy should prima facie be the same as that used in the home market, though some adaptations may be forced by local circumstances.

If a satisfactory positioning for the product appears to exist, the main problem remains that of choosing a local agent or distributor. The issues there are the same as those discussed in Chapter 14; the distributor should be able to reach the target segment, should be efficient and financially sound, and should if possible be in tune with the exporter's strategic thinking. The dilemma for the distributor remains that if they are too successful, the manufacturer may decide to take over the business directly.

In practice, many firms develop only slowly into exporting, sometimes almost by accident. Frequently, the initiative comes from the importer, and the exporter responds reactively. Successful experience may then lead to a more proactive development of further markets. In these early stages, help is often sought from others, such as government agencies, or from groups of like-minded firms; the latter occurs especially among smaller enterprises.

Licensing

Licensing involves making an agreement with one or more foreign firms, allowing them to exploit a particular technology, usually a patented one, in specific markets. For the home manufacturer it is a low-risk, low-involvement activity, and is attractive if there is a perceived shortage of top management time to devote to more active development of overseas markets. Licensing may also be attractive if the firm has insufficient capacity to export, if there is significant political risk, or where it is the fastest method. As a corollary, the returns are also likely to be low.

The choice of partner is still important, as the greatest danger is that the licensee will learn from the licensing agreement and develop their own technology, in time becoming a competitor and taking over the market share which has been built up. Licensing should be used with care, therefore, and not for a major part of proprietary technology or in countries in which it may be wished to market more directly later on.

Joint ventures and other alliances

In some ways, licensing, joint ventures and other forms of co-operation can all be termed alliances. There is now a huge range of alliances, in which firms share resources in international markets. As Bradley points out, the assets shared may be:

- Product-market knowledge
- Market access/distribution
- Know-how
  - product
  - process
- Manufacturing capacity
- Raw materials
- Management resources.

The form of the alliance may be:

- Marketing partnership
- Production agreements
- Franchising
- Licensing
- Joint ventures

(adapted from Bradley 1999: 313)

Marketing partnerships

These are an extension of exporting, in that they usually involve a home partner who continues to manufacture the product, and the 'importing' partner who provides the local marketing and distribution. The local partner is likely to be a manufacturer also active in the foreign market, rather than just an agent or distributor.

Production agreements

In a production agreement, the partners agree that the local partner should take over some or all of the manufacturing in the foreign market; there will probably be a transfer of know-how, rather than licensing of patented technology, although there may be a mixture of the two.

Franchising

Franchising has been particularly successful in retailing, with McDonald's, Benetton and IKEA leaders in their respective fields. This type of business format franchising offers the same benefits internationally as in a domestic market, i.e. the ability to expand more quickly than the franchisor's financial and management resources would otherwise allow.

Joint ventures

Joint ventures are formed when legal entities are set up by the partners to carry out the partnership's business; for example, two partners set up a third company to exploit particular product-market opportunities in selected countries. The motivation to do so may often be a wish to spread the risk, or may reflect capital demands which one partner alone would have difficulty in meeting. It may be a formalization or more permanent form of another type of relationship. Some host countries insist on JVs, with a local partner holding at least 50 per cent.

Temporary joint ventures are common in some industries, such as major contracting (civil engineering, construction, etc.) and international finance; in these industries, a joint venture will be set up to carry out a specific project, then dissolved again when it is complete.

In other cases, the joint venture is intended to be more permanent. In some industries, the growth of joint ventures has been such that what is called a 'spider's web' is created. If all the alliances in the world car industry are drawn, for example, the result looks like a complicated (if untidy) spider's web.

Strategic alliances of various sorts have grown enormously in the last few years. Some see them as the way of the future, with all partners benefiting from the exchange of technology and other know-how. In some industries it seems that one manufacturer in a single country is simply not capable of competing in world markets; alliances then offer a chance of survival. Others argue that many alliances in fact either fail (such as that between Dunlop and Pirelli), or end up with the stronger partner taking over the weaker. Some critics also argue that the Japanese are very good at getting more out of an alliance than their partner, and that they always seem to end up with the technological know-how which they then exploit themselves.

This may be mere chauvinism, but there is no doubt that, at best, alliances are uneven partnerships. Any firm thinking of entering into one must be absolutely clear about their objectives, and about the relative strengths and weaknesses of the partners.

The explosive growth in alliances has been a relatively recent phenomenon, and research is still continuing into their advantages and problems. They seem certain to be extremely important in some sectors for some time.

Foreign direct investment

Foreign direct investment means that the home firm owns and operates a direct subsidiary in the foreign market. Frequently this is a complete manufacturing and marketing operation, but it may be something less than that. It is the most permanent, and most expensive, commitment to a foreign country.

A major driver of FDI is manufacturing efficiency; that in its turn may be driven by scale, or by material or labour costs. We have seen in recent decades how manufacturing of some products has moved round the world in search of cheaper labour, as one country after another has become too expensive. Another major motive has been the need to avoid tariff barriers (a well-known example of this being the Japanese car manufacturers setting up inside the EU). For service companies, exporting offers limited opportunities, and FDI quickly becomes essential.

From a marketing point of view, the motivation must be to gain deeper knowledge of local markets, and better control of the implementation of strategy. When local agents or distributors are used, tight control may not be possible; and there is the ever-present problem of commitment mentioned above, in that the distributor may not want to be *too* successful, knowing that that will lead to FDI and loss of the business.

A medium-sized or large firm may, of course, have a variety of patterns of exploiting foreign markets: some FDI, some alliances, some licensing and some exporting. Many markets are too small to justify heavy investment, but may still offer profit opportunities if a low-cost way of reaching them can be found.

Organizational issues

Any company operating internationally will need to make some adjustments to its organization; the more deeply it is involved, and the more important international sales become as a proportion of the total, the greater the adjustment may have to be.

A firm with a small export business will need only a few people dealing with sales and the back-up functions of distribution, documentation, and accounting. Any international dealings involve new types of activity, in particular documentation and currency dealings, and new skills, if not new people, will be needed.

The really complicated issues arise when truly international marketing, as discussed in this chapter, is undertaken. Many companies retain a separate international division to deal with all their overseas business, even when that has grown very large. This has in the past been true especially of American firms, as the overseas sales, even if world-wide, have still seemed relatively unimportant compared with the huge home market. The international division allows direct control from head office over all subsidiaries; and as a corollary, may lack sensitivity to local conditions and flexibility to adapt.

Many British companies have, on the contrary, a tradition of allowing a great deal of freedom to their overseas subsidiaries. This allows them entrepreneurial opportunities, and gives local management real responsibilities; but on the other hand, co-ordination and control are difficult.

This remains the central issue of international marketing organization: how to reconcile local management responsibility with central co-ordination.

As previous sections have argued, the trend is towards greater harmonization of international strategies; this inevitably means some derogation from the responsibility of local management. How can the country chairman be held responsible for profit when some of the major marketing decisions are made elsewhere?

The solutions adopted by companies include matrix forms of organization, direct line control of a region or the world for a given product line, and various designs in between. The whole scene is changing rapidly, but the trend is definitely towards greater harmonization, at least on a regional basis. A typical development in consumer goods is the formation of European brand groups which develop the strategy for a group of brands across the region. The group may be in head office, or in a regional headquarters, or in one of the countries; it may have line authority, or some lesser power of co-ordination and guidance. The thrust is always to greater standardization of marketing strategy, concentrating on product and positioning.

Industrial products have fewer problems, and are more likely to be organized on a world-wide product basis, perhaps with regional subdivisions. What constitutes the regions seems to be based on history as much as logic, and different companies divide up the world quite differently. When reorganizations occur, market logic may be brought to bear, allowing resources to be focused on the most potentially rewarding markets.

Stages in internationalization

It is possible to categorize firms according to how far they have gone along the road to full globalization. The stages are:

- Wholly domestic
- Export
- International
- Multi-domestic
- Multinational
- Global
- Transnational.

(We should note that everyone does not use the terms in the same way, and several are used interchangeably, e.g. multinational and global.)

While we hear a great deal about globalization, few companies are truly global. Many stay wholly domestic, and are quite happy with that. Exporting, or dealing with a few countries through an international strategy, suits others. Some have businesses in many countries, but treat each as a separate domestic market, with no overlap or co-ordination. A multinational begins to co-ordinate some aspects of its marketing, and may deal with the world on a regional basis. To be called global, the firm should see the world as one market, and develop one overall strategy for its products; this does not rule out minor local variations, such as Coca-Cola's slight adjustments of flavour. Some commentators have argued that the final stage should be seen as transnational, when a company ceases to have a 'home' country (Bartlett and Ghoshal 1989). All companies, however large and however many countries they operate in, have a headquarters, usually (though not always) in the country they started in. Most of their board members are of the 'home' nationality. A true transnational belongs to the world, goes the argument. Some companies are perhaps approaching that condition, in that board members come from an increasing range of nationalities, and operational headquarters may be in a different country from the original base.

Key learning points

- **Companies develop international business for various reasons: a saturated home market; the need for further growth; excess capacity; the search for economies of scale; and competitive pressure.**

- **Whatever the motivation, a firm needs a sustainable competitive advantage in foreign markets.**

- **International marketing may be multi-domestic, that is, normal marketing practice is carried out independently in each country.**

- **Issues specific to international marketing frequently centre round the question of the extent to which marketing can be standardized or harmonized across many countries.**

- **The way in which environmental factors may be specifically international are discussed; culture is likely to be particularly important.**

- **Methods of entry to foreign markets are exporting, licensing, joint ventures and other alliances, and foreign direct investment. Alliances of various sorts are spreading rapidly.**

Further reading

Bradley, F. (1999) *International Marketing Strategy*, 3rd edition, London: Prentice Hall.
Keegan, W. (1999) *Global Marketing Management*, 6th edition, Upper Saddle River, NJ: Prentice Hall.
Mole, J. (1990) *Mind Your Manners*, London: Nicholas Brealey.

Case study: Finefilter Ltd 2

In the case study in Chapter 16, Finefilter was developing treatment systems applicable to a range of pollution problems. The board director from the venture capital company has started to argue that the markets are world-wide, and moreover that competitors are gearing up to take a global stance. He is worried that Finefilter will not be able to compete unless they too think internationally from the start.

He has suggested that a firm of outside consultants be brought in to study the problem and make recommendations, since the current management has neither the time nor the expertise.

Questions

1   Will pollution treatment become a world industry? Why (or why not)?

2   As the outside consultant, outline the strategic options available to Finefilter if it decides to go international. Which would you recommend (make any reasonable assumptions you need)?

3   How should Finefilter choose which markets to enter internationally?

Chapter 18

Putting it all together – marketing planning

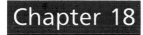

The process

Planning has received something of a bad name in some organizations, particularly amongst line managers. It has seemed intrusive, unnecessary, and unhelpful, especially when it has been imposed top-down in a bureaucratic way. In recent years, many markets have been very volatile, and managers argue that in fast-moving, unpredictable markets, planning is impossible. In practice, most firms use an annual budgeting process in which next year's sales are 'this year's plus 10 per cent', or something similar. Even when more sophisticated forecasting systems are used, this budgeting process is frequently unsatisfactory.

Problems of planning

A major study of marketing planning in British industry found that a number of problems were experienced:

1 Lost opportunities for profit

2 Meaningless numbers in long-range plans

3 Unrealistic objectives

4 Lack of actionable market information

5 Interfunctional strife

6 Management frustration

7 Proliferation of products and markets

8 Wasted promotional expenditure

9 Pricing confusion

10 Growing vulnerability to environmental change

11 Loss of control over the business.

(McDonald 1999)

Some or all of these problems will strike a chord with all experienced managers. Many of the problems stem from a basic lack of understanding of what the planning process is – or should be – about. As readers will appreciate, the stance taken in this book is that all marketing decisions should be based on thorough analysis of all relevant information about the factors which will influence events, a consideration of available options, and a logical conclusion about what action should be taken. The planning process takes this approach, and puts together all the lessons from the preceding chapters. Such a process needs to be formalized to make sure that nothing is overlooked, but it should not become rigid and mechanistic.

Benefits of planning

The same study quoted above showed that the benefits of a formal marketing planning system are:

1 Co-ordination of the activities of many individuals whose actions are interrelated over time.

2 Identification of expected developments.

3 Preparedness to meet changes when they occur.

4 Minimization of non-rational responses to the unexpected.

5 Better communication among executives.

6 Minimization of conflicts among individuals which would result in a subordination of the goals of the company to those of the individual.

(McDonald 1999)

Introducing a planning system

Introducing a planning system where none exists is not a simple or short project. It is as much a matter of changing ways of thinking as of designing new forms to be filled in. It must be supported by top management: this means not just encouraging managers to take part, but providing resources (for training, for example), and showing that the plans are expected to be acted on, not just put on a shelf. The planning system must be integrated into operational management, and the various parts of the planning (marketing, production, procurement, finance, human resources, etc.) must themselves be integrated. It seems likely that a new planning system will take up to three years to implement before it is working successfully.

Any detailed consideration of business planning is beyond the scope of this book. It should just be restated that marketing planning must inform, as well as being informed by, the overall business plan. The choice of product-market scope, which is a crucial part of the corporate plan, must take as input the views of marketing as to future developments and what is feasible, as well as giving the marketing function objectives to meet in its own detailed planning.

Company size

The exact form of the planning process will obviously depend to a large extent on the nature of the organization, in particular its size and complexity. In a small, homogeneous organization the process can be fairly simple; in a very large multi-divisional, multi-national company it will necessarily be more complicated, with many different levels and greater needs for communication and co-ordination. The larger the company size, and the greater the diversity of its products and markets, the more formal the planning process is likely to be, and it is in these organizations that the problems of over-formality and bureaucracy are likely to be most severe.

A fine balance must be struck between the need for co-ordination and control, and the necessity of encouraging creativity and radical thinking.

Any system which encourages managers to go through the motions every year, filling in superficial answers to a numbing series of forms, then forgetting them for another year, is doomed – and may actually harm performance by allowing opportunities and threats to develop unnoticed.

Any marketing planning process, therefore, whatever the size and shape of the firm, *must*:

- have active top management involvement
- be integrated into the overall business planning system
- be iterative, with feedback from lower levels to higher
- explore the possible impact of changes elsewhere in the firm (technology, finance, personnel) on marketing programmes, and vice versa
- be based on a deep understanding of the forces driving its markets
- have looked at possible changes in these forces
- examine the likely actions of existing and potential new competitors
- check the feasibility of its planned programmes against the firm's resources as well as external factors such as channels and buyers.

The planning cycle

Traditionally, the planning process is an annual one, tied into the firm's financial year. This is perfectly acceptable, unless the company's markets have a completely different pattern.

If the natural cycle of the market is from September to August, for example, while the financial year runs from April to March, there is no reason for not adapting the market's logic rather than the accountants' (though in practice considerable internal resistance might be expected).

There is also a longer-term planning horizon, normally five years. Again, this seems perfectly reasonable for most industries; it is about as far ahead as one can look with any degree of certainty. The long term must, however, be defined in relation to lead times, both production and marketing. If the lead time for the construction of new manufacturing capacity is ten years, then that must be the planning horizon. Some companies, such as utilities providers (gas, electricity, water) plan 30 years or more ahead. Equally, if the lead time for establishing a desired position in a market is longer than five years, then the marketing planning horizon must also be longer. The whole point about long-range planning is that it takes time to get from where we are now to where we want to be; but we must start now, and achieve all the intermediate steps year by year.

It follows that the annual planning process must integrate the long and short terms. Apart from achieving next year's short-term targets, the plan must show how the intermediate steps towards longer-term goals are going to be carried out.

The separation of long-term planning to some discrete organizational level or specialist department is disastrous; the people who have to carry out the plan must be part of the process of developing it.

The process, then, runs on an annual cycle, looking back at this year so far, and forward to next year and the years beyond. Human nature being what it is, and the day-to-day pressures on managers being unrelenting, it is helpful to have deadlines for each stage; how formal the system is will depend, as we have seen, on the nature of the organization. Put simply, planning consists of asking and answering these questions:

- Where are we now?
- Where do we want to go?
- How do we get there?

In a very small, simple firm, this framework may be sufficient, and the process may be fitted into a short period in the latter half of each year. For any firm of any normal size and complexity, however, the needs of communication up, down and sideways throughout the organization mean that much longer periods are needed.

The number and naming of stages may vary, but the following is representative of what needs to be done in most firms.

Stages in marketing planning

- Corporate objectives
- Situation analysis
  - environmental scan
  - marketing audit

- internal
- markets
- customers
- consumers
- competitors
- key SWOT

▪ Assumptions made about future changes in driving forces
- environmental
- markets
- customers
- consumers
- competitors

▪ Definition of critical success factors
▪ Marketing objectives
- long-term and next year

▪ Generation of alternative strategies
▪ Evaluation of strategies against objectives, situation analysis and assumptions
▪ Choice of strategy/ies
▪ Outline plan for five years
▪ Detailed planning for next year
- marketing mix for each segment
- costing

▪ Identification of possible blockages
▪ Contingency plans
▪ Design of measurement and control system
▪ Presentation and agreement of final plan
▪ Implementation and review.

Many of these stages could be elaborated in much greater detail, and in any given firm this will be the case, according to its particular needs. Equally, some organizations may be able to simplify or reduce the stages, as long as the essential thinking is done. The timing can then be set so that there is a smooth transition through the stages, allowing co-ordination with other functions and the corporate plan, to implementation. Typically, the earliest stage might start in April, with subsequent deadlines through, say, June and September, with final presentation in October/November for implementation in January to December of the following year. Clearly, the process is a rolling one, with review of the current year feeding in to planning for the next.

Equally clearly, the process must be iterative, with feedback from other levels in the hierarchy or from other departments leading to revision of earlier assumptions, objectives or plans.

Most of the stages have been discussed in earlier chapters and need no further elaboration; a few words are appropriate on those that have not.

The marketing audit takes its name by analogy from an accounting audit; it is an objective review of every aspect of the company's marketing resources, strategies and operations. The key word is 'objective', and the audit should examine the quality of everything the company does in the marketing field against some realistic benchmarks.

Kotler suggests (2000: 710) breaking the marketing audit down into:

Marketing Strategy Audit

- Business mission
- Marketing objectives and goals
- Strategy

Marketing Organization Audit

- Formal structure
- Functional efficiency
- Interface efficiency

Marketing Systems Audit

- Marketing information system
- Marketing planning system
- Marketing control system
- New-product development system

Marketing Productivity Audit

- Profitability analysis
- Cost-effectiveness analysis

Marketing Function Audit

- Products
- Price
- Distribution
- Advertising, sales promotion, publicity and direct marketing
- Sales force

This is a formidable list, and certainly, no firm needs to go through such a thoroug
every year. It is, however, a useful checklist of the areas that may crucially affect our
marketing success, and which we therefore need to check on now and again. The other
crucial area is competitor analysis (see Hooley *et al.* 1998).

A key SWOT is suggested, because a full SWOT analysis of a company usually
produces very long lists in each quadrant. Only a few of these are absolutely vital, and a
summary should try to reduce these to a very few, say three or four. This makes it much
easier to check back any strategy options against the SWOT analysis.

Critical success factors (CSFs, sometimes known as Key Factors for Success or KFSs)
are those things the firm *has to get right* to succeed in this market. They are those things
that differentiate winners and losers. In food retailing, we might define the CSFs as
location, relationships with suppliers, and supply chain management. For a lift manufacturer, rapid service is a CSF as well as design and manufacture. The purpose in defining
them is to make sure that managers focus on them during the year, rather than dissipating
their effort on less important matters.

The stage 'Generating alternative strategies' is an opportunity to challenge conventional
wisdom, and the way things are normally done. Human brains seem to get channelled into
well-worn paths: the more we know about our business, the harder it is to think of any
other way of doing things than the way we have always done them – yet it is the people and
firms who do something *different* who make the breakthroughs. Dell became a huge
business extremely quickly by selling computers direct (by phone, then over the Internet),
and ignoring the established channels. At this stage of the planning process, you can think
about any wild or unheard-of scheme, as it is completely risk-free (apart from a possible
danger of suggesting to a very staid management that you are dangerous, of course, but in
that case, you may be in the wrong firm). It is, in practice, very difficult to think of
different strategies, but it is worth making the effort, just in case someone comes up with
something revolutionary. Rational, objective analysis can come later.

Identification of blockages

The explicit identification of blockages is designed to bring out what we all know to be
true – that something will happen to prevent total success of any plan. Blockages may be
internal or external. Once identified, they can be classed as either 'Possible to do
something about' or 'Impossible to do anything about'; action can be planned for the
former, and the latter ignored (though borne in mind for explaining later what went
wrong).

Contingency plans

Similarly, contingency plans should be available for dealing with major changes in
circumstances. It is not sensible to spend time on detailed planning for every possible
combination of events, but a significant change in a major factor will alter the outcome of
your programme, and some thought should be given to what alternative action could be
adopted. The changes can of course be positive as well as negative, but better-than-
expected sales can be almost as much of a problem as sales which are worse than expected,
particularly if some system of rationing has to be introduced.

Measurement and control

Measurement and control are also important. Sales are the normal way of measuring a plan's success, but there may be other measures, either internal (margins, customer service levels achieved, number of returns or complaints) or external (levels of advertising recall, reputation of the sales force amongst buyers) which relate to the achievement of objectives. Without feedback measures, the plan cannot be said to be under control, and such measures need themselves to be planned rather than just wheeled out in an emergency.

Review

Finally, the review process must be built into the implementation phase, using the control measures. How frequently the reviews take place will depend on the nature of the business: in a rapidly changing business such as retailing, reviews may take place weekly and perhaps even daily; in other situations reviews may be needed only monthly, or even less often. The reviews should be diagnostic, in the sense that they should try to identify *why* sales (or whatever) are different from plan, so that sensible action can be taken.

The content

General Eisenhower, a great military planner, said that, 'Planning is everything, the plan is nothing'. What I take him to have meant is that what is important is the *process*: the analysis of information, the thinking through, the testing of ideas, the feedback and co-ordination, the use of creativity as well as logic; the final written document is less valuable. Even so, it should still be produced. Writing things down is a good discipline, and something needs to be kept permanently for future reference if the planning process is to mean anything.

The exact format of the written plan will reflect the needs of the particular organization. Certainly it need not contain all the details of every stage of the process that has produced it; much of that will remain as background data for the manager concerned. Many firms have a planning structure in which each annual plan for an individual brand or group of products is submitted on a form of one to three pages, consisting mainly of numbers. This may be acceptable *if* all the thinking has been done and the form merely summarizes the results of a rigorous process; if it represents mere form-filling, it is useless.

The minimum headings for a marketing plan ought to be:

1 Executive summary
2 Summary of situation analysis (including year-to-date results against last year's plan)
3 Objectives – next year, five years
4 Assumptions
5 Strategy/ies
6 Detailed plan for each element of the mix, including timing
7 Projected sales by period
8 Costs

9   Control measures.

Presentation to the immediate superior would be backed up by detailed argument based on the full analysis process, but only a summary document might then be passed on up the line.

Implementation and control

Many people feel that the real problems occur not in the formulation of strategy or the development of plans, but in their implementation. This is due not only to unforeseen and unpreventable circumstances, but sometimes to lack of skill on the part of the managers concerned, or to problems in the wider organization.

One study of the issues suggested that within each of the four levels of marketing implementation (actions, programmes, systems, policies) there are four ways by which effective implementation is achieved: interacting, allocating, monitoring, organizing. Examples are:

■ **Actions/interacting**   How are production and R&D colleagues encouraged to devote more time and effort to a single brand?

■ **Programmes/allocating**   How should prospects be selected for demonstration rides in a corporate jet?

■ **Systems/monitoring**   How does a mine machinery manufacturer monitor a major trade promotion expenditure?

■ **Policies/organizing**   How should the marketing team be reorganized by a company changing its 'theme'?

(Bonoma 1985)

Bonoma makes two further important points about the evaluation of marketing implementation:

1   Results are judged against expectations. The easiest way for a manager to look good is to set low objectives and then outperform them. The interaction between the objectives and targets set and their achievement is often a subtle one, especially in the marketing and sales area. Good senior managers will be aware of the pitfalls, and will set stretching but achievable goals.

2   The quality of execution of marketing plans may not be reflected immediately in measures such as market share or profit, because there are simply too many other factors affecting short-term results. Instead, Bonoma suggests, good marketing practice is 'quality performance in *coping with the inevitable execution crises that arise in every firm*, which threaten to short-circuit strategy's impact on the market place' (emphasis in original).

This may be true, and we still know relatively little about judging individual managers' performance objectively. It is certainly true that shocks and crises are inevitable. Marketing deals with people, both within the firm and among its customers, consumers and competitors; people are unpredictable, and plans will therefore never work out exactly. This reinforces the need expressed earlier for potential blockages to be identified, and reasonable control measures to be designed.

Some internal blockages, if identified and tackled, may be overcome. It is clear that the marketing function relies on other departments to deliver their part of the total effort, without the ability to control them directly; marketing cannot, for example, tell manufacturing or research how to allocate their resources. The personal skills of the marketing managers become important, but the organization structure may also either help or hinder their efforts.

It is up to senior management to diagnose and solve these problems, providing a structure which routinizes where possible, while allowing flexibility and creativity to flourish where they can. In particular, the structure should encourage co-ordination between functions; this is becoming more and more important in implementing marketing's tasks.

As to external factors, perhaps marketing directors should follow Napoleon; he wanted generals who, above all, were lucky. Apart from luck, good planning skills should help to identify most potential changes which might affect results, allied to a dash of flair. As Bonoma suggests, implementation skills may be different from strategic skills; if this is so, then the management structure needs to give support where it is needed, and to call on those people who do have the skills of execution and coping with crises when they are needed.

Key learning points

- **Installing a marketing planning system is difficult, but if done successfully brings a number of benefits.**
- **Short-term plans (next year) and longer-term plans (five years) are needed. The planning process itself needs to be planned.**
- **The stages in marketing planning and the content of a marketing plan are described.**
- **Implementation and control are crucial phases.**

Further reading

McDonald, M. (1999) *Marketing Plans: how to prepare them, how to use them*, 4th edition, London: Heinemann.
Piercy, N. (1992) *Market-led Strategic Change*, Oxford: Butterworth Heinemann.

Case study: Trowbridge Leisure Ltd

Muriel Stephens has just been appointed the first marketing director of Trowbridge Leisure Ltd, which owns two hundred pubs and fifteen hotels, mainly in the south and west of England. The company was set up as a result of the government's ruling that the large brewers should divest themselves of any tied pubs they owned over a figure of two thousand. In the ensuing turbulence in the industry, some brewers split themselves into two separate operations (brewing and pubs); some decided to concentrate on one or the other of these activities.

Trowbridge Leisure Ltd was formed from what had been a traditional, family-owned brewery, which had only recently been taken over by a larger competitor. The family had sold their shares, but some remained in management positions. TLL was formed by a management buy-out led by one of the old family.

Muriel had previously worked in the marketing departments of large consumer goods companies, most recently for a multinational drinks firm. She was thoroughly familiar with the techniques used in the marketing of brands, and with strategy and planning as practised in fast-moving consumer goods companies. She was uncomfortably aware of the fact that most people in TLL had never heard of concepts such as segmentation and positioning, and that no market research had ever been carried out.

Questions

1 Outline a programme of work for Muriel for the next six months. What should be her priorities?

2 Suggest how she should develop a strategy and a planning system for TLL. Produce an outline marketing plan for TLL for next year, giving headings and an indication of content.

3 Take a manageable piece of your organization, and produce a marketing plan for it, applying the approach described in this chapter. What difficulties did you have? What improvements could sensibly be made in the planning system?

Bibliography

Aaker, D.A. (1991) *Managing Brand Equity*, New York: The Free Press.

Abell, D. (1980) *Defining the Business: the starting point of strategic planning*, Englewood Cliffs, NJ: Prentice Hall.

Almquist, E.L., Turvill, I.H. and Roberts, K.J. (1998) 'Combining economic and image analysis for breakthrough brand management', *Journal of Brand Management*, 5 (5): 272–82.

Ambler, T. (1996) *Marketing from Advertising to Zen*, London: FT Pitman.

Ambler, T. and Barwise, P. (1998) 'The trouble with brand valuation', *Journal of Brand Management*, 5 (5): 367–77.

Ambler, T. and Styles, C. (2000) *The Silk Road to International Marketing*, Harlow: FT Prentice Hall.

Andersen (2000) *Leveraging Your Channel Partners in the Internet Economy*, Chicago, IL: Arthur Andersen.

Anderson, P.F. (1982) 'Marketing, Strategic Planning and the Theory of the Firm', *Journal of Marketing*, Spring: 15–26.

Ansoff, H.I. (1984) *Implanting Strategic Thinking*, Englewood Cliffs, NJ: Prentice Hall.

Ayal, I. and Zif, J. (1979) 'Market expansion strategies in multinational marketing', *Journal of Marketing*, 43: 84–94.

Baker, M. (1983) *Market Development*, London: Penguin.

Baker, S. (2000) 'What non-marketers think about you', 'Better Marketing Measurement', *Marketing Business*, September.

Bartlett, C.A. and Ghoshal, S. (1989) *Managing Across Borders*, Boston, MA: Harvard Business School Press.

Barwell, C. (1965) 'The Marketing Concept', in Wilson, A. (ed.), *The Marketing of Industrial Products*, London: Hutchinson.

Bateson, J.E.G. (1989) *Managing Services Marketing*, Chicago, IL: The Dryden Press.

Berman, B. (1996) *Marketing Channels*, New York: Wiley.

Bonoma, T.V. (1985) *The Marketing Edge: Making Strategies Work*, New York: The Free Press.

Boston Consulting Group (1970) *The Product Portfolio Concept*, Boston, MA: Boston Consulting Group.

– (1972) *Experience Curves as a Planning Tool*, Boston, MA: Boston Consulting Group.

Bradley, F. (1999) *International Marketing Strategy*, 3rd edition, London: Prentice Hall.

Brady, J. and Davis, I. (1993) 'Marketing's Mid-Life Crisis', *McKinsey Quarterly*, 2: 17–28.

Bullmore, J. (1999) private communication.

Buzzell, R. and Gale, B. (1987) *The PIMS Principles – Linking Strategy to Performance*, New York: The Free Press.

Buzzell, R. and Sultan, R. (1975) 'Market Share – a key to profitability', *Harvard Business Review*, Jan–Feb: 97–106.

Carroll, D.J., Green, P.E. and Schaffer, C.M. (1986) 'Interpoint distance comparisons in correspondence analysis', *Journal of Marketing Research*, 23: 271–80.

Chenecey, Sean Pillot de (2000) Unpublished manuscript.

Chisnall, P.M. (1975) *Marketing: a behavioural analysis*, London: McGraw Hill.

– (1995) *Consumer Behaviour*, 3rd edition, London: McGraw Hill.

– (1997) *Marketing Research*, 5th edition, London: McGraw Hill.

Christensen, C.M. (2000) *The Innovator's Dilemma*, reprint, New York: Harper Business.

Christopher, M., Payne, A. and Ballantyne, D. (1991) *Relationship Marketing*, Oxford: Butterworth Heinemann.

Cooper, R. (1998) *Product Leadership: Creating and Launching Superior New Products*, New York: Perseus Books.

Cooper, R. and Kleinschmidt, E.J. (1990) *New Products: The Key Factors in Success*, Chicago, IL: American Marketing Association.

Cox, K.K. and Enis, B. (1973) *Experimentation for Marketing Decisions*, Aylesbury: Intertext.

Craig, C.S. and Douglas, S.P. (2000) *International Marketing Research*, 2nd edition, Chichester: Wiley.

Crouch, S. and Housden, M. (1996) *Marketing Research for Managers*, 2nd edition, Oxford: Butterworth Heinemann.

Czepiel, J.A. (1992) *Competitive Marketing Strategy*, Englewood Cliffs, NJ: Prentice Hall.

Davidson, H. (1998) *Even More Offensive Marketing*, London: Penguin.

Day, G.S. (1981) 'Strategic Market Analysis: an integrated approach', *Strategic Management Journal*, 2: 281–99.

– (1990) *Market Driven Strategy: processes for creating value*, New York: The Free Press.

– (1984) 'The Capabilities of the Market-Driven Organization', *Journal of Marketing*, October: 38.

Day, G.S. and Montgomery, O.B. (1983) 'Diagnosing the Experience Curve', *Journal of Marketing*, 47 (Spring): 44–58.

Day, G.S. and Wensley, R. (1983) 'Marketing Theory with a Strategic Orientation', reprinted in Weitz, B.A. and Wensley, R. (1988) *Readings in Strategic Marketing*, New York: The Dryden Press.

Dhalla, N.K. and Yuspeh, S. (1976) 'Forget the Product Life Cycle', *Harvard Business Review*, Jan–Feb: 102–12.

Diamantopoulos, A. and Matthews, B. (1995) *Making Pricing Decisions: A Study of Managerial Practice*, London: Chapman and Hall.

Donaldson, B. (1998) *Sales Management: Theory and Practice*, 2nd edition, Basingstoke: Macmillan.

Doyle, P. (1989) 'The Strategic Options', in *The Brand Is the Business*, London: The Economist Conference Unit.

Drucker, P. (1967) *Managing for Results*, London: Pan Books.

– (1979) *Management*, London: Pan Books.

– (1985) *Innovation and Entrepreneurship*, London: Heinemann.

Ehrenberg, A. (1972) *Repeat Buying*, London: North-Holland.

– (1974) 'Repetitive Advertising and the Consumer', *Journal of Advertising Research*, 14, 2: 15–34.

– (1988) *Repeat Buying*, London: Griffin.

Evans, P. and Wurster, T.W. (2000) *Blown to Bits: how the economics of information transforms strategy*, Boston, MA: Harvard Business School Press.

Farley, J.U. and Ring, L.W. (1970) 'An Empirical Test of the Howard-Sheth Model of Buyer Behaviour', *Journal of Marketing Research*, 7, Nov.

Ford, D. (1997) *Understanding Business Markets*, 2nd edition, London: The Dryden Press.

Forrester (2000) *Online Grocers Diversity*, Amsterdam: Forrester Research Inc.

Frank, R.E., Massy, W.F. and Wind, Y. (1972) *Market Segmentation*, Englewood Cliffs, NJ: Prentice-Hall.

Gabor, A. (1977) *Pricing: principles and practice*, London: Heinemann.

Graham, J. (2000) *Beyond CRM*, www.clickz.com.

Grant, John (1999) *The New Marketing Manifesto*, London: Orion.

Haeckel, S.H. (1999) *Adaptive Enterprise: creating and leading sense-and-respond organizations*, Boston, MA: Harvard Business School Press.

Hamel, G. and Prahalad, C.K. (1994) *Competing for the Future*, Boston, MA: Harvard Business School Press.

Hamermesh, R.G. (1986) *Making Strategy Work*, New York: Wiley.

Hayes, R.H. and Abernathy, W.J. (1980) 'Managing Our Way to Economic Decline', *Harvard Business Review*, 58, Jul–Aug: 67–77.

Herman, G. (2000) *Making Data Warehouses Work*, London: Financial Times Retail and Consumer.

Hoffman, K.D. and Bateson, J.E.G. (1997) *Essentials of Services Marketing*, Fort Worth: Dryden.

Hooley, G. and Saunders, J. (1993) *Competitive Positioning*, London: Prentice Hall.

Hooley, G., Saunders, J. and Piercy, N. (1998) *Marketing Strategy and Competitive Positioning*, London: Prentice Hall.

Hutt, M.D. and Speh, T.W. (1997) *Business Marketing Management*, 6th edition, Fort Worth: The Dryden Press.

Johnson, T.H. and Kaplan, R. (1987) *Relevance Lost: the Rise and Fall of Management Accounting*, Cambridge, MA: Harvard Business School Press.

Jones, P.H. (1995) 'Advertising Accountability: measuring advertising's effectiveness', *Commercial Communications*, 1 (2): European Commission.

Kapferer, J.-N. (1997) *Strategic Brand Management*, 2nd edition, London: Kogan Page.

Keegan, W. (1999) *Global Marketing Management*, 6th edition, Upper Saddle River, NJ: Prentice Hall.

Keller, K.L. (1998) *Strategic Brand Management*, Upper Saddle River, NJ: Prentice Hall.

King, S. (1973) *Developing New Brands*, London: Pitman.

Klein, N. (2000) *No Logo*, London: Flamingo.

Kotler, P. (2000) *Marketing Management*, Millennium edition, Upper Saddle River, NJ: Prentice Hall.

Lauterborn, R. (1990) 'New Marketing Litany: 4Ps Passé; 4Cs Take Over', *Advertising Age*, Oct. 1: 26.

Levitt, T. (1960) 'Marketing Myopia', *Harvard Business Review*, Jul–Aug: 45–66.

– (1972) 'Production Line Approach to Service', *Harvard Business Review*, 50 (5): 41–52.

– (1983) 'The Globalization of Markets', *Harvard Business Review*, May–Jun: 92–102.

Lovelock, C.H. (1983) 'Classifying Services to Gain Strategic Marketing Insights', *Journal of Marketing*, Summer: 9–20.

Lunn, T. (1972) 'Segmenting and Constructing Markets', in Worcester, R. (ed.), *Consumer Market Research Handbook*, Maidenhead: McGraw Hill.

Macrae, C. (1991) *World Class Brands*, Wokingham: Addison Wesley.

– (1996) *The Brand Chartering Handbook*, Harlow: Addison Wesley Longman.

McCarthy, J. (1975) *Basic Marketing: a managerial approach*, Homewood, IL: Richard D. Irwin.

McCorkell, G. (1998) *Direct and Database Marketing*, London: Kogan Page.

McDonald, M. (1999) *Marketing Plans: how to prepare them, how to use them*, 4th edition, Oxford: Butterworth Heinemann.

McDonald, M. and Dunbar, I. (1998) *Market Segmentation*, 2nd edition, London: Palgrave.

Mitchell, A. (1999) 'The supertanker and the cat', speech at Information Resources conference, London.

Mole, J. (1990) *Mind Your Manners*, London: Nicholas Brealey.

Murphy, J. (ed.) (1989) *Brand Valuation*, London: Heinemann.

Nordan, M.M. (2000) *Online Grocers Diversify*, Amsterdam: Forrester Research.

Ortega, B. (1999) *In Sam We Trust*, London: Kogan Page.

Parasuraman, A., Zeithaml, V. and Berry, L. (1985) 'A Conceptual Model of Service Quality and its Implications for Future Research', *Journal of Marketing*, Fall: 41–50.

Pascale, R. (1990) *Managing on the Edge*, New York: Viking.

Pearce, L. (2000) 'Data Mining', lecture given to the Evening MBA, City University Business School.

Peters, T. (1989) *The Economist*, 4 Mar: 27–30.

Piercy, N. (1992) *Market-led Strategic Change*, Oxford: Butterworth Heinemann.

Porter, M.E. (1980) *Competitive Strategy*, New York: The Free Press.

– (1985) *Competitive Advantage*, New York: The Free Press.

– (1990) *The Competitive Advantage of Nations*, New York: The Free Press.

– (1996) 'What Is Strategy?', *Harvard Business Review*, Nov–Dec: 61–78.

Prahalad, C.K. and Hamel, G. (1990) 'The Core Competence of the Corporation', *Harvard Business Review*, May–June: 79–91.

Quinn, J.B. (1985) 'Managing Innovation; controlled chaos', *Harvard Business Review*, May–Jun: 73–84.

Randall, G. (1992) *Review of International Business and Management*, London: Council for National Academic Awards.

– (1994) *Trade Marketing Strategies*, Oxford: Butterworth Heinemann.

– (1997) *Marketing Strategy and Management*, distance learning text, Kingston: Kingston University.

– (2000) *Branding*, 2nd edition, London: Kogan Page.

Reichheld, F.E. (1994) 'Loyalty and the Renaissance of Marketing', *Marketing Management*, 2: 4.

– (1996) *The Loyalty Effect*, Boston, MA: Harvard Business School Press.

Ries, A. and Ries, L. (2000) *11 Immutable Laws of Internet Branding*, New York: HarperCollins.

Ries, A. and Trout, J. (1982) *Positioning*, New York: McGraw Hill.

– (1986) *Marketing Warfare*, New York: McGraw Hill.

– (1989) *Bottom-Up Marketing*, New York: McGraw Hill.

Robinson, B., Faris, S. and Wind, Y. (1967) *Industrial Buying and Creative Marketing*, Boston, MA: Allyn and Bacon.

Rogers, E. (1962) *Diffusion of Innovation*, London: Collier-Macmillan.

Shapiro, B., Dolan, J. and Quelch, J. (1985) *Marketing Management*, Homewood, IL: Richard D. Irwin.

Shaw, R. and Stone, M. (1988) *Database Marketing*, Aldershot: Gower.

Sheth, J. (1973) 'A model of industrial buyer behaviour', *Journal of Marketing*, 37 (4) Oct.

Sheth, J.N., Gardner, D.M. and Garrett, D.E. (1988) *Marketing Theory: evolution and evaluation*, New York: Wiley.

Stevens, M. (1991) *Handbook of Telemarketing Strategies for Implementation and Management*, London: Kogan Page.

Strafford, J. and Grant, C. (1987) *Effective Sales Management*, London: Heinemann.

Tuck, M. (1976) *How Do We Choose?*, London: Methuen.

Ward, R. and Perrier, R. (1998) 'Brand valuation: the times are a-changing', *Journal of Brand Management*, 5 (4): 283–99.

Vakratsas, D. and Ambler, T. (1999) 'How Advertising Works: What Do We Really Know?', *Journal of Marketing*, Jan: 26–43.

Webster, F.E. (1991) *Industrial Marketing Strategy*, Englewood Cliffs, NJ: Prentice Hall.

Webster, F.E. and Wind, Y. (1973) *Organizational Buying Behaviour*, Englewood Cliffs, NJ: Prentice Hall.

Wensley, R. (1981) 'Strategic Marketing: Betas, Boxes or Basics', *Journal of Marketing*, Summer: 173–82.

Wildstrom, R. (1998) *Business Week*, June.

Willigan, G.E. (1992) 'High-Performance Marketing: An Interview with Nike's Phil Knight', *Harvard Business Review*, Jun–Jul: 92.

Wind, Y. (1982) *Product Policy: Concepts, Methods and Strategy*, Reading, MA: Addison-Wesley.

Winkler, J. (1983) *Pricing for Results*, London: Heinemann.

Woo, C.Y. and Cooper, A.C. (1982) 'The Surprising Case for Low Market Share', *Harvard Business Review*, Nov–Dec: 106–13.

Zeithaml, V.A. and Bitner, M.J. (2000) *Services Marketing: integrating customer focus across the firm*, 2nd edition, New York: McGraw Hill.

INDEX

Index